M000009238

Taking the Leap

How to Build a World-Class Coaching Business

By Kasia Wezowski

NICHOLAS BREALEY
PUBLISHING

BOSTON • LONDON

First published in 2017 by Nicholas Brealey Publishing
An imprint of John Murray Press

An Hachette company

23   22   21   20   19   18   17   1   2   3   4   5   6   7   8   9   10

Copyright © Kasia Wezowski 2017

The right of Kasia Wezowski to be identified as the Author of the Work has been
asserted by her in accordance with the Copyright, Designs and Patents Act 1988.

All rights reserved. No part of this publication may be reproduced, stored in a
retrieval system, or transmitted, in any form or by any means without the prior
written permission of the publisher, nor be otherwise circulated in any form of
binding or cover other than that in which it is published and without a similar
condition being imposed on the subsequent purchaser.

A CIP catalogue record for this title is available from the British Library

Library of Congress Control Number: 2017944260

ISBN 978-1-47365-749-6
US eBook ISBN 978-1-47365-751-9
UK eBook ISBN 978-1-47365-750-2

Printed in the United States of America

Nicholas Brealey Publishing policy is to use papers that are natural, renewable
and recyclable products and made from wood grown in sustainable forests. The
logging and manufacturing processes are expected to conform to the environmental
regulations of the country of origin.

Nicholas Brealey Publishing   Nicholas Brealey Publishing
Carmelite House   Hachette Book Group
50 Victoria Embankment   53 State Street
London EC4Y 0DZ   Boston, MA 02109, USA
Tel: 020 3122 6000   Tel: (617) 523 3801

www.nicholasbrealey.com
www.coachingmovie.com

Contents

Part Two: Finding Your Clients

Introduction

KASIA WEZOWSKI

Any list of the most successful coaches in the world must include Marshall Goldsmith. He was ranked by *INC* magazine as the No. 1 executive coach in America. The *Economist* called him one of the most credible thought leaders in the field of business. He counts a former CEO of Ford Motor Company and the twelfth president of the World Bank as friends and clients.

Most coaches, of course, are not as successful as Marshall. Some may struggle to make ends meet. They spend days on end working on marketing and sitting on social media when they'd rather be spending time with their clients. They charge less than they are worth because they don't have the confidence to recognize their own value.

When my husband, Patryk, and I asked Marshall why so many coaches are struggling, his answer was simple: *"Many of the people in the coaching profession are really good coaches, but they are awful businesspeople."*

This book is about becoming *both* a good coach *and* a good businessperson. It's about ensuring that, as you help your clients thrive in their businesses, you are thriving, too! It's about helping you become a model of success for your clients, so they look at you not just for advice, but as an example of what happens when the attitudes and principles of coaching are successfully applied.

In our society, we naturally associate the *value* of any professional with how successful they have become. If you had to find a dentist and the first practitioner you visited had an empty waiting room and a snarling receptionist, you'd be unlikely to have confidence in their professional skill. On the other hand, if you found a dentist with a packed waiting room, a smiling receptionist, and happy patients, you'd likely conclude that this was a competent professional whom you could trust.

It could be that both dentists attended the same school, got the same grades, and have roughly the same level of skill. For whatever reason, however, one had become successful at the *business* of running a dental practice, and the other hadn't. As a patient, your trust immediately follows the trappings of success, and you feel more confident giving your business to the practitioner with the packed waiting room, smiling receptionist, and happy patients.

On some level, we are intuitively aware that the value of a dentist, a lawyer, or a banker isn't exclusively connected to the amount of training they have received, or even to their level of professional skill. It's about more than that. It's about how they have managed their business and their life to become holistically successful.

This distinction matters for every profession, but for coaches it's even more important. Our value and credibility as coaches is directly linked to our own level of personal and financial satisfaction. You wouldn't trust a toothless dentist, and yet many coaches who are dissatisfied with their own lives or careers expect clients to come to them for advice.

As a coach, it's not enough that you ask the right questions of your clients. It's not enough to care deeply about their problems and to wish them to succeed. You will not be the best coach you can be unless you find and recognize your own unique value and use this to create a level of success *for yourself* before you create it for your clients.

For those willing to develop themselves, now is a fantastic time to enter the coaching profession. The coaching industry around the world has grown 19 percent since 2011. In 2016, the total revenue of coaches around the world was US$2.35 billion.[1] Once considered a luxury for the business elite, more and more people now realize the value of coaching.

Awareness of coaching is on the rise among young people, with two-thirds of 24- to 35-year-olds familiar with the industry.[2] About 75 percent of coaches working today expect an increase of clients and revenue during the next 12 months. This means there are strong opportunities for new coaches to make their mark on the profession and for established coaches to have long and rewarding careers.

Today, the average annual income for coaches around the world is US$51,000.[3] That's almost *exactly* the same as the national average income in the U.S. It's also much less than most coaches deserve. Coaches who can develop and hone a specialization, who have established strong reputations, and who have the business skills to capitalize on this are capable of earning six or even seven figures per year.

When you learn the *business* and personal development skills to build a thriving life for yourself, you'll be able to shine as a coach and speak from a position of authority and confidence. This book sets out to help you achieve this—to become the kind of coach whose value is immediately obvious to everyone you meet, who attracts the right kind of clients, and who exudes success in everything you do.

Inside this book:

- You'll learn how to quantify the impact of your coaching so that you can charge high fees with integrity, with both you and your clients confident that you're worth every cent.
- You'll learn how to design your specialization so that you attract the right kind of clients, positively impact their lives or businesses, and become recognized locally or even internationally as *the* expert in your field.
- You'll learn how to live life as a successful coach, able to overcome your own barriers and evolve as a person while helping your clients do the same.

This book presents wisdom directly from some of the most successful coaches in the world. Many of the people you'll hear from are millionaires. Some are celebrities. But they all started off exactly where you are now.

There was a moment in the life of each of these coaches when they realized that making a difference for other people also means being successful yourself. We hope that their stories and advice will help you *take your leap* and become the kind of coach who inspires your clients not just because of what you do, but also because of who you are.

Congratulations on taking the first step, and I can't wait to embark on this journey together.

Kasia Wezowski, July 2017

Part One:
Finding Yourself
and Your Purpose

Inner Wisdom

The *Yin* and *Yang* of Building a Thriving Coaching Business

MARC STEINBERG

Marc Steinberg is an accredited International Coach Federation Master Certified Coach (MCC) with more than thirty years of international experience in coaching, teaching, and mentoring. He is the founder of Creative Consciousness International and its ACTP Coaching Academies, which are represented in Europe, Russia, South Africa, and the United States. He has helped thousands of entrepreneurs and worked with numerous corporate clients including L'Oréal, MasterFoods, and Harley Davidson.

As a coach, you help other people overcome barriers to success. In this chapter, you'll learn how to overcome your own obstacles and grow your coaching business through an understanding of both Eastern and Western philosophy.

The United States has a strong culture of "go-getter" entrepreneurial core competencies. There are many amazing teachers who explain the practical skills you need to start, grow, and market a business. Several of those teachers are featured in this book. As a coach, it is essential that you have these skills, but it's also important to realize that this go-getter approach to building a coaching business is only part of the picture.

Twice in my life, I have worked to create a coaching business from nothing. The first time was in Germany in the 1990s. Ten years later, after taking time out for a personal sabbatical and to upgrade my coaching credentials, I again started from scratch and began my second coaching business in South Africa, Creative Consciousness International, which today has a global presence.

Each time my team and I set out to build a coaching business, we were successful not just because of business skills and hard work, but also because of an awareness of where the attitudes and techniques of the modern business culture fall short.

In this chapter, we'll explore a few concepts that draw on Eastern and Western philosophy to fill some of the gaps in our understanding of personal and business success. You'll learn how succeeding and thriving as a coach isn't only about your skill as a businessperson, but also about your ability to balance the power of *yang*, making things happen, with *yin*, the disciplined *nonattachment* of letting things happen.

Embracing these ideas will not only help you reach new heights of success, but will also protect you from burnout, loss of passion, and the dangerous complacency that so often comes when the first summits of success have been achieved.

WHERE OUR UNDERSTANDING OF SUCCESS FALLS SHORT

In the West, entrepreneurial core competencies focus on *making* things happen. The techniques focus on personal power. They are about building *bigger, faster, better* businesses. This is important, but it's limited.

There are only twenty-four hours in a day, so there's a limit to how much you can simply *make happen*. You're limited in the number of clients you can see every day. You're limited in the number of networking meetings you can attend, the number of phone calls you can make, the number of books you can write.

If you focus only on *making things* happen, then you're only functioning at 50 percent of your real potential capacity. To access the full 100 percent, you need to combine *making* things happen with *letting* things happen.

THE POWER OF *LETTING* THINGS HAPPEN

When you read biographies of successful leaders, you may be surprised to realize how little *work* some of them actually did. Many achieved amazing things, but more than a few of them seem to have spent more time on the golf course or walking along the beach than on hard work. Isn't success about constant hard work and a good dose of luck? That's what many of us in the West are taught. The Western concepts of creating success are powerful and valid but represent only 50 percent of a human being's power to create. The other 50 percent belong to the Eastern way of creating success. The way of *letting things* happen.

From a holistic perspective one can posit that human beings are composed of two energies: the male energy and the female energy. The male energy, *yang*, is about *making things* happen. The female energy, *yin*, is about *letting things* happen. With both of these energies awakened and in balance, you can move mountains and become holistically and fantastically successful.

Many people fall short of success time and again because our Western culture has given too little attention to the female energy of success. We lose because we focus only on *making things* happen, without being open to the possibilities that arise when we begin to simply *let things* happen.

UNDERSTANDING THE MALE AND FEMALE ENERGY

Male (*yang*): Personal power. Attachment. Commitment. Vision. Taking a stand. Perseverance. Persuasion.

Female (*yin*): Nonattachment. Serenity. Freedom. Openness. Receptivity. Fortunate circumstances. Unexpected support. Being at the right place at the right time.

None of the great achievers in history achieved their success through personal power alone. Consciously or unconsciously, they used the power of *letting things* happen, also known as the law of attraction. By balancing hard work with the ability to attract and be open to unforeseen fortunate circumstances, they propelled themselves to greater heights of success.

THE PROBLEM OF ATTACHMENT

Everything I have accomplished in my life started out with a decision, with a commitment. But, through my understanding and awareness of Eastern and Western philosophy, I learned that if you become too attached to the decision and forget to open yourself to simply *letting things* happen, then you will sabotage your own success. This is the problem of attachment.

We've all had experiences that show us that the more we want something and feel internal pressure—expectations, needs, burning desire—the less likely we are to get it. The harder you try to be charming at the next dinner party you attend, the less likely you are to come off as authentic and likeable. The harder you try to close that deal over the phone, the more likely you are to come across as desperate and off-putting. As I tell my clients, you can't make a rose grow faster by pulling on it.

Cats are particularly sensitive to the energy of attachment, and their natural reaction is a stunning mirror. If you approach a cat and start stroking it, hoping that it will like it and play with you, then chances are the fur ball is going to flick its tail and rush away. But when you return to the couch, pick up a good book and forget all about the cat, that's exactly when it's going to start purring and rubbing against your leg.

Whatever you believe you absolutely need in life, the universe, like cats, has its ways of showing you that you don't. The philosopher Jiddu Krishnamurti said: "Freedom is not at the end; freedom is at the very first step."[4] Freedom is the natural state that we reach when we are not attached. Letting go of attachment to the desired outcome is therefore as powerful as it is important.

While it may seem counterintuitive, it is possible to be fully committed and engaged in powerful action while at the same time being nonattached, but it requires a conscious act of surrendering the notion of control. Remember, be free first, then engage with the world. Be clear on what your goals are, while not being attached to whether or not you achieve them.

THE CONCEPT IN PRACTICE

Next time you have a meeting or phone call with a potential client, keep in mind this constant search for balance between *making* happen and *letting* happen, between *commitment* and *detachment*. Before your meeting, be clear on your purpose: to create a new coaching client from this conversation. But do not become overly attached. Make peace with all possible outcomes. They may become a client, they may not. Be happy with either option.

Here's a powerful mantra: *"Some will. Some won't. So what? Who's next?"*

To detach, it helps to first *embrace* the worst-case scenario. Know that even if the worst-case scenario transpires, you will get through it. From the moment you accept this possibility and move beyond fear, you can arrive at a more natural place, a place of balance. When you are no longer attached to success, you are very likely to acquire it.

THE LAW OF RESONANCE

A powerful concept that helps us to balance both male and female energies when it comes to pursuing our goals is the law of resonance. If you've felt stuck at a certain plateau with your business, or if you've been hesitating before taking the leap to the next level, then the problem could be that you are not in *resonance* with where you need to be.

The law of resonance states that we attract into our lives the things we are in *resonance* with. To be in resonance with something means to be able to completely regard it as true for you in your consciousness. You are, you have, and you attract only that which you regard as true for yourself and thus place yourself in resonance with. You miss out on those things that you are not able to regard as true and are therefore not in resonance with.

Hermes Trismegistus, a mythological figure, said, "As within so without, as above so below." When you regard something as true in your consciousness, you bring it into your life because like attracts like. Happy people magnetize other happy people around them but, as the old saying goes, misery also loves company.

There are many social and political reasons why the rich get richer and the poor get poorer, but the law of resonance is a factor. Wealthy people find it easy to *believe in* their own wealth. They are in resonance with being rich. Poor people, on the other hand, often stay poor because they cannot make the idea of being wealthy true for them in their own minds.

Nearly one-third of lottery winners eventually lose all their riches and declare bankruptcy.[5] Could this be because, even though their bank balance changed, the fundamental, deep-seated beliefs and attitudes they carried throughout their whole lives remained the same? They may have been millionaires on paper, but in their minds they were still not *in resonance* with wealth. This caused them to make poor financial decisions, and soon they arrived back at where they were in the beginning, or even worse.

If you want something to happen, then you must first make it real for you in your mind. It doesn't work the other way around.

ARE YOUR GOALS TRUE FOR YOU IN YOUR MIND?

In my early twenties, I financed my spiritual studies and travels through modeling and commercial acting. I had some success and was soon earning DM4,000–5,000 every month. That was good money in those days, but I wondered why I wasn't making more. I had it all going for me, but every month my bookings seemed to be invisibly capped at the magic DM5,000 line. Unable to find external explanations, I approached a mental trainer named Richard, and I asked him what I would need to do in order to break through this barrier and make as much as DM10,000 or DM15,000 each month.

Richard said I would not be able to earn this much until I could clearly *imagine it and internally regard it as true*. He warned me that thinking and believing are entirely different domains. Thinking about a million dollars doesn't do anything for you, even if you think about it all day long. To be in resonance with it, you need to believe it. Of course, my next question to the mental trainer was, "OK, so how do I get myself to believe?"

First, I had to vividly imagine that DM10,000 in all possible formats, including a pile of coins, a stack of crisp notes, stock certificates, glimmering gold bars. The fine details were particularly important. How do those notes smell? How heavy are the gold bars? What is the feel of the engravings on the coins? It had to be completely real in my head, involving all five senses.

I would visualize every morning and every night for twenty minutes, changing the details in subtle ways to keep it fresh and interesting. Richard taught me not to *think* about the images I created in my mind but to *experience* them, to see them, to feel them, as if they were real.

To my delight this actually worked; and it didn't take long before more and better-paid jobs found me, and soon I reached the five-digit monthly income mark. Ever since, whenever I desire something and can't believe in it, I get busy practicing this way of visualizing until my mind starts believing.

LET'S APPLY THIS TO YOUR COACHING BUSINESS

You must internally regard something as 100 percent true for you before the power of attraction can help you manifest it in reality.

What you are not able to believe in is not likely to happen.

Think about the level of success you want to achieve as a coach. What symbolizes that success for you? A certain bank balance? The smiling, happy faces of your family? A transformed client? Waking up every morning, looking in the mirror, and knowing with certainty that you are on the right path and looking forward to another beautiful day?

Whatever this is for you, practice visualizing it as vividly and powerfully as possible, using all five senses, until you can internally regard it as true for yourself. Commit to doing this for twenty minutes every morning until it becomes a habit. It will get easier with time and will eventually become an exercise that you look forward to and enjoy.

When you are doing this, do not get sidetracked by thinking about how to make this come true. Focus on the what and the why; make it absolutely real for yourself in your consciousness; then relax, detach, and let it happen. But don't drop the energy of being connected to the what and why. This is the paradox that so many readers of *The Secret* struggle with. The *yin-yang* symbol is the power; you won't find just the *yin* or just the *yang*.

By doing this exercise you are placing yourself *in resonance* with what you want, which is closely connected to the concept of *letting* it happen. Deciding to place yourself in resonance with what you want is like making a commitment. It comes from *yang*, the male energy. Being in resonance with what you want and *letting* it happen comes from *yin*, the female energy. Both powers need to be energetically fueled. In essence, you are practicing the *action* of attached engagement while remaining nonattached.

YOU GET WHAT YOU GIVE

There's a famous story of a woman who took her son to see Mahatma Gandhi. The child had diabetes, but no matter how many times his mother pleaded, he wouldn't stop eating sugar. The woman asked the great guru to tell her son to stop eating sugar.

Our story goes that Gandhi looked at the woman and said simply, "Come back in three months." The woman was confused, but she trusted in the guru and led her son away. Three months later she returned with her son. Gandhi gazed at the boy for a moment before calmly saying, "Stop eating sugar." The boy nodded his head in agreement.

The woman was surprised. She asked her teacher, "Why didn't you simply say this three months ago?" Gandhi's famous reply: "Madam, three months ago I myself was eating sugar."[6]

Mahatma Gandhi understood that being in resonance with what you want from the world means accepting that you only get what you are willing to give. As we discovered above, the law of resonance states that *like* attracts *like*. Happiness attracts happiness, wealth attracts wealth. Before Gandhi could authentically and powerfully tell the boy not to eat sugar, he had to be *in resonance* with not eating sugar himself. As Gandhi himself said, you have to "*be* the change you want to see in the world."

HOW THIS WORKS IN PRACTICE

Look at your relationships, both your romantic relationships and the relationships you have with your clients, your business partners, your friends. Think about what you feel is *missing* from those relationships. What is it that you want, but they are refusing to give? Trust? Commitment? Respect? Inspiration? Loyalty? Pleasure? Then ask whether you yourself are *giving* this to them. As Gandhi shows us in the above story, we cannot expect to get that which we are not willing to give.

In the same way that Gandhi was unwilling to tell the boy to stop eating sugar before he himself stopped eating sugar, think about the situations in your life where you want something from other people that, until now, they haven't been willing to give. And then, go there first and get in resonance with that yourself. Be willing to give and believe fully in something yourself before you expect others to do the same.

OUR RELATIONSHIP WITH TIME: *CHRONOS* & *CHYROS*

One of the most significant areas in which the Western emphasis on *making happen* and *attachment* causes us to sabotage ourselves is in the area of time. In our culture, we have lost the sense of the right timing. We focus only on time quantity, without focusing on time *quality*. The opposing concepts of *chronos* and *chyros* help us to understand this.

Chronos represents the male energy in relationship to time. *Chronos* is about time quantity. The number of hours in a day, the number of working days in a week. It's about commitment, deadlines, certain outcomes being delivered at a certain time. It's about the past and the future.

Chyros, from the ancient Greek word *kairos*, meaning the right or opportune moment, represents the female energy in relationship to time. *Chyros* is about time quality. It's about the here and now. It's about having the necessary trust to allow things to happen *at the right time* without always needing to force them to happen when you want.

Our business culture is so focused on the male energy of *chronos*, making certain things happen at a certain time, that we suffer greatly by missing out on *chyros*, letting things happen when they are meant to happen. To be successful, you need to have both.

When you are overly attached, fearful, and constantly rushing to get things done, you are experiencing time only from the perspective of *chronos*. When you place yourself *in resonance* with what you want, as described in the sections above, then you open yourself up to the possibilities and opportunities presented by *chyros*.

Once you open yourself to *chyros*, you start to notice opportunities that you would otherwise have missed. You experience the present moment, the here and now, more richly. You are less anxious about the past, less fearful about the future.

THE CONCEPT IN PRACTICE

Let's say that you're a speaker from New York and you've decided to expand your speaking business internationally. You give yourself seven days to come up with a plan, execute it, and land your first paid speaking gig in London.

For the first three days you work solidly, finding leads in London, introducing people to your profile, researching potential events that would be a match. You still haven't landed the gig, but you have four days to go and you're working hard to reach your goal before the deadline.

Then, on the third afternoon, you get a phone call from an old friend whom you haven't seen in years. He's in town just for the one night, and he asks if you want to grab a drink. This could be a distraction that will prevent you from accomplishing your goal. Or, it could be the hand of *chyros* offering you an opportunity.

The more aligned you are with your purpose, the more you are in resonance with what you need, the more easily you will be able to notice the opportunities presented to you by the world, and the better you'll be able to tell the difference between unexpected opportunities and unnecessary distractions.

In this example, you decide to go for it. You finish your day early and meet up with your friend. You tell him that you've decided to expand your speaking business to London. It could be that he has a friend or colleague who is right now putting together an event in the city and is looking for a speaker who matches your expertise. And if we are really talking *chyros* here, then your friend is a messenger telling you where the fast lane is to be found. *It's only day three of seven, but you've already achieved your goal!*

HOW TOTALITY HELPS YOU OPEN TO *CHYROS*

The key to being open to the opportunities presented by *chyros* without being sidetracked is to keep your life complete. Tie up loose ends so that, when new things present themselves, there's more likelihood that they'll be an opportunity rather than a distraction. Go light!

When you're busy working on things that matter to you, it will become more natural to keep things complete. Never break a promise or commit to anything that you won't follow through on. Communicate clearly, honestly, and sincerely. This way, when you go to bed at the end of the day, there should be no thoughts left over from the day's work—absolutely nothing—because you will have completed every action that day in the moment. You did not resist, hesitate, or withhold. You gave it all 100 percent. If you feel like resting, rest 100 percent. If you decide to call prospects, do it 100 percent. Don't go to the fridge, don't look at your e-mails, and don't let your mind take you on a world tour.

Break down your time commitments into smaller units, like ten- or twenty-minute blocks—and spend these in totality. Add another block if you want to, but only after you have completed the current time block. This way you successfully avoid the overwhelming feeling that can happen when you take on too much.

This is what I call *totality*. Water only boils at 100° degrees Celsius, not 99. Ninety-nine percent is not good enough. Today is the only time that exists anyway. The past and the future exist only in your imagination. So, do not compromise on today. If you can live this kind of life, then *chyros* will come knocking on your door, showing you the golden path.

Summary and Your "To Do" List

By striking that balance between the entrepreneurial drive of *making things* happen and the peaceful acceptance of *letting things* happen, you open yourself up to new, greater levels of possibility, not just as a coach but in every aspect of your life. Search for balance to become a better coach.

- **Expand your focus:** Don't limit your focus only to making things happen. That's only half of the story. Combine *making things* happen with *letting things* happen, also known as the law of attraction.

- **Let go:** Letting go of any attachment to a desired outcome is as powerful as it is important. Surrender the notion of control, and embrace the worst-case scenario. Be free first, then engage with the world.
- **Understand the law of resonance:** You attract into your life the things you are in resonance with. To be in resonance means you must completely regard it as true for you in your consciousness. Like attracts like. Make the idea of what you want true in your mind.
- **Open yourself to *chyros*:** *Chyros* is about time quality, having the necessary trust to allow things to happen at the right time without having to force them to happen. When you are open to *chyros*, you will notice opportunities you otherwise would have missed.

Emotional Intelligence

Boost Your EQ to Lead in Business and with Your Clients

RELLY NADLER

Dr. Relly Nadler is a licensed psychologist and Master Certified Coach (MCC) with the ICF. He has been coaching CEOs and their teams as well as training leaders and coaches in emotional intelligence strategies for more than twenty years. He has worked with the U.S. Navy, BMW, DreamWorks Animation, and Vanguard Healthcare and as a senior faculty member for a coaching school for fifteen years. He the author of *Leading with Emotional Intelligence*.

Emotional intelligence is increasingly recognized as the key factor in determining business success. As a coach, emotional intelligence can help you master the moment to avoid sabotaging your own success, and better lead your clients with empathy, insight, and compassion. In this chapter, you'll discover emotional intelligence tools to improve your performance as a coach.

Emotional intelligence is where empathy meets insight. It's your ability to understand and manage yourself, multiplied by your ability to understand and manage others. Corporations are increasingly realizing the essential role EQ—as opposed to just IQ—plays in business success.

Research shows organizations that emphasize emotional intelligence are three times as effective at leadership development as those who don't.[7] As a coach, you need emotional intelligence to *master the moment* and succeed not just with your clients, but also with yourself.

Prior to my time as a practicing psychologist, I was involved in leadership programs for young people, such as Outward Bound. Corporations became interested in the programs we were running, and I noticed a real need for leadership training that emphasized emotional intelligence in the corporate sector. Merging my passions for leadership training and psychology, I founded a solution-focused coaching practice. Since then, we've worked with individuals, CEOs, and presidents, as well as a wide range of organizations, including Anheuser-Busch, BMW, Anthem Health, and General Motors.

Emotional intelligence isn't important only for the corporate world. Emotional intelligence is essential for a coach in terms of your own self-development, as well as how you interact with your clients and partners. Emotions happen in a split second, and how you react in that moment can make the difference between a productive solution and a wasted opportunity.

In this chapter, we'll look at some simple emotional intelligence tools to help you boost your EQ and increase your success as a coach. We'll begin by looking at the first pillar of emotional intelligence—your awareness and understanding of yourself—before looking at applying emotional intelligence to your interactions with your clients and others.

MASTER THE MOMENT: EMOTIONAL INTELLIGENCE TO UNDERSTAND AND MANAGE YOURSELF

How are you feeling right now? Check your emotional thermostat. Emotions play a powerful role in our lives, our behaviors, and our decisions, yet we often let them run unchecked in the background. By learning how to understand our own patterns and triggers and then working to improve this understanding, we can significantly boost our own emotional intelligence. This will not only make you happier and less stressed but also wiser in business and more influential with your clients.

Your emotional state influences others. In the same sense that you can instantly notice it when your partner comes home stressed and this makes you uncomfortable, your coaching clients will also pick up on the signals that you send to them. In the coaching environment, they look to you for leadership and in less than a second they decide if they can trust you. If you're hoping to close a potential new coaching deal but your emotional signals are off-putting to the potential client, they are unlikely to trust you or feel good about working with you.

To manage your emotions, it helps first to improve your **self-talk** so you can face the world with a baseline of positivity.

Self-Talk: Managing Your Internal Google Search

We all constantly talk to ourselves in our heads, thousands of times a day. The trouble is, most people have *negative* self-talk. They judge themselves, self-criticize, and punish themselves for mistakes. By filling your mind with negative self-talk, you're that much more on edge, and that much more likely to fall into a negative emotional state.

Negative self-talk results from judging ourselves too harshly. We ask things like, "How could I be so stupid?" "Why did I blow it with that client?" "When am I finally going to get my business together?" These questions run in our minds like an internal Google search. If you Google "cats," you're going to get results about cats. Likewise, if you unconsciously tell your mind to search for *negative things* about you, you're going to find them, and believe them.

Instead of searching for negative things, be more intentional. Program your internal Google search to provide you with more positive self-talk. If something goes wrong with a client, don't ask, "Why do I always blow it!" Instead, think: "What can I learn from this?" "How can I grow and do better next time?" You want to turn the beatings in learnings. This way your mind will search for solutions, not problems.

It takes practice and time, but when your head is full of positive self-talk instead of judgment and criticism, you'll have much more creativity and energy to face the world. Be on your own side, not on your case! Use the daily sentences percolating in your head to direct the incredible resources of your mind toward your own growth and development, instead of engaging in negative judgments that can rule your thoughts.

The Emotional Hijack: Managing Your Triggers

The most dangerous way emotions can undermine your success as a coach is through a lack of impulse control. When was the last time you lost it and reacted out of anger with your family, with a client, or with a business partner? Did your emotional reaction solve your problem and improve the situation? Chances are, it didn't.

When we start reacting with anger, the part of our brain known as the amygdala takes over. Instead of the rational intelligence of the prefrontal cortex, the amygdala asserts what's known as privileged position. This means that we react out of instinct, out of fear instead of rationality.

These situations when your amygdala takes over are called the *emotional hijack*. During these moments, we are significantly less intelligent than normal: Your prefrontal cortex is out to lunch temporarily, taking a heavy chunk of your IQ points with it. Instead of "consider, evaluate, decide," it's the four Fs: fight, flight, faint, or freeze.

To bring back these lost IQ points and act intelligently, even when surprised or under stress, I teach my clients to perform an emotional audit. This process helps you wrest back control from your amygdala and reassert your rational mind.

The Emotional Audit

Think of the last situation in which you were irritated or angry. It could have been when you were dealing with a difficult client or a demanding business partner. Imagine yourself in that situation, and run through these five strategic questions below:

1. "What am I thinking?'"
   The most important step toward reasserting rational control over yourself is *awareness*. This question immediately helps get you out of your emotions and into your head. Notice your self-talk, your opinions. It's fine if it's negative—just be aware, don't judge.

2. "What am I feeling?"

    These first two questions will help reveal your patterns. Asking your-self this question brings your emotional state into conscious focus. It helps you understand exactly what's going on in the moment and become aware of your own triggers. All of this can happen in just a few seconds.

3. "What do I want now?"

    In the same way that you learned to change your self-talk by asking positive questions instead of negative ones, this question immediately begins to shift your focus. You're already aware of what you *don't want*, the trigger that caused you to feel this way. Now it's time to focus on what you *do* want. A prompt end to the meeting? The client to understand your point of view? Be clear about the positive end you wish to achieve.

4. "How am I getting in my own way now?"

    Now that you're aware of your thoughts and feelings, you can start to notice how this affects your behavior. Is your voice raised? Are you pacing? In what way is your behavior betraying your emotions? This question will help reveal your patterns.

5. "What do I do now?"

    Now that you have all this information, how can you be more inten-tional? With your prefrontal cortex back in the room and the hijack over, what do you do now? Perhaps you could calmly redirect atten-tion to the goal of the conversation, or carefully explain to the client the benefits of the solution you are proposing.

Understand Your Triggers: What Sets You Off?

By allowing yourself to be hijacked emotionally, you haven't mastered the moment. You have destroyed the moment. In less than five seconds, you could have lost all your credibility with an existing client, or sabotaged your chances of forming a new and profitable business relationship. The emotional audit helps you rescue yourself from the brink of chaos. Knowing your triggers helps you prepare so that next time you're able to prevent the hijack before it begins.

Think back to the example you used in the exercise above. Remember the trigger that set you off. Now try to remember other situations in which you have acted out of emotion and suffered negative consequences. Think about the triggers in those situations. Was it the way someone spoke to you? A particular business problem that drives you crazy? An attitude or opinion that always gets you going?

Be aware of this pattern within yourself, and practice going through the emotional audit in your mind, remembering past situations. Imagine yourself handling those past instances better. Think about what you should have done, and practice more-positive resolutions. This helps you train yourself to automatically respond to triggers in a healthier, productive manner.

Managing your self-talk and preventing "emotional hijacks" takes you a long way toward boosting your personal emotional intelligence. Now let's focus on the second pillar of emotional intelligence: how you work with others.

Master the Meeting: Emotional Intelligence to Understand and Manage Others

Interacting with others in an emotionally intelligent way gives you a tremendous advantage as a coach. You'll be able to act more sensitively while helping clients effectively overcome problems. You'll be able to form business relationships by leading others strategically. The first step toward managing others is simply to manage yourself, as you learned in the section above.

Your emotions have a profound influence on those around you, particularly those with whom you occupy a position of trust or authority, like your clients. By managing your own emotions *first*, you've already made huge progress toward improving your relationships.

Developing the emotional intelligence to manage yourself is about understanding your self-talk and your triggers. Developing the emotional intelligence to manage others also begins with *understanding*. When it comes to the emotions of others, this understanding is known as *empathy*.

The Empathy Audit: A Quick Way to Get Inside the Feelings of Someone Else

Before beginning your next coaching session or meeting with a potential client, take a moment and go through the same five questions you learned for the emotional audit above. This time, however, instead of making the questions about you, make it about *them*. This will give you quick yet profound insight into how they are feeling in the moment, helping you better connect with and lead them. Let's run through this:

1. "What are *they* thinking?"
   They've just walked into your office for a coaching session. Put yourself in their position, and imagine what might be going on in their head.
2. "What are they feeling?"
   Are they likely to be nervous, stressed, excited?
3. "What do they want now?"
   Understanding someone's motivation in any given situation is essential for leading them toward a desired outcome. Why are they there? What are they hoping to achieve?
4. "How are they getting in their own way?"
   They're coming to see you because they have some kind of problem they cannot solve on their own. Think about how their behavior may be sabotaging their own success, and what you can do to help.
5. "What do they do now?"
   Because of your interaction and coaching with them and the help you're about to provide, how will they behave differently?

The empathy audit won't provide you with as much information as the emotional audit—after all, you're just guessing, really. Don't use this to form concrete conclusions, because the *data* you gain later may contradict this. Instead, use this guessing phase to help orient yourself away from your own mind and toward theirs. When it comes to interacting with others, the bedrock of emotional intelligence is your ability to *understand and empathize*. This exercise helps you kick-start the process of developing empathy.

Empty the Bucket Before Giving Advice

Many of us become coaches because we like giving advice. We've spent years studying and learning and have developed amazing strategies for achieving success, and we want to share this with others right out of the gate. Emotional intelligence shows us that before people are ready to receive advice—even good advice—they must first empty their own solutions.

Imagine that each of your clients has a bucket full of ideas, thoughts, and feelings. You also have a bucket full of advice, wisdom, and practical steps for them to take to improve their lives. But before you can pour your ideas into their bucket, you first need to create some room. You have to empty their bucket. Before you fill their bucket, take the time to *ask and drain* before you tell and fill. Let them talk, without interruption, until they've exhausted everything they came there to say.

Another phrase I use to describe this process is *connect before you direct*. Begin your conversation by checking in with them. Ask open questions, and pay attention to the information they provide to you. Are their eyes red from crying? Do they look tired? What are they particularly hesitant about saying? Use the data they are providing to confirm or correct the guesses you made when you completed the empathy audit. Think about what you're learning about them, and how you can use this information to better lead and help.

Stay in Their Story

A good coach SITS more than talks. SITS stands for "*Stay in Their Story.*"

As they're emptying their bucket, you have a great opportunity to truly enhance your understanding of them and their situation. Most people don't really listen. They ask questions but are actually looking for opportunities to jump in and offer advice or opinion. Instead of listening *with intent to reply*, practice *truly* listening.

I tell my corporate training groups, "No one knows you SEE their perspective until you SAY their perspective." As your client is talking, pay attention to the key emotional words they use to express their feelings, the words that really jump out at you. I call these *blinking words*. For example, they may say, "I'm really *upset* about this situation." Feed those blinking words back to them to let them know they are being heard and understood: "I can understand how *upsetting* that must be."

The key to staying in their story is to be truly curious about them and their situation. Understanding, as I've said earlier, is the essence of emotional intelligence, and curiosity is the gateway to understanding. Be genuinely interested in their situation, and ask meaningful questions that allow them to go deeper into what they are saying.

Don't let an interesting comment hang in the air. When a blinking word jumps out at you, feed this word back to them in the form of a question that doubles down and allows them to reveal more: "I can understand how *upsetting* that situation must be for you; you've really been working hard on this. What are you thinking of doing now?"

Allow them to talk, and listen sincerely and with curiosity until they have fully exhausted their story. Only once their bucket is empty can you jump in and start filling it up again with your ideas, suggestions, and stories from your own perspective. By this time, thanks to the empathy audit and the data they have provided to you, you will be able to more intelligently assess their situation and offer advice that really hits the spot and helps them move forward.

Summary and Your "To Do" List

In this chapter, we've looked at a series of techniques and principles to help you increase your emotional intelligence and be more effective as a leader in business and with your coaching clients. Increasing your emotional intelligence can help you master the moment to avoid sabotaging your own success, while empowering you to better lead your clients with empathy, insight, and compassion. Emotional intelligence is something you have, not just something you do.

- **Improve your self-talk:** Reprogram your internal Google search by training your mind to search for solutions, not problems. Ask yourself, "What can I learn from this? How can I grow and do better next time?"

- **Understand your own triggers:** Avoid the emotional hijack and rescue yourself from chaos by performing an emotional audit to reassert your rational mind.
- **Practice your emotional and empathy audits:** Ask the five strategic questions, first of yourself and then of your clients (What am I thinking? What am I feeling? What do I want? How am I getting in my own way now? What do I do now?)
- **Connect before you direct:** By staying in your client's story, you allow them to "empty the bucket." This helps you gain meaningful data, and it prepares them to be receptive to the advice you have to offer.
- **Practice your techniques:** Emotional intelligence isn't something you do, it's something you have. Practice these techniques and principles until they become second nature, and you'll find that people are receptive to your ideas, you're calmer and focused, and you're able to make a bigger difference as a coach.

Self-Mastery

7 Critical Areas Where You Can Grow Yourself to Grow Your Business

DAVID TAYLOR-KLAUS

David Taylor-Klaus cofounded an internet strategy and web development firm back in the earliest days of the internet reinventing himself and the company multiple times before discovering coaching in 2008. David is an accredited International Coach Federation Professional Certified Coach (PCC), a Certified Professional Co-active Coach (CPCC), one of the first to become a Certified Team Performance Coach (CTPC), and a Certified Conversational Intelligence Coach (CC-IQC).

Before you can do your work in the world, you have to do some work on yourself. From the way you think about money to the way you schedule your calendar, David Taylor-Klaus identifies the seven critical areas of self-mastery.

Entrepreneur and author Jim Rohn said, "The key to becoming successful is to work harder on yourself than on your business." To grow your business, find balance in your life, and help your clients grow and succeed, you must work on yourself *first*. Along my journey, I've noticed a dramatic leap in my business performance every time I've made progress in my own self-development.

About a dozen years ago, I was in a downward spiral. I knew that if I didn't change something, there was only so much further I could fall. In 2005, I was almost literally standing on a bridge, about to lose everything, when I chose that point as my rock bottom. I decided I wasn't going to let myself fall any lower. I declared to myself that it was time for a change. I was going to do the work, get clear, get focused, and turn my life around.

As I gained clarity on what I wanted from life and pulled together the resources and support systems to make it happen, I became aware of how common it is for people to wait until they hit rock bottom, until they've lost everything, before they make a change. I wanted to help people make that change *sooner*—before they lost connections with family, with community, and with their purpose.

With this powerful "why" in mind and clarity on what I wanted, I quickly built my coaching practice to over six figures in revenue. I felt like I was in a groove. But this groove turned into a rut. My business grew stagnant because I had stopped moving forward myself. It was time to do the work on myself again. I started embracing the idea that *achieving more requires becoming more.* This is what really allowed me to thrive—and has kept me moving forward ever since.

When you do the work of mastering yourself, you are better suited to do your work out in the world. Through my years of work as a coach, I have found there are seven areas that hold the key to growing into yourself and thriving, both as a coach *and* in your life. While they are in no particular order, the acronym MASTERY is an apt reminder:

Money

Alignment

Support

Time

Energy

Resources

Yourself

As we examine each of these seven areas in detail, I'll share the tips and discoveries that will empower you to thrive as an individual, a parent, a spouse, a community member—and a coach.

MONEY: FOCUS ON THE **WHY**, NOT THE **WHAT**

People have the concept of work-life balance backward. When did it become okay to put work first?! That simple language choice is the mistake that reveals the institutionally misaligned priorities.

Yet people do it all the time because they're not aware of the difference they want to make in the world. So, they tend to measure their goals in terms of dollars. Here's the catch: We're not on this planet to make money. Money is not the most important thing, but it touches everything that is. We make money to pay for the life we want to live.

Mastering money is about designing the life you want and then architecting your *business* to support that *life*. Yes, intentionally designing your life comes first. When people aren't clear about what they want, they default to thinking about money. When we're not clear on our "why," we default to replacing it with a "what."

Defining Your Life Like a CEO

To gain clarity and get the order right—life first, and then work for balance—the first question you need to ask is: *What do you want your life to look like?* Choose a point six or seven years in the future and build a clear, resonant picture of what you want your life to look like. There are three aspects to this, and it helps to think about it in terms of seeing yourself as the CEO of your life: the Cultural, Emotional, and Operational aspects of your life.

The Operational side is the one we all tend to focus on much of the time. This is what you're doing and how you're doing it. Where you work, what you do in the office, the day-to-day activity of your life. The Emotional field is about how you're feeling and not feeling, the emotions that are being triggered, the ethos of what you want to create and how it shows up for you. The Cultural side speaks to the people with whom you associate.

Once you've imagined the Cultural, Emotional, and Operational aspects of how you want your life to be, then you can turn your attention to the financial side. The question becomes: What does your business need to be generating in order for you to be able to live the life you've imagined?

At this point, it becomes much easier for you to identify what you want to earn because now you know what you're earning it for.

Having an income doesn't make you successful. Having an income that supports you living the life you want to live—*that's* success.

ALIGNMENT: BUILD A BUSINESS THAT SUPPORTS YOUR CORE VALUES

Happiness and success come when you build a business that supports your core values. I recently struggled in this area after following some advice given to me by an old mentor, advice that was out of sync with my values. I was so focused on growing my business and making it bigger that I lost touch with what was important to me, the impact that I was having, and the impact I wanted to continue to have. It took some time for me to notice what had happened and correct my course.

My original mission as a coach was to work with successful entrepreneurs and reintroduce them to their families. My mentor persuaded me to start a second area of my business marketing to "wannapreneurs" and "prepreneurs"—people in that early, scrappy, scarcity-driven phase of building a business. I had been there in previous businesses, and I knew that it has a tendency to be a hellacious, toxic place. Reaching out to and working with struggling entrepreneurs did fit my value of being of service. But reconnecting with those unpleasant ways of feeling and living required a tremendous amount of self-management and consumed a huge amount of energy, so it did not fit my value of self-care.

This shift to focusing on an audience that was out of sync with my values not only failed, it had a toxic impact on my existing market. By following someone else's values instead of my own, I had done real damage to myself and my business. It took me two years to build my business back to the level of trust and congruence that it once had. On the upside, I gained clarity, along with a deeper understanding of my own values and stronger commitment to them.

The key here is personal focus, staying in touch with what you truly know and doing what feels right to you. There's a Swahili expression, "Pole, pole" (*poh-lay, poh-lay*). It means *Slow, slow*. The message is that oftentimes you need to slow down to speed up. The race to get to your next milestone can blind you to your values and distract you from your intuition. Instead, work with your coaches, your mentors, and your colleagues to get clarification and feedback. Communicate what your values are to others, and this will help you clarify them for yourself.

Be accountable to your action steps, but also be accountable to yourself, to your core. As coaches, we lead our clients through processes to help them find their values and purpose, but all too often we forget to do (or skip doing) this work on ourselves. When you do the work, you'll experience a tremendous leap of clarity, insight, and momentum.

SUPPORT: BUILD A TEAM AND LEARN TO DELEGATE

Building a team requires a tremendous amount of trust. Many of us are guilty of thinking, "It takes longer to explain it than to do it myself," or, "If I want it done properly, I have to do it myself." The fact is, you can't do everything yourself, and you shouldn't try. The superhero cape won't fit. If you want to grow, you have to scale your business. Define the needs you have, find the right people, share your vision, teach them the current processes, and trust them to take some of the work off your shoulders—and even to make the work better.

I have many examples of learning this lesson the hard way. I have thirty years of marketing experience, so I thought I could make my own website for my coaching practice. In the end, I spent so much time playing with the website that I was neglecting other, more important areas—like talking to clients. As a leader, I had to learn to focus on that which only I can do and delegate the rest.

Nearly two decades ago, I was advised by my business coaching group that the first thing I should do is hire an assistant. I thought, "But this is a non-revenue-generating position—no way!" I held on to that opinion with a death grip. Later I learned better. For my current business, I hired an assistant early on, and it was one of the best decisions I've made.

In a perfect world, we'd all function like Frank Sinatra. He walked on stage, picked up the mic, and sang. That's it. He did only that for which he was uniquely qualified. He didn't book stadiums. He didn't print tickets. He didn't do the books. He didn't market. He didn't play the drums. He *sang*, and he did it better than anyone else could have done. You're a coach. So *coach*. Identify those who are uniquely suited to help you take care of the rest, and let them do it.

Time It Right

Hire a team before you're overwhelmed, but only when you have the cash flow and liquidity to be able to pay them. Your first hire is probably not going to be a full-time employee. A great solution is to begin with a virtual assistant. This person can work for you for just five or ten hours a week, at hourly rates much lower than you might expect. As your business grows, you can gradually scale up their hours, until you're ready to bring someone on full-time.

It takes time to hire and train your new employees. The employee onboarding process is where most entrepreneurs—and for that matter most companies—fail. The more time you put into training your team, the higher the chances of success, theirs and yours.

Action Step:

Ask yourself these questions:

- What are you doing that you should be delegating?
- What are you holding on to that is keeping you from having the impact and the expanded business that you want?

TIME: YOUR CALENDAR REVEALS YOUR PRIORITIES

Your calendar will give away your secrets. It tells what you're prioritizing. The growth edge here is congruency: Are the things that you're prioritizing (the things on your calendar) congruent with your values and goals?

Your calendar never lies. If you value sleep, but you book things late in the evening and early in the morning, then your calendar will reveal your inconsistency. If you say that exercise is important, but you're not scheduling any time for it, then your calendar will reflect your true intention. If you say that family is important, but you aren't blocking out time in the morning to drive your kids to school or time for family dinner (or whatever it would look like for you), then your calendar may be revealing an uncomfortable truth about what you're making a priority—or not.

You may say one thing to yourself about your values and your priorities, but is it consistent with the way you spend your time? If it's truly important to you, schedule it. As author, speaker, and motivator Stephen Covey says, "How different our lives are when we really know what is deeply important to us, and keeping that picture in mind, we manage ourselves each day to be and to do what really matters most."

Work on Your Business, Not Just in Your Business

This is really about life-work integration, about carving out time for working *on* your business as well as working *in* your business.

When you're working in the business, you're working with your clients, you're close to the issues, and you're thinking tactically. It's absolutely essential for the health of your business. But if it's all you're doing, it's incomplete.

You also need to make sure you're creating time to work the business, to think strategically and creatively. Structure time for planning, for clarifying your priorities, and for ensuring that your schedule reflects them. You should place time for working on your business on your calendar every week to avoid getting stuck in the weeds. This structure will provide support and growth in all areas of your life.

I recall once looking at my calendar and noticing that 90 percent of it was work-related—and I wondered why I had no social life! You have to block out chunks of time based on the priorities of you and your company. Now, my regularly scheduled clients are all stacked on Tuesdays, Wednesdays, and Thursdays, before 3:00 P.M. This means that Mondays, Fridays, and afternoons are set aside for working *on* the business, not just *in* it.

Not everyone's schedule goes perfectly, and you still need some flexibility, but I know that I have time for marketing, personal issues, and team building. I keep my schedule clear and consistent so I can manage my time and my energy throughout the day and throughout the week.

ENERGY: FUEL YOURSELF TO HAVE AN IMPACT

The first three things that an entrepreneur loses are sleep, exercise, and something that feeds you, that nurtures your soul. Once you lose these things, your energy plummets and you thwart your ability to work effectively. The key here is self-care: You can't give what you don't have. Do the things that regulate your brain and fuel your body so that you can deliver on your promise to your clients and the world. Let's dive into each of these.

Sleep. The sleep issue befuddles most people. It's not just about the number of hours you sleep, it's about your sleep quality. One of the best ways to improve your sleep quality is to establish a consistent routine. This means going to sleep at the same time every night, and waking up at the same time in the morning. By honoring the way your body is designed to work, you sleep better, and when you sleep better, your brain works better. It's better to get the same seven hours of sleep every night than six hours one night, eight the next, five the next, or trying to "catch up" on weekends. Getting into that consistent same-time-down-and-same-time-up routine is food for your brain.

The concept is simple. Putting it into practice can be, too. It takes five simple steps: commit, calendar, communicate, collaborate, celebrate.

Commit: make the decision. Nothing will change until you do. Calendar: block out time for sleep on your calendar. Communicate: share the commitment out loud. Making it public will make it real. Collaborate: recruit an accountability partner. For those of you who share your bed, enroll your partner. Help each other and share the benefits. For those of you who don't have a regular bedmate, enroll a friend. I've even seen people use their social media communities to hold them accountable. Celebrate: acknowledge and mark each of your wins. Success breeds success.

Exercise. We're not built to be sedentary, even though we tend to be. Our daily lives no longer require the activity levels they once did. We sit behind a desk instead of running in pursuit of food. You have to choose to exercise and set aside time for it, and it's not always an inviting choice. We think that exercise costs energy when, over the long term, it provides energy. I had a bike accident a couple years ago and had to go almost nine months without my chosen form of exercise, which made it particularly difficult to choose to engage at all. The loss in energy and focus—and the toll it took on my mood (and my relationships)—was noticeable to me and to my whole family.

Use the exact same steps I shared for shifting to a better sleep pattern (commit, calendar, communicate, collaborate, celebrate) to integrate exercise.

Something that feeds you. Find something that nourishes your soul. It doesn't matter whether it's a hobby, spiritual practice, meditation, or healthy cooking. Your brain is a machine that runs off the fuel you give it, and that goes beyond the physical to the metaphysical. Pay attention to what makes you feel grounded, solid, and centered. Make sure there's something in your life that brings you joy, that fills your cup, that brings you satisfaction and fulfillment.

Do the things that give you energy, so you can create the shift you're here to create.

RESOURCES: SURROUND YOURSELF WITH THE RIGHT PEOPLE

Your resources are all the people in your life who support you or challenge you constructively. This includes your coaches, your mentors, your colleagues. It's about making sure that you're connected to community. It's like developing a human resources strategy for your own life.

The key to effective use of resources is thinking in terms of lifelong learning. We are never done. We are always in progress. As long as you have a pulse, you still have time to learn, to create, or to redefine your world. If you don't keep feeding yourself, you'll stagnate.

Your resources are the people you surround yourself with—the people who inspire you and make you want to grow. Former President Theodore Roosevelt said, "Comparison is the thief of joy." Don't compare yourself to others; rather, compare yourself today with who you were yesterday. As Ernest Hemingway put it, "There is nothing noble in being superior to your fellow man; true nobility is being superior to your former self."

You never want to be the smartest person in the room. When you are, you won't learn anything. The greatest thought leaders and experts know that there's always more to learn, there's always room to grow. There's *always* something to work on with a coach. There's always something to make yourself better. You want to constantly challenge yourself through the people who surround you.

In personal relationships, I've noticed a phenomenon with coaches that I call the "falling away." As coaches advance, some of the people who have been in their lives begin to fall away. It's a kind of natural attrition. As coaches spend time among others who are growing, learning, and raising the bar, the cast of characters in their personal world can get smaller. They seek out others who are actively engaged in personal development, and they may find it difficult to connect to those who are not similarly engaged in personal growth.

This makes it more important to seek out community, to connect consciously, and to be intentional about whom you surround yourself with. Remember, as your world changes inside, it also changes outside.

YOURSELF: INTEGRATE YOUR INTERNAL VOICES

We all have a chorus of voices in our head, and our challenge is to harness the full constellation of these internal messages and use them to our full advantage. There is something positive available even in the most negative of voices, and if we dismiss them, ignore them, or silence them, we risk losing their gift.

All of us have our gremlins, or saboteurs—those internal voices that criticize, condemn, and derail us. If anyone ever spoke to my children the way my inner voice sometimes speaks to me, wow, I would be furious! Before we experience coaching, many of us tend to hear those voices and believe the lies we tell ourselves.

But those inner voices are part of who we are. Our job isn't to silence them, it's to be in relationship with them, even though 98 percent of what they say is garbage. The trick is to look for the 2 percent of truth. I tend to think of saboteurs as misguided angels. While their messages can stop us in our tracks, their intention is to be helpful in some way. The challenge is to find the gift.

Getting into a relationship with those little voices requires you to dig for pearls of truth. If I'm about to give a talk and my internal voices are screaming, "You have no idea what you're doing; who's going to listen to you?" I have two choices. I can listen to the saboteur and shrink back from the opportunity to have impact. Or I can reframe and look for the saboteur's accidental gift. I can use that as a reminder to stay on message, to be clear, to come from a place where I focus on what I want for the audience. Instead of believing the negative chatter, I can choose to keep my focus on the shift I want to create. Those negative voices can either knock you off track, or they can remind you of what really matters. It's up to you.

The key here is integration—for coaches to do your own work to integrate your chorus of voices, supportive and otherwise. You're a much more powerful, formidable coach when you are in active relationship with all of yourself. When you bring everything together, you bring a lot more power to face the world. Get clear on who and what your saboteurs are, and know the difference between meaningless criticism and helpful awareness. Listen to the positive voices that are reassuring, helpful, and connecting. Sometimes it can be much harder for us to hear the positive voices over the negative. When you integrate everything, when you listen closely to the real truth of the messages, the value begins to shine through.

"Tell me, what is it you plan to do with your one wild and precious life?"

~ Mary Oliver, *The Summer Day*

Summary and Your "To Do" List

You can achieve MASTERY by being in a relationship with all of who you are. When you make progress in any one of the seven key areas, your business will manifest the reward. Do the work on yourself so you can do your work in the world.

- **(Money) Build a picture:** Build a clear, resonant picture of what you want your life to look like six or seven years in the future. See yourself as the CEO, where you control the **C**ultural, **E**motional, and **O**perational aspects of your life.
- **(Alignment) Support your core values:** Stay in touch with what you truly know and what feels right to you. Communicate your values to others to help clarify them for yourself.
- **(Support) Build a team and delegate:** You can't do everything yourself, and you shouldn't try. Define the needs you have, find the right people, share your vision, teach them the current processes, and trust them to take some of the work off your shoulders.

- **(Time) Schedule what's important:** Your calendar never lies. What is yours saying about you? Schedule what is truly important to you. Carve out time to work *on* your business as well as *in* your business.

- **(Energy) Regulate your brain and fuel your body:** Find a consistent sleep routine that provides sleep quality. Choose to exercise and set aside time for it. Find something that nourishes your soul (spirituality, meditation, nourishing food, etc.). Pay attention to what makes you feel solid and grounded.

- **(Resources) Seek out your support:** Think in terms of being a lifelong learner, and surround yourself with the right people— smart people who inspire you and make you grow.

- **(Yourself) Integrate those internal voices:** Dig for the pearls of truth behind all that noise in your head. Reframe negative thoughts and ideas in a way that provides you focus, clarity, or confidence.

The Passionate Coach

Tap into Passion to Increase Your Influence, Stay Focused, and Build a Business You Love

SAM MARKEWICH

Sam Markewich is a psychotherapist turned business coach who works with small businesses and entrepreneurs in Vermont. Throughout his career, Sam has discovered that durable success can be created only out of passion and purpose. With his clients, he focuses on showing up with integrity and helping them succeed and grow by designing all their actions based on a set of meaningful core values.

All the business strategies and techniques in the world won't help you if you don't have passion for your clients and your business. Learn how to deliver unique value, grow your business with excitement and focus, and find a community that you can serve with passion.

The key to delivering unique value to your community is *passion*. There are a lot of business techniques and words of advice out there. A lot of it is great. But nothing will work for you if you do not show up every day with passion and purpose.

My business plan starts with integrity, and I believe I'm successful because I'm constantly committed to delivering unique value to my community. You cannot be the best coach in the world to everyone, but you can find a specific community of people that you can help in a way no one else can. This is how you'll build a coaching business that you love and become a critical part of a community you value.

As a kid, I had challenges that stopped me from doing many of the things I wanted to do. As an adult, I've set out to make up for what I missed, to prove to myself that *there are no limits*. One of the most important lessons I learned was that, while there are people who will help you and support you on your journey, ultimately success or failure comes down to you.

I learned this lesson when I got meningitis at the age of five and had to spend three months in a hospital room that looked out over a local cemetery. At that young age, I had to stare at my own mortality every day, and I was scared. Although I had the love of my family and a team of doctors looking after me, I came to realize that my inner survival was make or break.

No matter how many others were by my side rooting for and helping me, my attitude and drive to thrive was my responsibility, and mine alone. I took this lesson with me into adulthood and became a psychotherapist so I could help others find strength and enrich their own lives.

Several years ago I was on an endurance bike ride around the hills of the San Francisco Bay. I'd set the huge goal of conquering the 14 steepest hills in the area. It was a 65-mile journey, with 14,500 feet of climbing on a bike loaded with gear that weighed 85 pounds—all in one day. The expansive feeling that this challenge gave me was something I wanted to have in my life every single day.

As I was biking the hills, it clicked: I didn't just want to help people overcome problems, I wanted to empower them to go further and achieve their dreams. I wanted to partner with people and help them push the boundaries and do big things. I closed my psychotherapy practice and set about finding a community I could serve with passion. This is how I became a business coach.

In this chapter, we'll look at how to find a community you can serve with passion, and how you can discover your voice as a coach to deliver unique value, stay energized, and build a coaching business you love.

FINDING A COMMUNITY YOU CAN
SERVE WITH PASSION

Trying to be something to everyone will quickly make you lose your core sense of self. Instead of spreading yourself thin, find one community you can serve with passion, and love it as much as you love your spouse, your child, your god, or whomever it is that you love the most.

The community I live to serve is small business owners who operate according to my personal sense of ethics. We're a great match, but I didn't stumble into this by accident. Discovering the community I wanted to serve was a long process. To figure it out, I had to figure out what I wanted to do every day and find a way I could stay excited and passionate 365 days a year.

The Ultimate Challenge Question

Before I could find the community I wanted to serve as a coach, I spent a long time dabbling in different fields. I tried fitness coaching, health coaching, mindfulness coaching for depression. Noble work though it may have been, none of this felt complete or challenging enough to me. It wasn't difficult and ever-expansive enough. It wasn't *evolutionary* for me.

I found that I was being pulled into other people's coaching styles because my passion was insufficiently tapped. I wanted to be able to show up *as myself* and coach people in that ideal meeting place of my passion and the unique needs of the community I love.

It took time to get there. I did a lot of inner exploring. I got coaches of my own. Eventually, I settled on the most important question: *"What is the ultimate challenge I can tackle as a coach?"*

For me, this is coaching small businesses and entrepreneurs. I know how hard it is to build something from the ground up. It's sink or swim. People won't stop you from failing in business—it's all on you. And growth in business can go as far as you as a business owner and your team can take it. I *love* a challenge that sits on an infinite curve. I wanted to be there for small business owners and help them succeed as far along that curve as their dreams would take them. So I became a business coach.

Action Step: What Is Your Ultimate Challenge?

Instead of chasing the money as a coach, reorient yourself so that you are chasing your *passion*. I realized what motivates me the most while riding my bike over the hills in San Francisco, and I discovered my community after many months of reflection and experimentation.

Ask yourself, "What is the biggest challenge I can take on as a coach?" Focus on what you find inspiring, motivating, and, yes, maybe a little scary. Then show up, and be there for the people in that community.

Forming Relationships Inside Your Community

When you've decided upon the community you want to serve as a coach, show up with the intention of *adding value*. Form deep connections with the goal of helping people to achieve their goals. Talk about *them*, not *you*. Discover their challenges and their fears.

The most effective way of forming a connection and leading it into a coaching relationship is simple. Just say, "Hey, I'd like to find out more about you and how I can help you. Shall we meet up for coffee (or on Skype)?" That, and deeply caring, is really all there is to it.

You won't form meaningful relationships unless you stay *focused*. At the start of your coaching career, it's tempting to say yes to everyone and coach anyone who will have you. To really succeed, you must focus and be the No. 1 person to *one* community. My business works because I have a very small number of highly motivated clients. I can make a real impact in these people's lives, and this keeps me passionate about them.

Know the kind of people you want to work with, and *say no to everyone else*. It will be hard at first, especially when you're building your business and struggling to make ends meet, but it will pay off. Say no until your tongue bleeds, and then *keep saying no!* The value you have is going to be essential only to a small group of people. Show up for the few people you can truly be passionate about, and give them something unique. For everyone else, *say no!*

The Concept in Practice

Succeeding as a coach is about finding the community you can serve with passion. This community is likely to be in a field that challenges you to bring in everything you have. For me, the community is small business owners who operate with integrity. Your community could be centered around fitness and health, or entrepreneurship, or technology, or leadership, or anything at all where there's a group of people who share a common interest and whom you have the skill and desire to help.

Once you have found your community, focus on them to the exclusion of everything else. Say no to anyone who does not meet your criteria. You need to be there 100 percent for the people who matter to you, and you can't do that if you say yes to everyone who shows up at your practice.

FINDING YOUR VOICE AS A COACH

Once you've found a community you're passionate about, the next step is to figure out how to serve it in a way that no one else can.

You can't provide unique value until you know how your community is already being served. Get out there, ask around, and do some research. When I decided to become a coach to the small business community, I took all the money I had in savings and spent it on business coaching from a number of different coaches—from the "gurus" all the way down to the "little guys." I had to become a client and look out into the world to see what was already there. With this information and firsthand experience, I could decide what *unique* value I could offer the field.

Look at the Value You've Already Contributed

Finding your unique value as a coach is about two things:

1. Finding out what is already out there in the community so you can discover a gap the community wants filled
2. Looking at the impact *you have already had* on your community or your other clients, so you can realize your unique value as a coach

To discover the impact you have already had on your clients requires a combination of what I call the *asking self* and the *observing self*. The observing self looks out into the community and at your existing clients, noticing the changes they are enjoying because of your work. The *asking self* challenges you to go deeper by deliberately searching for the ways in which your coaching has been of value, as well as where your integrity requires you to improve.

The Three Questions

If you already have coaching clients, or if there are people connected to your community you have already helped in any way, create an opportunity to ask them these three questions. The answers will help you get a clear sense of the *unique value* that you can provide, as well as where you need to improve. Once you're aware of this, you'll be able to approach your chosen community with more focus and greater confidence.

1. How was your time working with me?
2. Was there anything you did not like and would not want me to do again?
3. Was there anything I could have done to make this a more useful experience for you?

Ask these question to your clients at the end of every coaching session, coaching group, retreat, workshop, mastermind, or speaking engagement that you offer. You will get valuable feedback about the kind of impact you have as a coach.

It may feel scary to make yourself vulnerable to feedback from others. But as a coach, you are asking your clients to be vulnerable, and you must model what you ask if you wish for your clients to achieve the phenomenal results that coaching is about. It may sound cheesy, but it's true: *Integrity always starts with I.*

The Concept in Practice

Delivering unique value to your community requires you to know what's already out there—and to be aware of the ways in which your work as a coach most helps your clients.

Use the three questions above to get a better sense of your usefulness and the ways in which your work best serves the clients you already have. Be willing to *become a client* and experience the other options in your market firsthand. That way, you'll know how your community is currently being served, and you can recognize any gaps that need to be filled.

Take feedback in. Be honest with yourself. Always strive to do better—and *do* better. Be the authentic self that your community needs you to be.

GROWING YOUR BUSINESS WITH PASSION

If you're a coach, then chances are there's also an entrepreneur in you somewhere. Many coaches fail at the business side because while they're passionate about coaching, they are not passionate about *business*. Finding a community you love to serve and to whom you have something unique to offer makes the business side much more fulfilling.

Running your business means you have more opportunities to show up and serve your community, so you can therefore be as passionate about *business* as you are about *coaching*!

Creating a Business Plan that Actually Works

Growing a business requires concrete, reality-based actions that you will do *every day*. It's all very well to create a business plan, but you need *passion* to excitedly show up and execute this plan each and every working day of your life. If you've learned your business plan from somebody else, and you're not excited about the actions that you have to take, then you *will not do them consistently!*

There's no way I would have pedaled up those fourteen huge hills on such a heavy bike if I wasn't passionate about cycling *uphill*. Growing a business is hard work, and it takes two to five years before most small business owners can even pay themselves a salary. Therefore, if you aren't passionate, you are not going to succeed.

You absolutely can earn six or seven figures as a coach. But the truth is that it's not likely to happen right away. You have to stay firmly planted in the driver's seat, eyes fixed on the lane you want to take, foot on the accelerator. Yes, you need a great support team, but no one on it will ever be the one behind the wheel. You are the driver of your own destiny!

Check in with yourself, and create a simple, action-focused business plan that you will love to "drive off the lot" and keep on driving forward. Don't give yourself a hundred tasks to do every day. Instead, focus on just two or three high-impact things you can do, things that are consistent with your values and your passion.

If you hate marketing online, then don't force yourself to do thirty Twitter updates every day! You may prefer face-to-face marketing approaches, such as public speaking or in-person networking. If that's the case, make it your daily goal to book public speaking events or attend the networking events where you'll find the people in the community you serve, or wish to serve.

Don't just do something because someone else has told you that you should. There are thousands of business gurus out there, and not all of them are as successful as they seem to be in their online glitz. Take advice and have an open mind, but ultimately *you* are the one who is going to grow your business and be responsible for your success or failure, not them. Be selective about what you believe and whom you believe, and ultimately create an action and business plan that is true for *you and your coaching success.*

What Is Your Bottom Line?

Why did you make the decision to become a coach? What is it about running your coaching business that is more important to you than anything else? Whatever this is, design your business around guaranteeing yourself this *no matter what.*

For me, I'm passionate about being a *leader*, not a worker or manager. This means I have to run my own business based on my own values and integrity and not work for somebody else. This was put to the test recently when I experienced a major health issue that forced me to reevaluate how I approach and market my coaching business.

Under pressure, I had to work on protecting my *bottom line*: the freedom and leadership that coaching gives me. Because I knew my bottom line early on and structured my plan around it in the first place, protecting this wasn't too difficult even under high pressure that caused me to make a big pivot.

I won't say I wasn't scared for a quick minute. But, because I know my bottom line so well and will always protect it like a warrior, I was able to rapidly move from a quick minute of fear into a new business model that:

- Excites me to no end
- Honors my passion
- Serves my community
- Rides the waves of success that I've nurtured over the years

Know your bottom line, and your waves of success will keep rising. There is no better way to avoid a crash!

The Concept in Practice

Like answering your "ultimate challenge" question and discovering the unique value that you provide to your clients, understanding your bottom line is something only you can do. Think about the reasons why you became a coach—your *why*—and how you want your life to look.

Ask yourself what is the *one thing* that matters more to you than anything else, whether it's a certain kind of freedom, a set of values, or a lifestyle factor, such as spending more time with your family or having enough time for travel. Then ask yourself what action you need to take to make this happen. It could be to save a certain percentage of your income so you always have something in the bank. It could be to practice saying no to clients who do not fit your value system. It could be to get out there and network in person. Put these actions front and center in your business plan, and practice them consistently.

You'll no doubt read a lot about creating a business plan. Study business and take others' advice, but remember that ultimately implementing your plan comes down to you. Choose two or three things you will be able to do every day *with passion and excitement*, rather than a hundred things that you probably wouldn't do anyway. This way, you end up creating a short list of powerful actions that you will do every day, without even having to think about it.

Summary and Your "To Do" List

Find your passion and use it as fuel to find a community, give it value, and stick to your plan.

- **Find your community:** Find a community you can serve with passion, and say no to everyone else. Your ideal community will depend on your own values and the "ultimate challenge" that motivates you the most. Ask yourself what *challenges and inspires you*, and let this lead you to a community you will be excited to serve.
- **Look around:** Look at those who are already serving your chosen community, and notice what is already out there.
- **Carve your niche:** Spend some time with your existing clients to discover the ways in which your coaching has the most value. Based on this information, figure out how you can serve your community in a way that no one else can.
- **Customize your business plan:** Instead of a hundred actions a day, make a list of two or three things you will happily do each day of the week. Structure your business plan around protecting your bottom line, that thing that made you become a coach and that you value and wish to protect over anything else.
- **Embrace your passion:** When your No. 1 driving force is *passion* for your community and for your business, every day will be a new adventure. Despite the challenges, you'll protect your *bottom line* and keep moving forward because this passion will motivate you to overcome every obstacle.

Leading as a Coach

Self-Awareness and Leadership Skills for Coaches and Clients

BETH J. MASTERMAN

Beth J. Masterman earned a juris doctorate from Boston University School of Law; a master of arts from Boston University School of Psychology; and a bachelor of arts, cum laude, from Wesleyan University. Prior to establishing Masterman Executive Coaching, she served in multiple advisory roles for business owners, senior executives, elected officials, and government relations board committees. As an executive coach, Beth helps leaders cultivate deeper self-awareness to improve the quality of their professional lives and heighten their effectiveness, impact, and enjoyment at work.

When you are present as a coach, your whole being is fully committed to the success of your clients. But before you can really be there for others, you have to be there for yourself. Learn how to develop self-awareness so you can take the opportunity to serve others as a coach and lead as a coach and in your business.

S uccess is usually about more than self-advancement—it's also about self-awareness. As a coach and businessperson, ambition focused primarily on advancement and position—unless you find that focus alone deeply fulfilling—can get you only so far. There comes a point when you need to make the effort to honestly figure out what you do well, what your gifts are, and what is important to you. Heightened self-awareness equates to personal sovereignty, which will assist you in optimizing profitability and growth as well as maintaining your sense of humor and satisfaction at work. Self-awareness helps you control your presence, your emotions, and your "self," making it possible for you to lead and guide others with poise and confidence.

Some people might fear they're stepping back when they step out on their own. For some, revenue might drop. Others could lose the prestige that comes from being associated with an ongoing, well-established business. However, I believe this is simply a different kind of step forward. By shifting directions, you do exactly that: You step forward into a new professional realm.

The most effective coaches are those who have hands-on experience in other industries, enabling them to apply their knowledge and maturity to assisting others.

I trained in psychology and enjoyed success as a lawyer and as a public affairs consultant for both business and government before deciding to step forward as an executive coach, putting my skills and experience to work. For me, becoming a coach was the integration of everything I'd done up to that point, letting me bring together my experience in psychology, law, and business.

Few people grow up dreaming of becoming an executive coach. A lot of people don't even know such an occupation exists until well into their careers. Executive coaches are professionals who discover their coach within and allow it to surface through layers of experience. This discovery is coupled with awareness that in some ways they have always been coaching by developing, supporting, and listening to others.

As a coach, your entire being becomes an antenna. Every part of you must be engaged in what your client is saying, how it is said, how your client is behaving, and in full alignment with *their potential* and their vision of success. For example, with my legal background, I often notice issues or concerns that could have legal ramifications for my clients. Usually, unless my client is an attorney, they have not considered that dimension. This heightened awareness is not something you can easily achieve on your own. An executive coach listens, observes, and notices nuances or contradictions, and, with the client, thinks through many angles that help get to the core of challenging issues and how to approach them.

If a coach is not self-aware, it is much harder to fully engage, own the moment with your clients, and maintain compassionate objectivity. Only by training and disciplining your *self* can you develop and utilize awareness and emotional strength to be fully present for your clients, hold them accountable, and positively influence them toward insight.

In this chapter, we'll look at principles and techniques of self-awareness and leadership. You can use these ideas to lead and grow as a coach. When you apply and practice these ideas, you'll be able to handle more situations with confidence, authority, and grace, guiding your clients toward new levels of clarity.

DEVELOPING SELF-AWARENESS AS A COACH

Focus on Self-Awareness, Not Just Self-Advancement

A former client of mine was an academic who had spent twenty years working her way up the university ladder. She was promoted to assistant provost, a big career high, but she was uneasy. She was highly respected by others but felt unsure and overwhelmed. Things were the same and somehow completely different at the same time. There was an unfamiliar type of pressure and stress from the challenges of her new role. Her behavior started to change, her enjoyment started to plummet, she became less tolerant of others, and the quality of her communications declined.

Although proud of her achievement, many of her colleagues had advanced much sooner to even higher positions (president and provost), and she was privately frustrated. Retirement was approaching, and she was focused on the gap between her expectations and her present reality. Many people can identify with that feeling of frustration in their own lives and careers. Self-advancement is the default way in which we face the world, but it often distracts us from what we do best and need most in order to be fulfilled.

With this client, I didn't focus on giving advice or emotional comfort. Instead, through assessments I provided her with new frameworks through which she could think about herself anew. Then I listened. I became her partner and guide on the journey toward self-awareness. She told me her story. We talked about the organization, its culture, her roles, and the personnel challenges.

Things began to change. Gradually, my client realized that she had, in fact, enjoyed a great career and achieved more than she had once imagined she might. She began to orient herself away from the default pursuit of *advancement* and toward regaining her core pride, competence, and confidence. Part of that involved accepting that there were certain aspects about those coveted, prestige positions that she did not want at all. In addition, she admitted aloud that she had been more resistant to those opportunities than she realized and could have been sending mixed signals, which got in the way of promotions.

These insights coalesced when she was promoted again from assistant to interim provost of the college. A few months later, she was offered the role of provost. This was the position of her dreams, but she turned it down. She had learned that self-awareness can be more important than self-advancement. She was able to acknowledge that she will always wish she had been president or provost, but that ambition was the result of external values and expectations more than it was what she wanted and needed to have a long, impactful, and honorable career.

Executive coaches teach and support their clients' discovery of technical and adaptive solutions to their problems. In a strong coaching relationship, the coach becomes the client's trusted ally. Together, we think through challenges; two minds, working to help one person identify and achieve their goals. The coach asks questions; the client finds possibilities and answers. Coaches feel the client's emotions, identify with their struggles, while maintaining the objectivity to help articulate thoughts and feelings that may be too tangled up with anxiety, emotion, habit, or fatigue for the client to think clearly, just as we read about above with my academic client. This act of pure, empathetic *listening and questioning* is what makes coaching a generous and rewarding practice.

My clients often describe the simple ability to discuss situations with a trusted adviser to be invaluable. Why? Because a coach can apply reasoning, problem solving, and planning to help a client create, pursue, and evaluate their goals. As a side effect, when speaking with others, we often end up with more clarity ourselves.

Are You Advancing with Purpose or by Default?

There's nothing wrong with the purposeful pursuit of advancement in your career. Ambition can be healthy when you're honestly motivated by your values and staying true to yourself. It is also possible to be caught up in momentum and expectations. Advancement in an organization is a reflection of perceived or actual worth to the company. It is natural that you might feel you should and want to advance with your peers, as my client felt. As social beings, we cannot easily opt out of caring about belonging and being valued by the people in the organizations we are part of. In addition, we all have bills to pay. *External* pressure to keep climbing the ladder is a great motivator if you fundamentally enjoy your work. But when habit, fear, and pressure fuel uncomfortable commitment to prior choices, then you run the risk of feeling frustrated, dissatisfied, and ultimately disengaged and unproductive.

At some stage in your journey, it is wise to pause and look again at what has taken you to where you are now, and what you need to do or care about to move forward. How have your experiences changed you? Coaches support the process by listening, questioning, and providing the opportunity to achieve greater clarity. By explaining their feelings and challenges to a coach, clients are in fact revealed *to themselves*. It's hard to achieve this level of self-awareness on your own. If you're struggling with a specific area of your business or your life, you might benefit from seeking out a coach to help you critically analyze the big picture and determine next steps that reflect your values and aspirations. Such assistance could lead to your breakthrough.

Self-Awareness Can Help You Grow Your Coaching Business

When I made the transition from lawyer to consultant and then to executive coach, I initially struggled with my own branding. I didn't know how to create a recognizable *business* that would attract the kind of clients I wished to work with. I sought out a branding coach. He listened, helped me articulate my feelings, aspirations, and expertise. We then looked deeper into what I could offer as a coach that would benefit clients. We developed a repeatable program based upon the expertise I bring to the table. Finally, we discussed what kind of person or organization would be most likely to benefit from my style and approach.

Marketing and branding a coaching business requires the ability to *put into words* what you do and why. Networking and promotion simply amplify that core message. Today, I put my energy into the evolution of my services and brand, as opposed to trying to figure out what to say and how to say it in reaction to my perception of the potential client. I am confident that if I clearly present what I do, how I do it, and why, I will continue to attract clients and do great work together with them. With a program, I am able to listen to prospects present their situation and then explain my approach and how or whether it would be a good match. Far more than the *techniques* of branding, what I got most from my branding coach was self-awareness.

The Concept in Practice

Self-awareness has a double benefit.

1. It makes you happier, more genuine, and more confident as a coach.
2. It enhances your ability to communicate what you do in a way that will make it easier for a potential client to know that you are right for them. As a result, you will attract more of the business that is right for you. You will enjoy it more and succeed with your clients when you are doing what you do best and they have some idea what to expect.

Take a few moments to reflect on your current *awareness* level when it comes to your coaching business:

- Are you confident about what you do?
- Are you happy that you have chosen to become a coach?
- Do you look forward to continuing to learn through practice and study?
- Can you articulate what you do, how you do it, and why?
- Is it easy to understand?
- Will it help people self-identify as the perfect client for you?

If not, find someone to talk to. Get a coach. The process of *articulating* to your coach what you do—answering their questions and telling your story to them—will help you reach a deeper level of understanding and help you know what to do next.

HOW SELF-AWARENESS HELPS YOU LEAD AS A COACH

In today's world with so much information at our fingertips, we as individuals have the power to make a greater impact than ever before. Your personal sovereignty—the extent to which you know and own your feelings, your values, your actions—is critical for your success as a coach. In order to lead others, you need first to develop *self-awareness* and couple it with intention.

There are many coaches, and someone will choose to hire and work with you. From a deeper level of self-knowledge and confidence, you can help a client choose you and then accelerate a client's trust and confidence in you and your partnership with them. This will help you inspire them to look to you for leadership, guidance, and reassurance through the coaching journey you are on together.

There's an old Afghan proverb: *If you think you're leading and no one is following you, then you're only taking a walk.* As a coach looking to grow your business, you have to assert your personal sovereignty and be willing to lead in two key ways:

Lead from Behind: Lead your clients by guiding them toward their own self-awareness and by helping them reach their goals in a way that can be sustained in your absence.

Lead from the Front: Know your business, be your business, promote what you do. Inspire your employee(s), even if the only employee is you.

In each working day of your life as a coach, you will be presented with various opportunities to lead. Having self-awareness gives you the personal power to seize those opportunities and use them to make a strong impression, lift others up, create a positive work culture, and better influence others' perspectives so that you can attract more clients.

Coaching Your Clients to Lead

In my work as a coach, I help executives develop and use self-awareness to become better leaders and inspire loyalty, productivity, and engagement in their employees. It takes self-awareness and self-respect to be a successful leader, one able to respond positively to the unanticipated challenges that emerge over the course of a busy working day.

When someone asks you for help, they call upon you to lead, and that needs to be honored. Some days, these situations can be irritating. It could be at the end of a long day when someone calls you with a problem. It could be an employee interrupting you to ask for guidance. Your first response may be emotional. You may be tempted to resist, snap, deflect, or brush them aside. While it is important to have boundaries, it is also important to recognize *leadership opportunities* when they arise.

It is acceptable to feel all of the negative emotions and the impatience, but not to be at the mercy of your emotions in these situations. Leaders learn to sharpen their self-awareness, which enables them to focus on the bigger implications of the moment and think granularly about their interactions. With self-awareness and personal sovereignty, you have the power to reframe these interruptions, problems, and challenges as leadership opportunities; seize them, own your role as a leader, inspire loyalty in your team members, and validate their trust.

This is the same dynamic that operates in coaching, because much of the day is dedicated to listening. A coach focuses on challenge after challenge through the eyes of their clients. Sometimes you just want to give advice and solve the problem. Urgency, impatience, and fatigue can work against a coach's commitment to objective presence in service of the client's agenda. Through the development and discipline of self-awareness, a coach can feel these emotions taking over and utilize techniques to mitigate their effects on the quality of the coaching conversation.

Noticing and embracing opportunities to lead helps inspire loyalty, build rapport, and foster a sense of community and common purpose with others. In the context of coaching, your clients will be reassured that you have their interests in mind and are a stable, dependable resource.

You become a role model for your clients by demonstrating how to be present and clear-minded, and how to handle sensitive information. As a coach, you demonstrate the power of personal sovereignty and the value of exercising strategic, respectful, enlightened self-advancement.

Coaching Fitness

A coach's presence, their entire being, is their antenna. Self-awareness enables a coach to tune into your client's world. Emotions inform your coaching and do not distract you from your work. When a client speaks to you, you must be right there in the moment with them. Being fully absorbed in a client's world takes a huge amount of emotional strength and composure.

Elite coaches must constantly develop themselves in ways similar to elite athletes. By continuing to work on yourselves as coaches, you enhance emotional awareness, physical awareness, and behavior awareness. This is coaching fitness. This fitness helps you become better coaches.

The best athletes work with a coach to raise awareness and alter habits, beliefs, and assumptions when warranted. Athletes need to constantly refine their techniques and adapt to the challenges presented by their bodies, by the opposing team, or by other circumstances surrounding the competition. A great coach evolves like an athlete. A great coach understands the physical, emotional, and psychological pressures and how they vary from person to person or day to day. A great coach must feel connected, yet know when and where boundaries are needed. This is achieved by having a firm grip on who you are. This is self-awareness.

Summary and Your "To Do" List

To succeed as a coach, pursue self-awareness alongside ambitious self-advancement. Align your antenna so that it captures all the signals and also has a positive impact on others; get reintroduced to yourself. Seek out self-awareness, and the rewards will be profound.

- **Find what's important to you:** Articulate your situation and your state of mind with someone who can listen to you and help you deconstruct your situation. Speaking aloud that which is in your head can deliver clarity and insight.

- **Clarify your brand:** Branding and marketing are just self-awareness amplified. If you're struggling, consider a branding coach, who can help you discover who you are and what you offer.

- **Embrace opportunities to lead:** Embrace challenges not as obstacles, but as opportunities. Instead of being ruled by your emotions, take a step back, assert your personal sovereignty, and own the occasion. Be there for yourself so you can be there for others.

Mastering Change

How to Grow as a Coach by Getting Out of Your Comfort Zone

MELINDA FOUTS

Dr. Melinda Fouts has twenty years of experience as a personal and executive coach. She helps her clients recognize and tap into unknown potential through self-awareness and the affirming belief that "success starts with you." She holds a doctorate in Jungian psychology from Saybrook University, and she is a member of the Forbes Coaches Council, an invitation-only organization for successful business and career coaches.

Coaching is about helping others make profound, positive changes. Too often, however, we refuse to make the meaningful changes in our own life. Discovering practical ways to deliberately pursue change as a pathway to personal and professional growth is essential.

The late entrepreneur and author Jim Rohn once said, "Your life does not get better by chance, it gets better by change." To grow as a coach—a facilitator of change for your clients—you have to embrace change in your own life as well. Most of us resist change, defaulting to familiar habits and patterns that keep us stuck, often without even realizing it. Change can come to us deliberately, or out of the blue. It can be confusing, confronting, and even scary. But it also can be empowering and exhilarating. And it is the *only* path toward growth, success, and self-actualization.

Psychologist Abraham Maslow put self-actualization at the top of his hierarchy of human needs. When we become the best possible version of ourselves and *realize* the person we want to become, we have reached the pinnacle of our potential. Self-actualization isn't something that simply happens to us, however. It's something we need to *choose* to create. It arises out of our deliberate refusal to accept the dissatisfying status quo, our refusal to stay in our comfort zone, and our aggressive pursuit of change and self-improvement, despite the risk and uncertainty this presents.

My first encounter with real, deliberate change came out of desperation, and it led me on the path to becoming a psychotherapist and then an executive coach. I was a single mother, working hard to put food on the table. Despite a profound love for my daughter, I was deeply unhappy with my situation. I would walk along the beach in the evenings, raging at the universe, fed up with my life. And yet for a long time, despite my unhappiness, I failed to change. The situation continued. This is a familiar story for many of us. Even if our situation is awful, we stick to what we know rather than risking the uncertainty of *moving into uncharted territory*.

One evening I was walking along the beach again. It was a few miles down, and a few miles back. On the way down, I silently raged at the world, as I did on so many evenings. I thought to the world, *"Why don't you answer me?"* And for the first time, I seemed to hear a reply: *"Because you only talk, you don't listen."* On the way back, I found myself automatically reaching down and picking up the broken shards of glass that had been washed up by the tide. On the way down I hadn't noticed them, but by the time I was back at the start, my hands were full of glass fragments, smoothed over by the ocean.

The answer was now clear to me. I would become a coach and work to put other people's lives back together, as I restored my own. I didn't know how to become a coach, but I had the drive to improve myself, to change my circumstances, and to build a better life for my family, my clients, and myself.

Without the willingness to change, you will never reach your potential as a coach. In this chapter, we'll explore how you can accept, pursue, and embrace positive changes in your life and career.

LAYING THE GROUNDWORK FOR POSITIVE CHANGE

Change begins in the mind. Before I could transform my life and establish myself as a coach, I had to be open to the *idea* of changing my circumstances and walking a new path. Many of us may consider ourselves open-minded, but in fact we may feel threatened by new perspectives. It's possible that, without even realizing it, you've been rejecting the very ideas that would enable you to grow and thrive in your life and your coaching business.

The other day, I was walking with my daughter and she noticed that, despite it being daylight, the moon was visible in the sky. She said, "Mom, I don't like it when the moon and the sun are in the sky at the same time." I asked her why, and she replied, "Because the sun is melting the moon." Now, I knew her answer was not scientifically true, but I felt this was a wonderful, poetic way of looking at the universe. I didn't take on her perspective or reject my own understanding of science, but I enjoyed picking up her idea, playing with it, taking it seriously, and trying it on.

The Concept in Practice

As you've been reading this book so far, have there been any moments when you've thought to yourself, "Hmm, this all sounds well and good, but this concept would never work for me"? How many times have you *disagreed* with a potential new idea or perspective presented to you by anyone in the past month? How about just today, or even in this chapter so far?

It's natural to be skeptical of new things. It keeps you safe, and it protects you from mistakes and falsehoods. But it's also possible that this protection is keeping you *too safe*—and is in fact keeping you stuck, preventing you from embracing the ideas that could help you grow.

As an experiment throughout the rest of this book, practice adopting an attitude of acceptance. You don't have to agree with everything, but be prepared to give ideas that you may otherwise reject a second look. Ask yourself, "If I believed this, how would it feel?" You may find that some of the ideas you may have previously rejected could help you reach new levels of personal or professional success.

Learning How to Think Slow

Embracing change by practicing the above exercise is the first step toward growth and self-actualization. It prepares you to accept change on the level of *ideas*. The next step is to accept and practice making positive changes on the level of *behavior*.

In his book *Thinking Fast and Slow*, Daniel Kahneman describes the concept of "cognitive ease." This is what happens when you are so accustomed to a certain task or pattern of behavior that you can do it without even thinking about it. This is fine when it applies to simple, everyday tasks like brushing your teeth or tying your shoes. But this can hold you back when you choose cognitive ease in complex situations, such as talking to your clients or executing marketing campaigns for your business.

Overcoming Your Default Patterns

Cognitive ease helps you complete familiar tasks quickly and easily, but it can also prevent you from learning. When you're operating at the level of cognitive ease, you're on autopilot. You're doing the same thing you did yesterday and the day before. This can become particularly damaging in important situations when you fall into default patterns rather than reaching for a more challenging, creative solution. Let's take a closer look at how your default patterns could be holding you back.

A client of mine is a high-powered executive, and she's the only female at the highest rung of a large corporation. One of her default patterns is to act aggressively when challenged or stressed. When she discovered that some of her subordinates feared her because of her harsh managerial style, she decided to make the effort to break this pattern. This wasn't easy for her to do. We sat in my office, rehearsing situations in which her default pattern of aggressive behavior would come up.

I'd ask her: "If a subordinate acts like this, how do you react?" She'd say something aggressive or angry, falling into her old patterns. I'd tell her, "That's an F-grade answer. Try again." We kept at it until, finally, she was able to come up with an alternative, improved response. We rehearsed another scenario. "If you're in an important meeting and your boss derails the conversation, what do you do?" Again, her first few answers were F-grade, reflective of her old patterns. It took a long time before we could train her to overcome this deeply ingrained pattern and reach for more empowering, creative responses.

The Concept in Practice

When faced with challenges, people default to what I refer to as their "go-to" style. Instead of developing new responses, they fall into cognitive ease and act on autopilot. In some situations, this is fine; your default responses won't all be bad. Plus, it would be exhausting to have to learn new responses to every situation you encounter with your clients and in your life. But defaulting to cognitive ease can stop you from growing. It prevents you from broadening your tool kit, and it can cause you to over-rely on strategies and behaviors that are no longer useful.

To grow and change, think about how you react to common challenges in your life as a coach. What do you do if a client causes issues for you, or if a business partner isn't holding up their end of the deal? Is there a default style or behavior pattern that you over-employ, such as becoming aggressive, or agreeing with the other person even if you don't like what they are saying? If you could change this behavior pattern, would it help you grow as a coach? If so, mentally rehearse new, creative responses to these challenges.

It won't always be easy to come up with new solutions, as your ingrained default responses will fight to retain the No. 1 spot in your mind. Keep forcing yourself to come up with new responses. Think *slowly*, not quickly, and be open to the new ideas and possibilities that come to you. You'll likely find that the creative solutions you're able to come up with will achieve far better results than the autopilot responses you have been relying on.

Shake Up Your Routine to Stimulate Change

A great way to help your mind come up with new, creative responses to challenges is to start small: begin by simply altering your daily routine. I find this a great way to help myself and my clients get the creative ideas flowing. Interrupting your old patterns in small ways loosens up your mind, and it becomes easier to think in new ways about the bigger challenges you face.

You may find that making small changes to your habits can be harder than you expect. When I suggested to one of my clients that he shake things up in small ways, such as by reading a different morning paper and sitting on the opposite side of the breakfast table, his initial reaction was, "No way!" I often suggest changing up the morning routine, such as taking a different route to work or sitting in a different room and chair when drinking your coffee. Being conscious of the change in habit is what is important.

Often, we practice our daily routines for years and perform 99 percent of the functions completely on autopilot. Changing this can be confronting and upsetting, but it's great practice for making the bigger, creative changes that hold the potential for real growth and development.

If you aren't choosing to change, you're choosing to stay stuck. When I walked along the beach each evening, furious with my situation in life but failing to make any real effort to change it, I was unwittingly choosing to stay stuck each and every day. You are in the driver's seat. It may not be easy, but you can choose to invite in new perspectives and ideas you may have previously rejected. You can break habits and even shake up the routines that have become second nature to you. Start small and let the momentum ricochet throughout your life.

CHALLENGING YOURSELF TO CHANGE AND GROW

The deliberate, fearless pursuit of change is essential for your growth and development as a coach. It gives you the opportunity to become *more* than you have been in the past. But beyond the habits and default behaviors that you're aware of and you notice every day, where else can you find opportunities for change? Let's look at the two basic kinds of learning and how an over-reliance on your existing strengths could be holding you back.

Capitalization vs. Compensation Learning

Are you spending your time developing new skills, growing in new directions, and challenging yourself? Or are you cruising by on what you already have?

As an executive coach, one of the greatest joys I experience is helping someone manage a transition in their career. Often people with technical expertise, such as programmers or designers, are rewarded for their abilities with promotion to a management position. The skills they relied on are not enough and may no longer be needed. Instead of technical expertise, they need to become leaders and managers. Developing managerial skills is a new and exciting area of growth—provided you have the right attitude and are willing to look at your limitations and work on them. If so, growth and self-development are inevitable.

When change isn't forced on us from the top down, however, we tend not to set out in the pursuit of new skills. Instead, we stick to what is familiar and focus on improving and honing the abilities we already have. In his book *David and Goliath*, author and journalist Malcolm Gladwell explains the difference between *capitalization* learning and *compensation* learning. Capitalization learning is when you take your existing skills and make them better. If you're a great listener as a coach, then capitalization learning would involve you further enhancing your listening skills and becoming even more empathic and attentive. If you are a great talker, then capitalization learning would involve you becoming more eloquent and persuasive.

Capitalization learning is common. It's *growth without change*. You improve, but you stay in your comfort zone. Real progress comes through *compensation* learning, which is much more challenging. In compensation learning, you take your gaps, or your weaknesses, and focus on transforming them into strengths. If you're a great listener but a hesitant speaker, then compensation learning would involve making a deliberate effort to improve your communication skills, tell better stories, and speak more persuasively.

The Concept in Practice

Compensation learning is challenging not only because it forces you out of your comfort zone, but also because it requires you to admit your weaknesses. This isn't always easy, but without the willingness to acknowledge your own limitations, you'll never be able to overcome them.

Think about your work as a coach and your journey toward building a coaching business—even if this journey is just getting started. Think about the areas in which you are struggling, or the aspects of your business you have been ignoring. Is there a gap in your skill set when it comes to sales and marketing, or a particular aspect of the coaching process where you've been underperforming? It's possible that you've been neglecting opportunities to develop new skills in challenging areas, and instead you've been cruising by with the abilities you already have.

Stop cruising and make the decision to improve yourself as a coach. How?

Decide on a handful of weaknesses that you want to turn into strengths. Adopt the attitude that you have nothing to lose. If you fail to turn these weaknesses into strengths and they remain weaknesses, you get the satisfaction of having tried, and you're no worse off than you were in the first place. If you succeed, then you've taken a huge step toward your own personal growth and improved yourself as a coach. Sign up to take the EQi–2.0 assessment and go over the results with a coach. It will amplify your strengths and what needs developing. I also recommend that you role-play with your coach. Role-playing is an effective tool to stretch you beyond how you normally respond to developing a different approach, expanding your skills. When role-playing, my clients ask me how they can receive an A+ answer. I tell them when they give me a "never before thought of" answer. Now that's getting out of your comfort zone.

By trying these new approaches, you'll have proven to yourself that you are not bound by the limitations of your past, and you will have added a powerful new tool to your coaching repertoire. You'll become an example to your clients, showing them what is possible when you refuse to accept the status quo, honestly assess your limitations, and aggressively set out to improve yourself. After all, how can you expect your clients to make changes if you're not willing to make them yourself?

Summary and Your "To Do" List

Becoming your best self and reaching peak performance as a coach requires the deliberate pursuit of change. Change challenges, it prevents you from stagnation, and gives you the chance to develop in areas you may have previously neglected, thereby unlocking your fullest potential. Deliberately pursue change to grow as a coach.

- **Shake up your routine:** Practice opening yourself to new perspectives, and be willing to "try on" ideas that you may have rejected in the past.
- **Mentally rehearse:** Rehearse alternative responses to problems that you would like to handle better.
- **Adopt a nothing-to-lose attitude:** Be willing to overcome your limitations. Honestly assess your own weaknesses and make a deliberate effort to develop yourself in new and challenging ways.
- **Befriend uncertainty:** To achieve success as a coach and get closer to realizing your potential, befriend the uncertainty and make a habit of pursuing change whenever the opportunity arises.

Coaching with Heart

How to Build a Coaching Business by Listening to Your Body and Following Your Intuition

KATHERINE MCINTOSH

Katherine McIntosh works with clients to help them identify and overcome the unconscious blockages held in their bodies. An author and widely sought international speaker, her work has inspired everybody from royalty to Hollywood celebrities to reach higher levels of personal and professional success.

We spend most of our time trying to use our rational mind to solve our problems and achieve our goals, but that greatly limits us. To achieve success as a coach and in life, learn to listen to the wisdom contained not just in your mind, but throughout your whole body.

Albert Einstein is often quoted as saying, *"No problem can be solved from the same level of consciousness that created it."* Most of us go through our lives trying to use the conscious, rational mind to solve our problems and achieve our goals. We are taught to think everything through and follow careful, calculated business plans. Rational thinking and careful planning are essential to succeeding as a coach, but they're just part of the picture. You also need self-belief. You need to follow your intuition by listening to your body.

I believe our bodies contain all our gifts and everything we have ever known. It's inside of us at a level beyond reach of the conscious mind. The things that happen to us are kept in our bodies, even if we don't remember them constantly. When triggered, we feel fear, and sometimes we don't know why. By focusing on the wisdom contained within our bodies, we can overcome the limitations that have been holding us back and soar to new heights as a coach.

When I was in my twenties, I became ill. Despite visits to doctors and specialists, no one could identify the problem. I spent nine months dealing with hospitals, doctors, medical tests, and lots of different medications. Nothing worked. No one knew what was wrong with me. One day, out of desperation, I went to an alternative healer. She put her hands on my body and asked me what I knew about my body and what my body was trying to tell me. It was the first time anyone had ever asked my body or me what I knew. Within one hour 50 percent of my symptoms disappeared.

That experience was my first encounter of discovering the body has a consciousness and wisdom of its own. I learned to trust my body and let go of the fears that I had kept bottled inside. The hidden emotions, sensations, and stresses were manifesting themselves as physical ailments. I learned the importance of trusting my intuition, which has been a guiding force throughout my coaching career.

As a coach, I help clients tap into the intuitive wisdom contained within their bodies to make better decisions and free themselves from fear and hesitation. I've worked with Hollywood celebrities and millionaire business owners and leaders who have found that trusting their conscious minds took them far, but to really reach the heights they dreamed of, they had to move beyond logic and start trusting themselves on a deeper level.

To succeed as a coach, you need self-belief. You want to work passionately toward a vision that you can surrender to 100 percent and make decisions guided by pure perceived knowing, trusting that knowing is a window into a whole new possibility. In this chapter, we'll explore how you can learn to listen to your body and channel this wisdom and energy into your coaching business so you can begin to create a business beyond what you can perceive. The mind can only create limitation. The target is to listen to the subtle nuances so you can create a business beyond what you can conceive. Once you discover this in your own way, you will be able to help your clients go beyond their limitations, not by using the mind, but by listening to the body and its internal knowing.

LEARNING TO LISTEN TO YOUR BODY

Listening to your body can help you in two key ways:

One: By helping you to release fear and tension and overcome the barriers that may have been holding you back for years. Fear isn't real. It is an invention and limitation. How do I know? Fear and excitement have the exact same vibration. We've been taught that if we feel that particular vibrational frequency it is always fear. If you could have thought or talked your way out of your limitations you would have already done so. You will begin to discover the key is to stop thinking and start listening; your mind is a limitation.

Two: By helping you connect to the energetic frequencies of your vision, not just the logistical nuances of your future. Once you perceive these energetic frequencies, saying yes to anything that matches that energy will bring you closer to actualizing the vision of your future quicker than you ever imagined.

When clients ask how listening to their bodies can help them overcome blockages, I ask them to look out the window. The place where I live has a backyard that stretches for more than a hundred acres. Out of the window you can see my neighbor's cows and the grass they eat. Throughout most of the yard, the grass grows thick and green, but there are occasional flat patches where nothing grows.

If a cow lies down to sleep in the same spot for months on end, the ground acquires an impression. The soil becomes dense and compact, and it becomes harder and harder for the grass to grow. To restore that patch of soil, the farmer must till and aerate the land so that nutrients can return and the grass can start again. Our minds are the same. We get stuck holding on to impressions of things that have happened to us.

We cling to stress, to tension. Sometimes to heal, we simply need to ask our bodies to let go.

What Are You Holding On To?

The next time you have a few moments to yourself, sit quietly, relax, and ask your body if there's anything you've been holding on to that it's time to let go of. Think about your coaching business and the work you're doing with your clients. Are there areas in which you're holding yourself back? Perhaps you've been hesitant to market your service, to put yourself out there. Listen to your body, and give yourself permission to refresh, to till the soil, and start anew.

It takes practice to listen to your body; the idea seems strange and alien to us at first. We are so focused on trusting our minds, but the mind is part of the body, and everything is connected. Build a habit of *asking your body* for guidance, for direction, and you'll find it easier to tune in to its signals. When you do and you're able to let go of the tensions that may have been trapped in your body for years, the possible ramifications can be huge.

A client once came to me to overcome a fear of heights. Her phobia had been so severe that, when in college, she had to be rescued from her bunk bed. Despite being barely six feet above the ground, she was paralyzed with terror. No one ever bothered to ask her what her body knew. I asked her body where it was stuck in fear of heights. Immediately her body lit up, she could perceive the butterflies in her stomach, sweaty palms, and her body showed her a memory she didn't know was there. As soon as we acknowledged the energy, it started to shift in her body and the fear lessened. We repeated the process, and within five minutes her fear had completely changed. It was quick and lightning fast. Immediately she announced she was going to take a leap with the group and tackle a 300-foot-high zip line over the jungle floor in Costa Rica!

Without this fear of heights limiting her choices, my client's whole life changed. When you let go of a cellular imprint that's been holding a pattern in place, you can rewire the neurotransmitters in your body to create and fire a different pattern. Almost immediately after that incident, her dating life improved and her business reached new heights. She trusted herself better and made wiser choices, all because she had learned to listen to her body. The experience of watching her exuberant joy and elation zip lining was a moment I will never forget, and neither will she. That one choice changed her future and the way she was willing to see how risks and taking giant leaps into unknown territory can create more.

What Vision Do You Have of Your Future?

By the time I was pregnant with my son, I already had years of practice at listening to my body and following my intuition. While pregnant, I had the admittedly quirky practice of asking my son what he wanted his life to look like, what is his vision of our future? The vision he shared with me was the picture of us on stages all over the world, speaking to hundreds of people. I thought, "I have no idea how to make this happen!" But the vision was clear, I trusted it, and over time it became my reality. I could not have used my mind to create the life and living we currently have.

Like resolving tension, the best way to find the truest vision you have for the future is simply to ask yourself. Most people sabotage this process by involving the rational mind too much. You may get a vision of yourself as a best-selling author and think, "But I don't know how to write a book! This can't be my actual vision." But if the vision feels right to you, the conscious side is not important.

Business magnate and philanthropist Richard Branson said, "If somebody offers you an amazing opportunity but you are not sure you can do it, say yes—then learn how to do it later!" If your vision feels true to you, say YES and you will work out the details as you go.

Let's look at how to tune in to your vision and use your intuition to better guide your decisions.

TRUSTING YOURSELF TO BRING YOUR VISION TO LIFE

If you're like most people, you spend a lot of your time in your own head thinking, questioning, and judging. Learning to listen to your body can help you to trust yourself and make decisions using all the wisdom available to you, rather than just the rational mind.

Think about the vision of your future you tapped into earlier in this chapter, and follow these two steps to access the *feeling* that your vision creates in you. This feeling will be your compass, helping you make decisions and know when to say yes down the road.

1. Get in touch with the vision of what you want to create. Tune in to what that looks like. Trust your vision, get inside. Remember, don't worry about the practical side! This is literally about tuning in to the energetic components that don't always have words. It's the subtle energies that don't have words that will lead you to a greater future than you can imagine.
2. Tune in to the *felt* experience. Pay attention to the sensations you can perceive. Get in touch with the feelings or sensations that most closely match your vision. Say hi to those energies. Invite those energies to come play with you.

People and experiences will come into your life that match the sensations you discovered—the feelings that your vision brings about in you. Learn to say yes to anything that matches that. Especially when it doesn't make any cognitive sense.

Discover How to Find the Yeses in Your Life

Most people gather tension into their bodies and their lives by focusing on heaviness and negativity. They lie awake at night thinking about problems with money, difficult decisions, and tough clients. Instead of the heaviness we normally dwell on, focus on what is easy and light for you.

What are the things in your life that you would automatically say yes to? A marriage proposal from the love of your life? A free cruise to a tropical paradise? In the same way that you found the *felt experience* of your vision in the exercise above, focus on cultivating more of these easy, light, effortless things in your life by following the *feeling* that these effortless *yeses* give you.

To bring more of these light *yeses* into your life, think about the things you already love to do. Answer this question:

What are the two or three things you would do all day long, even if no one paid you for them?

These are the things you would happily say *yes* to doing. Then go back to that *feeling* you created and the vision of your future you thought of earlier. Do any of the things you would happily do all day long *for free*—and say yes to—connect with this vision? If not, do they connect with this feeling? These could be signs of an empowering new path for you to follow.

Connect Your Easy Yeses with Your Vision of the Future

When I was pregnant and had that vision of being a speaker who travels the world inspiring others, I had no idea how to make it happen. I'd been working as a hairdresser, and I would happily chat to my customers all day. My hairdressing customers would tell me their problems, and I'd talk to them about intuition and the body. These conversations changed the lives of many of my regulars. They came in for a haircut but left with a whole new vision of themselves and new motivation for the future.

Chatting with my customers and helping them with their lives was something I *loved* to do. I'd do it all day for free, it was an obvious *yes*. My vision for the future was of me speaking on stage and inspiring others. It didn't take long for me to realize the connection.

I considered coaching and reached out to the top coaches in my area for feedback. Making decisions by tapping into the *felt experience* of my vision, I created a life that was full of this easy lightness. Speaking at events is now a regular part of my work life, and I'm closer and closer to the vision I was aware of back when I was a hairdresser, when I had no clue as to how to make it happen.

How do your easy yeses connect with your vision? If you love helping people achieve big, meaningful goals, and your vision is of you as a high-flying business success, then executive coaching could be an ideal marriage of your passion and your vision. If you love art and creativity, and you have a vision of yourself surrounded by fulfilled, creative people, then art coaching could be a great direction for you. Only you know the answer to this. Don't force it. Check in with the *felt experience* of your vision, then practice saying yes, and you may find the path unexpectedly laid out before you.

To Grow as a Coach, Gradually Let Challenges into Your Life

Talking to others and helping them came easily to me—it was an obvious yes and connected to my vision—but some aspects of achieving my goal did not. I suffered from stage fright throughout my youth, and I lacked confidence in the financial side of the business. When I started, I wanted to earn minimally $100,000 a year as a coach but didn't have the confidence to demand such high rates of my clients initially.

To achieve your goals and grow as a coach, you also have to say yes to things that are *less easy* and less intuitive. Following your natural yeses helps keep things light. It lets you save your energy so you can gradually let in the things that are hard.

Listening to your body is a great way to prepare yourself to tackle these challenges. Ask your body to *prepare*, be open to receive the messages from your intuition, and you'll be on your way toward conquering your fear.

For example, if you've also struggled with public speaking but you are offered a speaking gig, say yes even if you don't think you'll be ready. Then imagine the speech, feeling the nerves and everything in your body. Ask your body what you need to do to *prepare yourself* to succeed at this event. The farther in advance you do this, the longer you'll have to prepare yourself and really bring everything you've got.

If you've been wrestling with fitness and want to start going to the gym, you'll experience this process vividly. The first step is to ask your body to prepare yourself for your new fitness regime. Imagine the process in your mind—getting up, finding your workout gear, getting in the car, driving to the gym, finding the equipment, *doing* the workout. When your alarm clock rings the next day, you'll already have practiced the entire process in your mind. Even if it's your first day at the gym, in some sense you'll already be familiar with the process.

Practice Taking Action to Make Your Vision Real

Once you've cultivated a life in which about 90 percent of your time is filled with what is easily connected to your vision, you're ready to prepare for the hard part: the 10 percent that forces you to grow and stretch yourself as a coach.

By asking your body what it is you need to do to *prepare yourself* for the upcoming challenge, you've taken an important first step. Chances are, you will want to *practice* in a safe environment. Practicing helps you integrate everything in your mind and body, and gradually makes what may have seemed hard become easier and more natural.

To overcome my problems with the financial side of growing my coaching business, I needed to *practice* charging my clients higher rates— rates that better reflected the value that I provided and would get me to the annual income level I wanted to achieve. Before speaking to a potential client, I'd ask my body what I needed to do to prepare. This would lead me to stand in front of the mirror and *quote my rates.* "My rates are $400 per day. My rates are $400 per day." Only by doing this could I confidently look my clients in the eye and congruently ask them to pay me this much.

Before tackling the areas of your coaching work that challenge and frighten you, try to fill your life with the things that come most easily and are connected with your desired vision of the future. Then, ask your body to *prepare* yourself to overcome a task that had previously seemed difficult or impossible. Practice in a safe environment, speaking in front of the mirror, with your family, rehearsing in your head. When it's time to face the challenge in the real world, you'll be coming from a place of strength and will find yourself prepared and ready.

Summary and Your "To Do" List

Opening to the wisdom beyond your mind lets you free yourself from obstacles and access greater levels of depth and insight. This can help you grow as a coach by getting in touch with what really matters to you and walking the easiest, lightest path toward that goal.

- **Listen to your body:** When we have a goal to achieve or a problem to solve, most of us default to using our rational minds. Rational thought is very important, but it's only part of the power that we have access to. Listen to your body to access the wisdom of your intuition and get in touch with what is important to you. There may be tensions that you have been holding on to for years, which you can now let go of.

- *"Ask* **your body and** *feel* **your vision:** It may seem silly at first, but practice asking your body to provide you with a *vision* of your future. Don't worry about whether it is possible or realistic. Get in touch with this vision, and focus on the feeling it creates in you. Let it guide your decisions. Ask your body to prepare you for challenges. Be willing to practice, and you'll be able to leave your comfort zone and grow without getting bogged down by stress.
- **Find the things you say yes to:** Think about the things in life that you love doing and would always say yes to. See if there's a connection between these things and the vision you have created. Fill your life with easy yeses, and from that position of strength, gradually let in the harder things.

Defining Your Dream

Creating an Empowering Vision of Your Future and Making It Happen

JOANN LYSIAK

Joann Lysiak had a successful career as a trainer in corporate America before going into business for herself. After thirteen years as an entrepreneur, she embraced her passion for personal growth and spirituality by becoming first a wellness practitioner and then a full-time coach. A certified nutritionist and a practitioner of quantum reflect analysis (QRA), Joann draws upon her life experience and personal history to help her clients define their dream and make it happen no matter what.

Your success as a coach will come down to four things: your vision for the future, your power over your limiting beliefs, your ability to align your mind-set to your vision, and taking action steps to fulfill your dream. Learn how to create an empowering vision of the future and make it happen no matter what.

When you have what author Napoleon Hill called a "burning desire" about your future, you will be empowered to make it happen *no matter what.* Setting goals is one thing, but this burning desire takes you deeper than you have ever gone before. Your burning desire is your driving force, your WHY.

Once you have defined your dream by creating this motivating, thrilling, and compelling vision of your future, you can orient your entire mind-set around making it happen. This involves looking at the deeply buried limiting beliefs that could be holding you back without you even realizing it, and making a conscious effort to release them and replace them with new beliefs that support your desires.

I started in corporate America as a sales manager with the cosmetics company Revlon, where I was tasked with putting together a training program for regional salespeople. Based on my success, I was then invited to participate in their national training programs, during which I discovered my passion for coaching and personal development.

With all the new business skills and knowledge I'd been acquiring, I decided to take the leap to pursue a longtime dream to go into business for myself as a fashion designer. During this time, I became more engaged with the spiritual side of personal development, and I learned how our beliefs and energy directly affect our lives.

Amid all this, I experienced a health-related wake-up call, which prompted me to delve deeper into how energy and belief can affect our lives. I learned that your subconscious beliefs determine everything. If you have the burning desire to be healthy and are congruent with this at all levels of your beliefs, then you stand the best chance of being well. I carried these learnings with me in a career as a wellness practitioner and then, finally, a healthy lifestyle and mind-set coach.

The mind-set techniques I discovered as a corporate trainer and then later as an entrepreneur can help you grow your coaching business. It's about *defining your dream*, knowing where you're going and understanding why you want to get there. Once you have this clarity, you can begin to clear your mind of the limiting beliefs that have been holding you back, and make the conscious effort to shift your mind-set. Let's look at each of these steps in detail.

DEFINE YOUR DREAM: CREATE A COMPELLING VISION OF YOUR FUTURE

Think about your coaching business and ask yourself: What do you really desire? This isn't simply about setting goals, it's about going deeper than you probably ever thought you could go and finding this burning desire that will empower you to overcome any obstacle life can throw at you.

Some time ago, when I had my significant health issue arise, my dream was on the line, and I knew that I had no choice but to take immediate action to correct my situation. I was diagnosed with heavy metal toxicity, which impacted my cognitive function and energy level to the point where I could not function as an entrepreneur doing my daily accomplishments. Instead of focusing on my health challenges, I focused on what I desired, my *burning desire*. I gained clarity on what wellness meant to me, and why I desired to be healthy. I imagined myself as fit, vital, and energetic. I visualized myself in the present and also in my eighties and nineties as healthy, surrounded by family, active, happy, and well, then took action in making it happen by living a healthy lifestyle that required changes in my mind-set and daily actions.

Make Your Dream More Powerful

Beyond the personal—the dream for myself—I also tried to find clarity on my bigger *why*. A vision is most powerful when it is beyond you. WHY do you want it? When you are committed to making a contribution beyond yourself, you tap into even greater energies of motivation and passion. For me, the dream is to change how people think about health and wellness around the world. I want to shift the paradigm to one of prevention as well as cure.

Because my vision of being well is so powerful, because my burning desire isn't just about me, but the whole world, I never waver in my efforts to be healthy. My dream for both myself and for others drives me; it keeps me going no matter what. Because this dream is driven by what I want rather than my fear of what I don't want, it empowers me with positive energy. Orient yourself toward what you desire, not what you fear. See it and feel it and you'll bring it to you and to your reality.

Action Step: Define Your Dream

Let's explore what you really desire. The idea is to create a vision of the future that fills you with excitement and inspires you to go the distance. Open your laptop or tablet, or get out a piece of paper and a pen, and answer these questions.

If money were no object and you knew you couldn't fail:

What would you be?

What would you do?

What would you have?

What would you give?

I like to divide my answers into four headings: health, wealth, love, and spirituality. I normally dedicate one piece of paper to each area of my life, and I answer all four questions for each of them. You can choose to divide your answer in whatever way feels right to you—you could have one piece of paper for your coaching business, and one for your family life. Everything is connected. It's impossible to zoom in on just one area of your life in a vacuum, which is why I find it helps to do this exercise for each area of my life that is important to me.

Be sure to include all four questions, because focusing not just on you, but on what you are *giving* and *contributing* to the world will make your dream that much more powerful. Do not restrict yourself by your current means. The goal is to create a burning desire that will motivate, empower, inspire, and drive you throughout your life. You may not be able to afford your ideal life now, but a sufficiently inspiring goal will make it much more likely that you'll get there one day.

You can read your answers back whenever you need another jolt of energy, or even repeat the exercise as often as you want. As you learn and grow, your dreams are likely to need some updating. Make this an exercise you treasure and enjoy, connected to the areas of your life that are most important to you.

OVERCOME YOUR SUBCONSCIOUS LIMITING BELIEFS

You have defined your dream, and you are empowered by your burning desire. The question now becomes, what is standing between you and this dream? In the gap between your present reality and your dream for your future, you'll find your limiting beliefs.

If you're like most people, then you're being held back by false beliefs that you are probably not even aware of. I believe that 95 percent of the negative things we believe about ourselves are not true. They enter our minds through the countless inputs we are exposed to every day and lurk unnoticed until they burst forth in the form of fear, doubt, or resistance.

The Concept in Practice: Your Coaching Business

Let's say you have defined your dream and have a clear and compelling vision of yourself as a successful, happy, influential coach. Your dream is beyond just yourself: You want to change the lives of your clients and help them succeed beyond *their* wildest dreams. In your conscious mind, you may feel that you are on the path to success. But things keep interrupting you—you feel anxious at the start of each working day, and you notice that fear keeps stopping you from seizing opportunities.

Although your conscious beliefs are in line with your success, subconsciously you may not believe you can do it. It may be that, during your childhood, you watched your father struggle to start his own business. You saw him fail and take out his frustrations on his family. Now, into adulthood, you've carried with you the belief that you cannot succeed in business.

In Bruce Lipton's book *The Biology of Belief*, the author explains how before the age of eight, we basically accept any inputs that come our way. It could be the words of a parent, the actions of a teacher, the background noise of the TV, the bullying voice of a school yard thug. These messages take deep root, and we are often unaware of their ongoing impact on our daily lives.

These beliefs don't exist to harm you. They exist to protect you, to keep you safe. Your subconscious mind is like a recording mechanism, keeping permanent record of every input you've ever received throughout your life. But often, the lessons you absorbed as a child are no longer doing you any favors now that you are an adult. They could be restricting you and holding you back in ways that, until now, you haven't even been aware of.

When you are faced with a negative belief in the course of your daily life, it's like coming up against a wall. You can push through the fear and break through the wall, but it's exhausting having to do so again and again. Instead of trying to crash through each wall, it's time to build a door. Look your limiting beliefs in the face, see them for what they are, and let yourself move on.

Action Step: How to Clear Your Limiting Beliefs

The key to overcoming these limiting beliefs is to bring them into the open. They say sunlight is the best disinfectant. By bringing your subconscious beliefs into the bright light of your conscious mind, you empower yourself to be free of them. They can't operate unnoticed and in the background any more. You can address them with all the intelligence of an adult and allow yourself to move on and be free.

Think about a situation in which you have negative feelings (fear, anger, or anxiety) that are getting in the way of your success. Imagine the moment when those feelings come up, and then ask yourself why. Be open—the first thing that pops into your head will be a clue. Ask yourself where that feeling comes from, reflect on it, and follow it to its source. Follow your intuition. For instance, if anxiety surfaces, ask why. Your intuition may bring up a memory of a time when you "failed," leaving you feeling anxious and believing that you can't succeed. Your subconscious mind, hardwired to keep you safe, protects you from failure by avoiding similar situations. You can replace that limiting belief with a new supportive belief, that you can succeed by implanting a recent success in your subconscious as evidence that you can do it. If you have done it before, you can do it again. You can state, "I am choosing to replace that belief with my new belief. I am capable of succeeding again. I am skilled in solving my client's needs, as I have with XYZ."

Don't dwell on the negative; instead, face it with the confidence and authority of a coach, and replace the negative with a positive. Give thanks for the lesson you have learned and the knowledge and experience you have gained. Remember your vision, your burning desire, and let this melt away the resistance created by your limiting belief.

The first step to freeing yourself from limiting beliefs is to accept that you have them. Be alert, and when negative feelings crop up, follow them to their source. When you get there, it's time to shine a light on them and let in the positive energy. Let's focus more on this step.

BECOME YOUR BELIEF: HOW TO FLOOD YOUR LIFE WITH POSITIVITY

You've defined your dream and learned how to identify the limiting beliefs that stand between you and where you want to be. The next step toward making this vision happen is to take conscious control of your inputs.

Many of your subconscious beliefs will have entered your mind during your childhood, when the information you were exposed to was largely beyond your control. Your parents and teachers told you what to believe, and the TV remote was out of your reach. Not anymore. These days, you can take control over what goes into your mind. In my experience, there's almost no better way to ensure your success than to deliberately surround yourself with uplifting, positive input.

Filling Your Life with Positive Input

To have a healthy body, you must nourish yourself with pure, nutritious food. It is the same with your mind: you must feed your mind with positive, empowering thoughts or input.

The inputs you receive include all the media you consume: the books you read, the audios you listen to while driving to work, the TV you watch at the end of a long day. When I committed myself to my dream of success, I made a deliberate effort to optimize all the media I consumed toward this goal.

Today, I read empowering books that inspire and uplift me every single day. I monitor my daily input of energy, choosing to flood my conscious and subconscious with positive energy. On the way to work, instead of listening to the radio, I listen to success-focused podcasts, interviews and audio programs such as Brian Tracy, Zig Ziglar, Tony Robbins, or Dr. Michael Beckwith. This means that every day, I am flooded with positive input.

The inputs you receive aren't limited to the media you consume. It also helps to take a look at the company you keep. In the same way that you can deliberately cultivate empowering input through what you read, watch, and listen to, you can make a deliberate effort to surround yourself with other positive, success-minded people. Joining a success club in my local area with other successful entrepreneurs was one of the best decisions I have ever made. When you are surrounded by positive people, you lift each other up and carry each other farther.

Become Your Belief: Live the Life of a Successful Coach

You've defined your dream, you're aware of the pitfalls of limiting beliefs, and you're making a deliberate effort to absorb positivity throughout your day. The next step toward making your dream a reality is simply to act as if it already is. All these steps so far have been about helping you do this: Start behaving and thinking like the successful coach you want to become.

This begins with your work space, how you dress, and how you hold yourself. Even if you have no clients coming over and are working at home all day, keep your work space tidy, put on a professional outfit, do you hair, shine your shoes, and look the part. If you look like a success, you will feel like a success.

Before you go to bed every night, set your intention on how you want to feel in your business and see what it looks like. Tap into your dream, your burning desire, and feel it as if it had already happened to you. Ask your subconscious mind to empower you to achieve your objectives, and feel this positive, empowering energy of success. When you wake up the next day, deliberately feed your mind with inputs that support, emphasize, and enhance these positive feelings.

My mentor, Dr. M. T. Morter, told me, "Things don't happen *to you*. They happen *for you*. They happen for you to learn the lesson." When you master your inputs and feed your mind with success, you're training yourself to tackle every situation you face in healthier, more empowering ways. If a client hangs up on you, you will learn not to put the emotion on yourself. Instead, you'll have enough motivation and positivity to look for the lesson and turn the negative into a positive.

Summary and Your "To Do" List

By creating an empowering dream for your future and designing your mind-set accordingly, your dream will become your reality. Your success as a coach is defined by your vision for the future, your power over your limiting beliefs, your ability to align your mind-set to your vision, and taking action steps to fulfill your dream.

- **Define your dream:** Divide your life into the areas that matter most for you, and answer these questions: If money were no object and you knew you couldn't fail, what would you be? What would you do? What would you have? What would you give?
- **Trace your limiting beliefs:** The inputs you receive as a child may be holding you back as an adult. When you encounter negative emotions, trace those feelings to their source. By bringing these subconscious limiting beliefs into focus, you can reduce their power over you.
- **Feed your mind with positivity:** Create an environment that supports your journey toward success. Surround yourself with positive, successful people. Read uplifting books. Listen to inspiring audio programs. Attend pivotal seminars, and find accomplished mentors to work with.
- **Hold on to your burning desire:** Believe that things will work out for you. Think, act, and feel as if you have already achieved your dreams. Take 100 percent responsibility for your life by creating your reality using the power of your mind to take action and achieve your dream business.

Possibility Coaching

Push Your Own Boundaries to Empower Your Clients and Grow Your Business

CLINTON CALLAHAN

Clinton Callahan is the originator of Possibility Coaching, Possibility Management, and *Expand the Box* trainings, and is the author of several books, including *Radiant Joy Brilliant Love*. Clinton has been developing his own perspectives and coaching methodologies for more than forty years. Along with twenty-five fellow coaches, Clinton delivers Possibility Coaching in Europe, the United States, and Asia.

Are you ready to be challenged? Creating change for your clients involves guiding them toward new possibilities, but most of us fail to embrace new ways of thinking in our own lives. Through Possibility Coaching, learn how to expand your own limitations to inspire your clients and attract more people to your coaching practice.

Your clients are developing new forms of relationships, new markets, new products, new services, and new ways of living. They are trying to create inspiring and satisfying lives in turbulent circumstances. They are working on the edge. They need to navigate new possibilities in order to accomplish their goals. To help them, you need skills for *navigating change on the edge*. These skills are the basis of *Possibility Coaching*.

Possibility Coaching specializes in making use of previously unnoticed possibilities. If you ask yourself, *"Where was my last great idea the instant before I found it?"* the answer is that it was already there, waiting for you in the same place brilliant new possibilities are waiting for you this very moment. You may not see many of these possibilities right now because you have hidden them from yourself behind a veil. We adopt these veils in our assumptions, expectations, beliefs, and stories about ourselves and others. We believe our own conclusions about what is possible for us in a world like this with people like "them." The veils wrap us into a "box" that serves as defense mechanisms to help us blend in, to survive. A Possibility Coach serves as a bridge for crossing through these veils and embracing wonderful new ways to grow and thrive.

Before you can help someone else navigate unfamiliar territory and utilize new possibilities, you need the skills to make the journey yourself. This is why the Possibility Coach goes first. Through personal experiences, you build the skill set to authentically guide your clients through their obstacles and uncertainties while they learn new ways of thinking, feeling, and behaving. This depends on you waking up and getting out of a fresh and newly discovered side of your bed each morning even if your bed only has four sides. How do you do that?

Since 1975, I have been researching practical ways that a coach can help others detect blocks and veils and turn them into bridges for accessing new possibilities. By the late 1980s, I had hundreds of pages of notes and diagrams for shift processes that enhanced a person's responsible effectiveness that I wanted to turn into a book, but something was stopping me. I was frustrated enough to go to the edge of my possibility box and visit a famous psychic who was holding an open event nearby. I nervously sat in the circle of people gathered around her feet and watched as person after person asked their most delicate questions and witnessed how she consistently delivered powerful distinctions that touched each person in ways that seemed to inspire them profoundly.

Finally I felt confident enough in her skills to ask my own question. I raised my hand. She said, *"Yes, young man?"* I said, *"Is it time for me to write my book?"* There was a pregnant pause of silence and stillness, but then she could no longer hold it in. She exploded in unstoppable laughter.

The who... question, but when I a... s of hilarity! I was horr... y a stretch for me, but... ice of staying open to a... ly, she caught her breat... *d you possibly think it is... to feel?"* This question...

The... ches come to face: *You...* By embracing new poss... also pave the way for al... themselves.

In thi... d techniques of Possibi... ess.

It is a fasci... of new possibilities in... s parroting answers, a... . How can you make i... not already known and... ket this? It helps when... ss, you are building a g...

A game... w rules of engagement... ld. Family is a gamewo... coaching practice into... empowering new context to o... your partners, and your clients to new possibilities for change.

Let's look at how to create your own gameworld.

Creating a Context of Radical Responsibility

If you regard yourself as a gameworld builder, then the first element you need is a context. Context is your gameworld's foundational relationship to consciousness and responsibility. As an example, think about modern business as a gameworld that is built, by most measures, in the context of the more you avoid responsibility, the more profit you make. Responsibility is applied consciousness. In this particular context, you are conscious that the more you can externalize costs to the environment, future generations, third-world countries, or government subsidies, the more successful you become. Winning comes from avoiding responsibility.

I would suggest that your coaching gameworld be based on an almost opposite context, the context of *radical responsibility*, meaning you provide the service of increasing your client's capacity for taking responsibility by increasing their awareness. If you establish your coaching business as a gameworld in the context of radical responsibility, then your clients benefit from learning to create successful results in a world without victims. They do not "win" by creating losers, or by finding someone else to blame, because in radical responsibility the concept of irresponsibility is an illusion. There is no such thing as a problem because your clients learn to avoid applying that label to any situation. Instead, your coaching empowers your clients to become skillful at creating possibilities and making new choices. Even if avoiding responsibility may seem "profitable" in the short-term, the glaring consequences of dumping toxins in your own drinking water or driving "competitors" to extinction make it clear that assuming radical responsibility creates a brighter future for your clients and therefore also for you, the coach.

Creating Your Gameworld

Step One: To start your gameworld, you need at least three people to agree on a context. If you are only one person, you will easily fool yourself. Your ego will take over the gameworld and dedicate it to confirming the story: *"I'm the best. I'm the most important."* Two people is also not sufficient because you end up in a battle of wills and opinions about who is right. For an effective gameworld, you need to begin with at least three.

Step Two: Once three people agree on a mutually beneficial context, then decide on what the purpose of your gameworld will be. The purpose of the Possibility Coaching gameworld I created with my team is *upgrading human thoughtware*. What is the purpose of your gameworld? This purpose should be consistent with the mission of your coaching business, inspiring people to live more fulfilling lives or helping executives make future-building choices.

Step Three: Distill which principles empower your gameworld. If your gameworld's power comes from your ego's resources, you may soon be exhausted and burned out. If your gameworld serves something greater than you, then it is empowered by what I call Bright Principles, which are archetypal forces of nature, facets of raw consciousness. The Bright Principles of Possibility Coaching are clarity, possibility, and love. What are the Bright Principles that empower your gameworld?

A person is attracted to a gameworld because one or more of their personal Bright Principles resonates with the gameworld's Bright Principles. When they come to your gameworld, they get nourished and fulfilled through the creative collaboration. If your gameworld is based around the principles of love and respect, then the coaching clients and participants who value love and respect will find you. Together you will create a powerful culture in which you all thrive.

BECOME A MAGNETIC CENTER

Achieving clarity about your gameworld's context, purpose, and Bright Principles turns your gameworld into a *magnetic center*. Your clients will be naturally pulled into the energy that you create, and they'll be motivated and inspired by sheer proximity to your gameworld due to the way you and fellow participants collaborate and communicate with each other.

Your excitement and joy in your work seems to curve space in your direction so more people naturally hear about you and are attracted to what you offer without you trying to convince them through flashy advertising programs. The deeper your clarity about your context, purpose, and Bright Principles, the further you curve space toward your gameworld and the more customers and clients seem to fall toward you.

Imagine a solar system. Planets orbit a star because the star pulls them in through gravity. In your coaching practice, you are the star and the planets are your clients. You pull your clients into your orbit and empower them by providing clarity, possibilities, and enthusiastic energy they can feed on and use to grow until they themselves become stars.

In the same way that planets need stars to hold them in orbit and prevent them from drifting out into space, stars also need planets. Without your clients, you are merely a lone wolf, a single fighter, perhaps shining gloriously but unable to to fulfill your mission as a coach delivering your true service to your community. Without your gameworld you stand there like a decorative ornament. With your customers and clients you have the opportunity to "walk your talk" and demonstrate how your coaching has practical value.

Action Step: Provide Energy to Those Who Orbit You

One obligation of the star is to provide inspiring new ideas and opportunities your clients, customers, and subscribers require to help them thrive in the gameworld you create together. They need the tools and distinctions to apply what you teach them for expanding their own possibilities and staying on track with their goals.

If you are regularly seeing a client, then maintaining this level of energy input will be easy because you can experience in action both their progress and their blocking patterns and can provide ongoing *tweaks*. A powerful tweaking force is to suggest specific nano-experiments your client can use to build inner resilience in their new skill sets. For example, you might be building their skill set to stop changing their assumptions into expectations which, when unfulfilled, create resentments that break down relationships. A powerful nano-experiment that you could suggest in this case would be to avoid assuming anything. Then, in the middle of your interactions you can peacefully ask, *"Do you think this might be an assumption? Have you made an expectation out of it? Could this be a resentment?"* In real time your coaching changes from theoretical to immediately practical. The contrast between what you ask for and what is delivered is sudden and irrefutable.

If you work remotely, or deal with customers with whom you have less frequent contact, one way to stay at the center of their world is simply to send out a regular monthly newsletter. Don't fill it with advertisements. Instead, fill it with short, empowering ideas and inspiring invitations to events, talks, and practice groups. This helps you maintain connection while also keeping relevant ideas, principles, and purposes at the forefront of their minds. Another practical way to provide energetic food for remote customers is to offer a half-hour weekly webinar in which you give a five-to-ten-minute presentation about a particular tool for creating nonlinear possibilities. For example, you could explain how to ask questions the answers to which do not exist within currently active perception limits, or how to receive and listen to and complete communications from employees or customers (or husbands and children . . .) that contain more energy than their personal stability can manage without getting triggered into emotionally reactive response patterns, or how to tap into resources that help them be prepared in circumstances for which they are totally unprepared, etc. Then open the webinar to questions. Your concern for each person's development will be felt and will inspire further confidence in your coaching methods. True skills aren't suddenly acquired during a coaching session. True skills emerge during periods of diligent practice. By consistently feeding your clients either in person or remotely you create *legend-making* change results in the field.

CREATE IMMEDIATE VALUE THROUGH LEGEND MAKING

Legend making means to create immediate value that takes people's breath away. It sends a chill of inspired enthusiasm down their spine. They feel more human and more alive because they are blown away by what is possible for a human being. How do they know the unbelievable is truly possible? Because they just experienced you doing it with them. They want to leap into life with their own flames blazing full-on, giving more than what is reasonable, creating more than what is possible. When people see that you use your own tools effectively, that you continue to do what inspires, what provokes, what brings people to laughter and to life, they will want more, and **they will tell their friends not to miss this!**

Legend making is like dropping a pebble into a still pond. The circular waves all go out from one central point into the global ethnosphere—that combined cloud of all the active gameworlds on Earth. The source of your waves remains visible because it is where the waves came from. Months, sometimes years later, your legend-making actions are still reflecting back to you. When the impulse is attractive, people surf the reflected waves back to their source. People will tell their friends about your exquisite and delightful coaching for days, months, or years after they experienced it for themselves.

The legend-making ripples you cause come back to you in the form of clients and customers, attracted to you by word-of-mouth recommendations. The story a happily surprised client tells someone else about you is not a simple recommendation, it is legendary. Through your astonishing actions you recruit passionate fans who want other people to experience the transformation and excitement just as purely as they did.

Let's look at some concrete ways for you to create your own legend.

Legend-Making Method One: Make Your Products Open Source

Make your products open code and free to copy. Whatever your product is, be it music CDs, rejuvenating natural skin care creams, audio books, massage methods, personal development or healing processes, social entrepreneur techniques, permaculture-style meeting technologies, recycled next-culture clothing patterns, etc., if you empower your clients to be able to create the product themselves instead of trying to protectively guard your "trade secrets," you instantly and automatically double your customer base. By freely empowering the creative commons, half your customers will happily want to obtain your products as you make them without further hassle. An additional wave of clients will want to learn from you how to create the products themselves. Your new product line is to teach your clients how to do that. If your products are functional, fun, and fabulous, the viral distribution of your work will catapult you into unimaginable success.

Rather than starting from a position of fear-based scarcity, start from a position of joyful abundance. Keep explaining to everyone that there is an unlimited source where your inspired creativity comes from for meal recipes, application program utilities, product distribution algorithms, communication network ecologies, massively multiplayer on- and-offline computer-game story lines, cloud-marketing strategies, recycled furniture designs, community empowerment formats, healing treatments, intimacy expansion experiments, thoughtware upgrades, political stability revisions, conflicted communication responses—on and on and on. Explain that if someone can understand and use any of your ideas, then it's theirs to freely use. If they understand it, they are licensed to make money by teaching it in classes, workshops, trainings, films, books, talks, anywhere. This is legend making.

Your thoughtware is your patterns of understanding and inner skills that determine how you interact with the world. Possibility Coaching thoughtware consists of tools, distinctions, processes, frameworks, and ways of thinking about what you are thinking about. Since our purpose is upgrading human thoughtware and the source of our thoughtware is abundant, then we can say, *"Please steal this thoughtware."* These possibilities are too abundant to be copyrighted. By the time you copyright one idea, five better ideas have emerged into common usage. These resources are for everyone's benefit. Please take all you can get. We win when our new, empowering thoughtware is distributed as widely and as quickly as possible.

By stepping out of the copyrighting game, we have inspired other people to step in and deliver Possibility Coaching for us. We now have a global network of coaches and trainers who are connected as a team, as a community, working together around the world supporting each other to do better.

By adopting the open code strategy, you automatically build a massive new customer base of people hungry for your products and services because they see a future for themselves in your open code gameworld. These customers are hungry to learn themselves how to deliver your products and services, so this gives you an entirely new set of customers— those who want to create their own businesses to deliver your products and services. And! This suddenly builds a further additional client base for you of those who want to train and support those who want to deliver your unique and powerful products and services.

The open code paradigm automatically opens massive new market spaces, often dwarfing the currently existing market spaces and making them irrelevant. As soon as you understand what I just said you will hardly be able to sleep at night because you will be so excited about creating your own open code gameworlds.

This is naturally good for your brand and your business because more people are exposed to your ideas and eager to trace them to their source, which is you, the ones who dropped the first stone into the pond.

Legend-Making Method Two: Give Away a Free Empowering Distinction

Each time you meet with someone, offer them a distinction that upgrades their thoughtware. What does this mean? A distinction differentiates something that before could not be differentiated. For example, when you can distinguish the true fans in your circle of clients from those who are there for consuming or complaining, you can feed your new categories of clients with different sets of opportunities more suitable to their inner needs and desires. If you can deliver this distinction to your own clients, they have new power to accurately serve their clients.

Distinctions create clarity. Clarity creates power. When you can empower someone with a new distinction they cannot make for themselves, they automatically become your client.

The way to create a legend-making distinction is not with a statement that claims to speak the truth about what is so, but rather by asking a question that introduces a valuable possibility that someone has not considered before. You are asking a question the answer to which lies in a space outside of a person's current thoughtware. You cannot ask such a question rhetorically. Instead wait and listen expectantly in such a way that you hold a vacuum into which they can give you their answer. By holding this vacuum space open within yourself, you learn something new from them that helps you respond more accurately to what they need, perhaps in ways they could not ask for before you asked them your questions.

One such vacuum question could be, *"In order to get to know you better, would you please explain to me how a person such as yourself could arrange to spend days and weeks of your life avoiding doing what you really want to do?"* Then you listen expectantly.

You could also ask, "Please explain something to me about yourself (or your business situation) that I don't see."

Or, "You know what results you are trying to create. What is in the way of better results?"

Or, "Please tell me what part of you (or your company) is starving and what you are starving for?"

Each answer you receive through your vacuum question and your open listening will probably create a space in your client into which you can deliver a distinction they probably never used before. By making this distinction for them they experience immediate value from you in this interaction. They have the experience of not having wasted their time with you. Quite the opposite, in fact. You have already given them a taste of your wares and also exposed them to the wealth of unknown possibilities that can be called into action through your ability to ask about and listen for possibilities. Through engaging your questions they get new distinctions to explore. This upgrades their thoughtware and shows them the endless utility and power of your basic calling card tools.

Legend-Making Method Three: Create Extraordinarily Attractive Possibilities

If you offer unexpected yet pleasantly startling experiences for free, it can create a huge positive legend. For example, put up two chairs at a shopping zone or a festival next to a sign that says *FREE POSSIBILITY*. Creating possibility is a coaching process that does not automatically assume a problem-solution mind-set. Instead, it uncovers desires and potentials and asks, *"What is really possible for you?"* and, *"What can become a gateway for you to enliven that potential?"* Rather than trying to repair current circumstances, it orients toward opening doors for shifting into entirely different circumstances. People rarely know the depth and breadth of their true potential.

Someone sits down and you say, *"What can I do for you?"* They explain what they are up against. Then you say, *"Interesting! I experience you as being a person who has resources that you are unaware of not using. Here is the evidence to support my observations. I saw you cause this . . . I saw you perceive that . . ."* Proceed to enthusiastically explain their unnoticed potentials in abundant and irrefutable detail. Invite them to shift their self-experience and to expand into their bigger potentials. I did this once with a client who complained to me that their relationship was stale. I said, *"Interesting! I experience you as being a person who is able to be radically honest; for example, you just told me that your relationship is stale. Could you please tell me your evidence for this story that your relationship is stale?"* She said, *"Yes, of course! When we talk I am bored. When we eat together, for example, at a restaurant, we hardly talk at all. When we have sex together, it is over so fast and always the same way."* I said, *"Again I thank you for your radical honesty. Could you please tell me the fears that drive you to make and hold such a story?"*

"Yes," she said. "I am afraid that this pattern will continue, and either I will have to numb myself like my mother did with alcohol and gossip, or I will have to leave the relationship to stay alive." I said, "Thank you. I trust your fear. I am asking you to trust your fear with the same radical honesty you have been demonstrating to me. [Note: This radical honesty is the resource she was not aware of having.] If you are willing to go numb to stay in the relationship, or to actually leave the relationship, are you willing to be radically honest in your relationship and to continuously say what you are noticing, what you feel, what you are starving for, and dare to reveal qualities of yourself to your partner that they never noticed about you?" This was a shocking and unexpected invitation. She was not sure she could do it. We then did a role-play in which I took on the character of her partner and simultaneously coached her degree of radical honesty. With tears of sorrow, rage, and joy she found her radical honesty skills were honed to a far higher degree then she imagined. She soon reported that her recently boring relationship had blossomed into entirely new levels of intimacy, especially when her partner began expanding his own skills with radical honesty.

This is a fun and energizing thing to do, by the way! At the end your clients stand up having discovered a new experience of themselves. This is not simply appreciation or affirmation. You have reflected clear evidence to them of their untapped potential.

Legend-Making Method Four: Make an Unreasonable Offer and Deliver on It

Ross Jackson, a friend and colleague who is the cofounder of the Global Ecovillage Network, published the book *Occupy World Street* in English. It was not available in German, the language most of my clients speak. During a Possibility Lab, I explained the situation and asked if anyone would join a team and translate the book into German by November of that year. Eight people joined the team and accomplished the translation by the deadline through pure enthusiasm and teamwork joy, for free.

Then I called the English publisher and asked if I could get the book published in German. They said the translation costs would be too high. I said, "Well, strangely enough, a team here in Germany was so enthusiastic about the book they made a German translation for free!" The translation team's purpose was to cause the book to exist in German in the shortest possible time. They succeeded. A few months later the book was published in German! Many people in the Global Ecovillage Network and associated gameworlds were touched and inspired by our totally unreasonable action. It created a massive wave of legitimate credibility and goodwill toward us, which continues to open doors to paid coaching engagements in these circles still today.

Think about ways in which you can create extraordinary, unprecedented value for current and potential clients. The ripples of these actions will return to you for many years to come.

SHIFT INTO EXPERIENTIAL REALITY

We were all born and raised in a culture that hammers us into verbal reality and excludes us from experiential reality.

From childhood, we are primarily rewarded for our ability to communicate in words. Modern schooling is focused on this. But if you compare the amount of things in the universe for which there are words with the total amount of things in the universe, our vocabulary box becomes barely visible. The rest is only accessible nonverbally, experientially.

So much happens experientially that we have not yet named, but in verbal reality, if you have no words for it, it does not exist. It becomes invisible. And as soon as you do find a word to name your experience, the intellectual understanding prevails and the experience diminishes.

This can be remedied. In fact, to serve as a coach you must somehow find ways to escape the rigid limitations of verbal reality and enter into direct fluid experience of the world in all its subtlety, variety, and swiftness. Coaches need access to experiential reality, where experience prevails. Then, when truly needed, you can intentionally revert back to using words.

To develop your talents for navigating experiential reality you can practice this exercise. Sit facing a partner. At first it is most practical if your partner is a fellow coach, because they will better understand and align with the purpose of the exercise: to improve your nonverbal sensing and communication skills. Partner A sits ordinarily without trying to do or not do anything. Partner B is the coach, who in this case pays attention to nonverbal states and communications from Partner A. Partner B experiences for fifteen to thirty seconds and then reports what they experience.

For example, Partner B might say, "You don't like eye contact. It makes you afraid. You fear I might see something about you that you do not see yourself. I might see that your personality is irrelevant. You are glad I said this because you are not so happy with your own personality. But you are also angry, because it is all you have. You disagree with me now. You do have more. Actually you are more, but I don't see it yet. There is a tension in your left shoulder. It hurts you. You both want and don't want me to see this. You trust me about 60 percent. You are projecting someone on me now. It looks like you are projecting your brother onto me whom you liked but who was never fully trustworthy . . .," etc. Whatever you pick up nonverbally. Partner A says nothing, but at each comment gives you a thumbs up to signal accuracy, thumbs down to signal inaccuracy, or a wavy hand to signal 50 percent accuracy. Then change roles.

Another exercise is to walk slowly with a fellow coach through a shopping zone, a neighborhood, a natural outdoors area, or a personal living space while one of you shares everything that you notice while scanning in experiential reality for ten minutes and the other listens. Then change roles.

Shifting into the expansive flowing world of experiential reality is perhaps the most difficult of coaching skills to develop but well worth the practice time because of the wide variety of information-sensing channels it opens up.

Sell Your Coaching Services by Painting the Beach

A particular use of experiential reality is to use words to paint a positive experience of the benefits of a particular service into the sensations of a potential client. This is called "painting the beach," referring to the idea that a travel agent does not explain that to get to Bali you will need to sit for fifteen hours next to some stinking sweaty man who snores, plus eat plastic-covered airplane food and breathe bad air only to get mosquito bites and sunburn.

Instead, the travel agent says, *"The tropical air in Bali is so moist and fragrant that it heals your soul from your first breath. Warm tropical waters lap at your feet while you sip fresh iced pineapple juice."* By then you already have a ticket in your hand.

Practice painting the beach about your coaching services. Practice giving your potential clients the sensation of being truly seen and supported in their personal and professional processes. Focus on building a safe place for them to experiment with unfolding their vast potentials. The more they trust your trust of them, the more they can trust themselves. One corporate manager had a lifelong vision of climbing the company hierarchy but spent all her spare time climbing snow-covered Alps in Austria and Switzerland. She lived alone in an apartment that matched an Ikea catalog more than it did her own soul. There was no place in her survival-oriented imagination for her authentic self to live, and her professional personality kept her from getting close to any partner. She felt extreme loneliness while thinking something was wrong with her. Finally she discovered Possibility Coaching. During the first few sessions she only became nauseous each time I started to paint the beach of what else was possible. Her nausea frightened her but it was totally acceptable to me as the coach. My acceptance allowed her to trust the process. The next session we did something nonlinear. I asked her to exchange roles. I became her and she became me. Suddenly it was up to her to paint the beach for me, to explain experientially what else was possible for me, the cold-hearted, self-isolating corporate manager. She did such an amazing job that both she and I could taste the tender aliveness of her new future. She discovered her true calling as a beach painter, and now she is self-employed as a highly sought Possibility Coach shifting corporate enclaves into human and Earth-nurturing environments. Plus she just moved out of her fifteen-year isolation apartment and into the home of a wonderful man friend.

Practice painting the beach over and over again, asking for feedback and coaching from your partners and also your clients. Try different approaches each time, and bring in more life with fresh word combinations. Accurately transfer the experience of coaching benefits to your potential clients until they can hear the seagulls screech and the waves gently crashing on the shore.

Summary and Your "To Do" List

Creating change for your clients involves guiding them toward new possibilities. Possibility Coaching specializes in making use of previously unnoticed possibilities. By expanding your own limitations, you will inspire your clients and attract people to your coaching practice.

- **Empower your clients:** Gather a team, deepen your context, clarify your purpose, connect to the Bright Principles, and create a vibrant gameworld. By following these steps, you will empower your clients to redefine their own experience of the world.
- **Expand your perception limits:** In the new playing field you create, you collaborate together to discover and apply the limitless possibilities hiding just beyond your current perception limits.
- **Build your legend:** As your gameworld empowers others to thrive, it becomes a legend even to strangers you have not met. Creating effective transformations tips people out of the everyday and into the limitless.
- **Enter new territory:** People are often afraid to take such bold, daring steps alone. The courage you use to enter new experiential territory and upgrade your own thoughtware isn't just for you. These efforts benefit your clients as well. Seeing that you are a learner makes your clients trust you even more.

Part Two:
Finding Your
Clients

Connecting with Experts

How to Partner with Influencers and Industry Leaders

MARK THOMPSON

Mark Thompson is the world's No. 1 growth company coach for thirty years. A *New York Times* best-selling author, Mark worked closely with legendary founders like Steve Jobs, Charles Schwab, Sir Richard Branson, Lyft's Logan Green, FitBit's Chris Park, and Pinterest's Ben Silbermann and Evan Sharp. In addition to his success in business and venture capital, Mark maintains close connections to the academic world as a visiting scholar at his alma mater, Stanford University, as well as John F. Kennedy University and the American Management Association.

Learn exactly how to grow your coaching business by forging close partnerships with influencers and industry leaders.

N o matter how good you are at coaching, business, or marketing, you will not get where you want to go without the *leadership* and support of the right people. Nobody does it alone. Partnering with experts and industry leaders completes your skill set, boosts your brand, and greatly expands your network of potential clients and customers. Most importantly, surrounding yourself with successful people in your industry is a fantastic source of inspiration, energy, and ideas. Together, you'll be able to achieve far more than you ever would have alone.

I grew up in Silicon Valley, at a time when this former farm town transformed as the epicenter of one of history's biggest, boldest ideas—shooting for the moon. The exuberance for the space program attracted the best and brightest thinkers from eighty nations. The sense of urgency was caffeinated by the endless optimism and possibilities created by technological innovation and accelerated by horrifying fears of the Cold War. Seemed as though every garage burst with imaginative start-ups and every backyard had a bomb shelter. For me, the decision was easy: I'd better build a start-up before we're all vaporized!

My twenty-five years in business have been defined by that sense of abundance and scarcity, so the community I built shared that sense of disruptive partnerships and continuous reinvention. I've been privileged to have worked with many visionaries who started with nothing and, in addition to changing the world, also became billionaires—Charles Schwab, Steve Jobs, and Sir Richard Branson—with whom I've been able to contribute more than I ever could have on my own.

Working with the people at the top of a range of industries has helped me to understand that the key to networking isn't about having the biggest contact list. It's about aligning based on a shared purpose and finding a way to contribute real value, authentically.

In this chapter, we'll explore how you can align yourself with the right influencers and leaders in your industry and form partnerships from which you both win.

THE SECRET TO NETWORKING IS GIVING VALUE

Before we jump in, let's dispel a few myths about networking.

Myth 1: Any Celebrity Will Do

Many people think that partnering with *any* celebrity—any face from the TV—will be a boost to their business. Whilst a well-placed celebrity endorsement can certainly help shift products, to really get things done you want to partner with people who share the same drive and mission as you. Instead of the heavily managed celebrities, focus on the rock stars *in your industry.*

Ask yourself: Who are the people who are transforming what you do and taking it to a level that you respect and cherish?

Myth 2: The More Contacts, the Better

The most successful coaches in the world are not necessarily those with the biggest network. In fact, the *quality* of your professional relationships is much more important than the quantity. Focus on the partnerships in which you can go deep and work together long-term toward a meaningful goal. You'll find this a far more valuable and authentic approach than simply scrambling for all the connections you can make.

Myth 3: It's All about Me

This is the biggest and most damaging misconception about networking out there. Partnering with celebrities and industry leaders will, of course, bring tremendous value to your business, but only if they're the right people, and you must not show up as a self-absorbed opportunist. If it's all about you, and you don't believe that what you're doing will add value to others, then people will smell your desperation a mile away. They'll reject your proposals like a virus. You cannot set out with your No. 1 goal being to help yourself. Your networking efforts will only truly succeed and bear fruit when you shift your No. 1 priority toward *helping them.* The rest of this chapter will explore a few ways you can make this happen.

When you understand that networking is about *giving,* not *taking,* you'll already be head and shoulders above most other coaches. Industry celebrities and influencers are already jaded. They have people calling them every day, and every one of those people *wants something from them!* They are starving for *authenticity,* for someone to show up without an agenda and sincerely offer value based on a shared mission.

Be Willing to Give before You Get

I've been a TED member for years, and often see my friend Al Gore, the Nobel laureate and former vice president who's transformed the way the world thinks about climate change. Last year during a networking event I asked him for his thoughts about how most people approach him. He sighed, shook his head, and said, "The only way to earn reciprocity from anyone else is for you to show generosity first."

Reciprocity is what happens when you do something for someone else, and human nature generally compels people to consider returning the favor. When it comes to networking, this means that before you can expect someone to do something for you, you must be willing to do something for them. Generosity always comes *first*.

Make the Effort to Understand What Matters to Them

Before you can offer real value and show generosity effectively, you first need to make a real effort to *understand* the person with whom you want to connect, and then figure out what it is they really want. We did extensive research about this for my *New York Times* best seller, *ADMIRED: 21 Ways to Double Your Value*. We learned that most people expect and hope to be valued by others, but ironically never do their homework to learn about what those people really care about. Why should they help you, or even value what you do, if you haven't bothered to find out what matters to them? If you have the opportunity to meet someone important to your future, the last thing you should do is immediately launch into a pitch or a plea for help. Instead, ask questions and sincerely strive to figure out what makes them tick, what they are trying to achieve, what drives them, and what they may be struggling with right now. How could you actually help them with that?

When seeking to understand how best to offer value, it helps to take the time to think about who *they* are accountable to. Do they have a boss or a CEO to whom they report? Do they have a community they need to recruit to their cause or mission? If they are a leader, what is their board expecting of them? Attempt to understand the criteria on which they are being evaluated.

The Right Way to Offer Support

How could you help them overcome a point of pain related to something they are working on right now? Think about how you can make them more effective at their goal—or even how to look good in the short term. What's going to make their mission stand out at that Monday meeting? What are they striving toward, and what is stopping them?

When it comes time to offer help, don't preach or give unsolicited advice. Instead of "making them eat their broccoli," gently introduce your proposed solution in a way that makes them feel good.

Let's say you have decided to seek a partnership with CEO Jane Smith, to make up an example. After doing your research and speaking to Jane, you discover that she is struggling to motivate her employees to increase productivity. You realize the problem is that Jane has not been taking the time to listen to her employees and find out what *their* needs are.

You could say, "Your employees aren't listening to you because you aren't listening to them. I can help you fix that," but this approach isn't likely to win you any friends. Instead of offering a prescription, offer an invitation. *"I know what it's like when your employees aren't motivated. I've recently overcome this problem in my own business. Let's put together a plan for solving this together. Here are a few case histories; perhaps some of these tools and tactics could help you."*

Why Richard Branson Sought Me Out

Take the approach of seeking to understand and offer value, and you will stand out as a contributor, not just another climber. My partnership with Richard Branson began because he's an expert at it!

I first met Sir Richard at the World Economic Forum when I was a board member of one of the world's largest consumer electronics retailers. He remembered my connection as a consumer expert when he was launching Virgin's mobile phone business. He called me one day from

Necker Island, and he sweetly reminded me who he was—although I don't know how anyone could ever possibly forget Branson! He said he was really inspired about how much I sincerely loved customer service and he shared my passion for advocating for clients. He asked for advice about how to break into the U.S. market with his edgy new Virgin phones. He wanted to transform the terrible service levels in the cell phone business, and Branson made a point to recruit me to his mission-driven, people-focused fresh way of promoting that business. But stop a moment now and think about what he was doing here: What makes visionaries like Sir Richard so powerful is not that they believe that they can do everything themselves, but that they actively seek out other experts who share their passion for manifesting similar goals. He's recruiting talented partners for bold ideas and new businesses, not promoting his stardom or leadership. It's very disarming and powerful to treat others with that kind of respect.

And the only reason he even knew about me was because I started by trying to figure out what he was striving for a year earlier when I met him at the forum in Switzerland. I admired him and intentionally thought about how I could add value to his world of interests and values. Turns out that we shared a passion for creating start-up incubators and entrepreneurship centers. I was leaning into something that he believed in, and it was something I believe in even if we had never met. When you find authentic common ground, that's when you get some traction.

We had a real relationship based on mutual values, not dependencies, not scarcity. That's why he knew who I was when he needed help. At that point, it was easy to think about his ambitions to move Virgin Mobile into the U.S., but more importantly, we were aligned toward a similar mission about helping the larger world. I'm always looking to do good and do well! Since then I've become one of the founding patrons of his Branson Entrepreneurship Centres, and that's a relationship that's built to last.

The Concept in Practice: Making This Approach Work for You

Physicians and concert masters *practice* what they do long after they've earned degrees and professional recognition. They're never done learning. As a coach, you're helping yourself get better at what you do every day. That's why you're reading this book. And you can learn something from everyone you meet. Making this approach to life and work manifest for you requires a fundamental shift in mind-set from how most people think about networking. Here's how it could look for you.

1. Research a small list of *industry* rock stars who are motivated by a similar mission to yours.
2. Do your research and seek to understand where they are going. Find out what highway they're on in their business, and seek to discover how you might mutually benefit from being in the same car pool.
3. Reach out with the express purpose of *offering value* and helping them to achieve their goal. Be authentic and sincere. After all, their mission is the same as yours.

Authenticity Is Essential

Let me reinforce this principle because it's so often ignored by the very people most anxious to have impact and influence in their career as a coach. If you merely offer value as a token means to an end, then you will come across as inauthentic. Successful people can sense phonies a mile off. Faking it may get you to the top for a year or two, but it will not keep you there for long because you simply cannot fool everyone. When you are sincerely aligned toward the same purpose, on the other hand, this will be radiantly obvious to the authenticity-starved influencers who will be *eager* to get to know you and discover what you can achieve together.

Jack Canfield, Marshall Goldsmith, and I were leading a management seminar for three days in Doha, Qatar, when we received a call from Patryk and Kasia Wezowski, who wanted us to be a part of their film *Leap*. Marshall and I have been coaching CEOs as partners at Walgreens, Intel, Pfizer, and many of the world's top companies, and Jack has been inspiring the public with his work for decades. We've long been friends who love working together, and we were struck with the special quality of the Wezowski family's sincere enthusiasm for professionalizing the role of coaching in the global lexicon. We were impressed at their authentic interest in our work and our impact on the world, and we're excited about how the themes expressed in *Leap* might help millions more people embrace their greater talents.

GOING DEEPER: ALIGN BASED ON A SHARED MISSION OR STRUGGLE

People who have long-term success are nearly always driven—at least in part—by a mission or sense of purpose that is far greater than themselves. To form deeper, more profound connections with the leaders in your industry, it helps to look *beyond* everyday business goals and find out what *contribution* they are trying to make to their community.

For my Businessweek best seller, *Success Built to Last*, the sequel to business classic *Built to Last*, thought leader Bonita Thompson and I conducted the world's first Global Success Survey in 110 nations. In partnership with the Wharton School's Professor Wind and Harvard researcher Howard Moskowitz, we asked highest achievers in almost every industry what success means to them. During the prior ten years, I'd been conducting face-to-face interviews with Nobel laureates, Academy Award winners, self-made billionaires—from Bill Gates to Nelson Mandela, from Oprah Winfrey to the Dalai Lama—and found most everyone has their own definition of success. Fortunately we discovered that those people who've achieved lasting success share three essential definitions:

1. I'm successful when I'm serving a cause larger than myself.
2. I'm successful when I set a goal and I achieve it.
3. I'm successful when I experience **all** of my passions.

What we found particularly interesting is that, of the people who had real long-term success—those who had been at the top of their industry for at least twenty years—at least 80 percent of them expressed some combination of *all three* of the above definitions. When one of the definitions wasn't being achieved, they were still supported and kept in balance by the other two.

This is extremely important information when you're seeking to understand and align yourself with the successful people in your niche. What stood out for us is how frequently the first answer (I'm successful when I'm serving a large cause.) came up, either on its own or in combination with the other two definitions. While there are exceptions, those who have success that lasts are overwhelmingly driven by a desire to help others and serve a cause that's larger than themselves as individuals.

When you get to know these successful people, you learn that this greater purpose is often born out of a personal struggle they have overcome in their own lives. Charles Schwab became a billionaire in the financial services industry, but I believe he was put on this world to help people with learning disabilities like those that he struggled through as a youth. This is a journey my wife, Bonita, and I share with Chuck Schwab. I was privileged to serve alongside him as he built a company with over $3 trillion in customer assets, but the biggest thrill was to help him start the Schwab foundation and to support his charity, All Kinds of Minds, helping people overcome dyslexia and live amazing lives. Because we have this common ground, this alignment, my connection with Chuck became much deeper, and our business relationship and the opportunities we created were multiplied a thousandfold.

The Concept in Practice: Give Your Time and Make a Difference

Go back to that list of influencers and industry leaders you created earlier in this chapter. Find out which charities they support with their time and money. If you sincerely believe in the cause, then show up and start giving your time. Nonprofits are hungry for help. As Jerry Yang, one of the founders of Yahoo!, said to me, "'No one will ever turn down your offer for genuine support for a worthy cause."

Don't expect your efforts to be rewarded with a partnership on day one. Make sure you are genuinely driven by belief in the charity you're helping and that you have a real, sincere passion for the work they do. Nonprofits need that support and that help. If it's real for you, the industry leaders will read that. They'll know. Give generously and completely, and you're likely to find the right people will notice your efforts.

Summary and Your "To Do" List

Partnering with experts and industry leaders can complete your skill set, boost your brand, and greatly expand your network of potential clients and customers. Forming partnerships with influencers and industry leaders is about *alignment* and *authenticity*. The key is aligning based on a shared purpose and finding a way to contribute real value in an authentic way.

- **Offer value at every opportunity:** Seek to generously offer value at every opportunity. Doing so requires you first and foremost to understand who they are, what they want, and what they may be struggling with.
- **Contribute to a bigger cause:** Find out how the successful people you emulate are serving their community, and if you have passions or interests in common, contribute your time and energy to help them. A sincere contribution that helps influencers advance something they believe in can win you a valuable connection.
- **Find the rock stars:** Research the industry rock stars who are motivated by a similar mission to yours. Try to understand where they are going. Reach out to them with the express purpose of offering value and helping them achieve their goal—and be authentic about it.

Confidence and Self-Belief

Your Self-Worth Determines Your Net Worth

PETER SAGE

Peter Sage has twenty-five years of experience as a business leader and entrepreneur. As a best-selling author and sought-after speaker, his ideas have inspired tens of thousands of people around the world to improve their businesses and live better lives. Peter's book *How to Master Your Life: The Four Keys to Excellence* has sold more than 150,000 copies. His businesses include the World Wide Health Corp. and the Energie Fitness Group.

Your success as a coach is a direct result of your self-worth. Clients are looking for certainty and will follow your lead when it comes to valuing your services. If you hold yourself in high regard, they will too.

Before you can attract your ideal coaching clients, you must first *become* the kind of coach your ideal client would want to hire. Everything begins with you. Clients don't buy "coaching" or a one-hour session: They are buying *you*. Your integrity, confidence, and certainty are everything. If you come from a place of unshakable faith in your own ability to transform their lives, then clients will be magnetized to you. If you have absolute belief in the value of your coaching, then clients will pay high fees without blinking. In the world of coaching, your self-worth directly determines your net worth.

In a twenty-five-year career as an entrepreneur and founder of a diverse range of businesses, I've had one consistent strategy: to *own* myself. Some of my ventures have been fantastic successes, some have failed majestically. Throughout all the ups and downs of a high-level entrepreneurial career, I've learned that self-worth directly translates to net worth. Your current level of earnings as a coach is directly equivalent to your current estimation of your own value. To earn more and grow your business, you must first increase your own sense of self-worth. It doesn't work the other way around.

My transition from entrepreneur to coach happened because of one phone call. As my businesses succeeded and I gained a reputation as a speaker on entrepreneurship, my phone started ringing with people asking for advice. My friends told me, "You should charge for this," and eventually I agreed. One day I got a phone call from an entrepreneur who wanted some help. He asked, "Do you offer a coaching package?" I told him I did, and (perhaps at some level wanting to price myself out of the market) replied, "It's £1,000 per month for one phone call a week." Somewhat to my surprise, he agreed on the spot and became my first coaching client.

After signing my first client based on this unexpected phone call, I decided to get a handful of additional clients and dedicate one day a week to coaching. With five clients, each paying £1,000 a month, this worked out to an additional £60,000 of revenue per year, which was nice to have! Many coaches reading this may think quoting such high prices for merely one weekly phone call is outrageous, but I was able to do so with congruence and always maintain a full, satisfied roster of clients because of one thing: I know my own value. My clients get more *back* in value than they give in fees. I know it, and they know it.

My No. 1 business strategy is to own myself. To succeed as a coach, you must stop looking for external validation and instead *own yourself* by increasing your sense of self-worth. With your newfound self-esteem, you can honestly assess the value you provide to your clients and charge accordingly. For most coaches, this will mean a significant increase in the fees you charge. To reassure clients and separate yourself from the competition, be willing put your money where your mouth is and *reverse the risk*.

Let's look at these concepts in detail.

OWN YOURSELF: THE RIGHT WAY TO INCREASE YOUR SELF-WORTH

No amount of skill can make up for a lack of certainty. Most coaches chase skills and certifications, believing that if they just take one more course and complete one more training program, this will give them the confidence they have been searching for. It doesn't work like that. Chasing skills in the hope that they will give you the *certainty* and *self-worth* you need is getting everything backward. Your certainty is the mother of your ability, not the other way around.

When people are vulnerable and looking to make a change, they gravitate toward *certainty*. Imagine you become ill and consult two doctors, who propose different treatments. One doctor confidently offers you a trial drug, saying that the initial results have been spectacular, and he's very optimistic about its chances. The other doctor hesitantly offers you surgery, saying, "Well, it may work, but we don't really know." Which doctor do you choose?

No matter how many certificates are on your wall, no matter how many techniques you learn, if you can't look your clients in the eye and confidently offer your services as the solution to their problem, then you will remain stuck as a coach. Your clients will not recognize your value or risk taking a chance on you if you do not have absolute, unequivocal belief in yourself. When I told my first coaching client *"I charge £1,000 per month for one phone call a week,"* I may not have been trying very hard, but I was *certain* of my own value. This certainty was communicated to my client, who accepted the offer without hesitation.

Instead of chasing external measures like training courses and certificates to give you this certainty from the outside, focus on building confidence from the inside out. The most important source of this certainty for coaches is your *intent*.

Mastering Your Intent as a Coach

Sure, we become coaches because we want to help others, but at the deepest level of your being, is that really the No. 1 reason you entered this world? When a lot of people say, "I want to help others and do good," there's something insincere there. You can tell that, really, they're in it for themselves. If you say, "I make my living helping people," the red flag is obvious—that sentence is about *you*, not the people you help.

If you claim to be working to help others but deep down you have a self-serving agenda, this will come through. You won't have true *certainty* because your intention will not be pure and direct. To succeed, you have to show up with the simple, clear objective to *serve* and *add value*. If this intention is strong in your mind, then it becomes the source of your confidence, the solid rock upon which you stand.

The Concept in Practice

To succeed as a coach, you need to have *certainty*. Your clients will read this certainty in you, trust you as a coach, and be comfortable paying high fees. The origin of this certainty is your *intent*. If your intent isn't genuine, then you will not have genuine *certainty* in the moment.

Look in the mirror, and be honest about your intentions, about your decision to become a coach and your motivations for doing so. Do you have an absolute, unequivocal belief in your desire to help your clients, in your desire to make the world better through the gift of you? If so, great. Double down. Own it. Make this intent part of you, nurture it, and carry it with you. Instead of seeking external validation to fuel your confidence, think on this *intent* of yours and this will provide energy, certainty, and passion that your clients will respond to.

If you find there is something murky about your intention, then that's okay. Accept that, make an honest appraisal of yourself, and be willing to work on it. A lot of coaches use their clients as proxies of themselves so they can avoid looking in the mirror and being honest about their own issues. That's a problem. On the other hand, it's healthy to accept your own limitations and honestly attempt to correct them. All good coaches have a coach of their own. If you don't, then *get one* and put this issue at the top of your agenda.

Once the issue of your genuine intention is solved, it's likely that the rest of your business will fall into place.

OWN YOUR VALUE: HOW TO UNDERSTAND AND EARN WHAT YOU'RE REALLY WORTH

Mastering your intention and having *certainty* in yourself as a coach means your clients will trust you and want to work with you. Your confidence reveals your own sense of value as a coach, which is the foundation of your entire business. Your clients won't want to pay you decent fees if they don't think you're worth it, and they won't believe in your value unless you believe it first.

But how do you know what to charge your clients, and how do you demand high fees without scaring away potential business? In the same way that resolving confidence is about zooming in on your intent, charging more as a coach is about recognizing the true *value* of what you offer.

How Much Is What You're Doing Really Worth?

I work with business leaders and CEOs. This means that it's easy for me to put a monetary value on the work I do. Although the figure of £1,000 that I charge my clients was more or less pulled out of the air, it is consistent with my assessment of the amount of *value* I could provide for the few hours of coaching I was offering. If a client of mine earns more than they pay me because of the work we do, then I'm worth it. It's that simple. But what if your specialization isn't directly connected to business or money?

Regardless of your niche, your value can be found at the intersection of your sense of self-worth—your confidence in the value you provide—and whatever it is your clients can afford. I'm confident that I can provide £1,000 of value, and my clients are businesspeople who can afford £1,000 in fees per month, so that price point fits perfectly.

This equation works in all niches, from executive coaching to fitness, relationships—whatever it is you happen to be doing. Most coaches undervalue their work and undercharge their clients because of issues with their self-worth. By making the shift, owning yourself and your value, you can probably charge two, three, four, or even ten times what you do right now, provided you've targeted a market segment that has the means to afford it.

The Concept in Practice

The story of a young protege of mine helps illustrate the direct connection between self-worth, the value of your coaching, and the fees you charge.

I was once contacted by a young Englishman who lives and works in China as a fitness coach. He was a fan of my speeches and online materials, and he really wanted to grow his business, but he was stuck at the same level and unable to reach the amount of income he aspired to. He reached out to a me via e-mail, and something about how he wrote connected with me. I replied with a few tips and a list of recommended books for him to read.

Unusually, he replied and said, "I bought the books, read them, this is how I'm applying what I've learned. This is what's changed. How can I thank you?" I told him he could buy me lunch when he was next in town, and we could chat further about his business. We met up and he told me that despite the new ideas and information he'd gained, he was still stuck. I asked him, "How much do you charge per hour?" He said $50. I said, "Why not charge $500 per hour?"

Stop for a second and imagine I'd asked you to increase your fees by tenfold. How would you react? The young man in question said what most coaches would probably say in that situation: "No one will pay it!" I replied: "It's not that there aren't people who will pay you this much. The issue is you don't think you are worth it."

To demonstrate this, I explained to him what he already knew: China's economy was growing fast, and a major market force in China is the idea of prestige, of significance. A lot of people like to demonstrate their wealth with their waistlines. Being chubby was once a sign of status, but culture is changing. The *prestige* of having a more expensive, exclusive fitness coach than one's peers would be a major selling point. Beyond that, the value of health and fitness is huge: the confidence in front of your rivals on the tennis court, the peace of mind that you'll be around to see your grandchildren go to school.

We drilled down into the *key benefits* of the service he provided. Think about this in your niche. What you provide isn't one hour of coaching, it's complete transformation. The value you put on this is limited only by your own mind. If you're a relationship coach, then you help people find and maintain love, feel good, raise a family. If you're a start-up coach, you help people turn their dreams into a reality. You don't provide "coaching." You provide transformation.

Your Fees Are Limited Only by Your Belief in Your Own Value

One year later I heard back from the young man. He'd followed my advice, taken the *leap*, and increased his coaching fees to $500 per hour. He was thriving, but that wasn't the end of the story. Another year later, I got an unexpected e-mail from him. There was a photo attached. He was in a first-class seat flying from Beijing to Shanghai, sitting next to his lifelong hero, the actor Keanu Reeves! He hadn't stopped at $500, but ended up increasing his fees to $5,000 *per hour!* All this for the exact same work that he had been doing for 1 percent of the price just two years before.

Your net worth is limited only by your self-worth. Think about the *transformation* that you create in your clients. Believe in your value, and be prepared to charge fees that are an honest reflection of this value.

REVERSE THE RISK: SEPARATE YOURSELF FROM THE CROWD

In a sea of competition, knowing your own value and having the confidence to back up your claims will go a long way toward making you stand out from the competition. Instead of having to relentlessly pursue clients, they will be magnetized to you by your self-belief, your intent to transform their lives, and your certainty that what you do has real value to them.

To help further separate yourself from the crowd, consider putting your newfound confidence to the test. Put your money where your mouth is and reverse the risk. Offer an ironclad guarantee: If your clients don't achieve the results you promise, they don't pay. Promise a clear, tangible, measurable result that quantifies the service you provide. If your clients don't lose a certain amount of weight, increase their income by a certain amount, achieve a certain level of peace or satisfaction, then you don't get paid.

When I began as a coach, I used risk reversal to validate my own skill set. I told my first clients, "I charge £1,000 per month, but I won't cash the first check until you tell me that you've received £1,000 in value." This gave my clients confidence—it proved my self-belief to them and demonstrated confidence in the value of my coaching.

Often this £1,000 worth of value was achieved before our first session was even complete. Once it took just sixteen seconds. At the start of the first coaching session, a client told me, "I really loved your introductory questionnaire. It inspired me to think differently about a business issue I've been dealing with and helped me close a £25,000 deal this morning." I said, "Oh, so is it OK for me to cash that check now?" Obviously, the answer was yes!

Summary and Your "To Do" List

Your self-belief is your value as a coach. True self-belief comes from the inside out, not from external sources.

- **Engage in introspection:** Take a close look at yourself and the reasons why you became a coach. Tap into your intention to serve and help your clients as a source of your confidence.
- **Charge fees based on value:** Charge an amount that honestly mirrors the massive impact of your work. The value you provide to your clients isn't your time. It's the transformation you help them create.
- **Reverse risk:** Back up your work, and put your money where your mouth is. Back up your work with an ironclad guarantee. Keep it simple: "If you don't feel like you've received XX dollars' worth of value, then I won't cash your check."
- **Think like your audience:** Focus on becoming the kind of person your ideal candidate would want to work with.

Specialization

How to Find Your Niche and Establish a Formidable Reputation in Your Field

KELVIN LIM

Kelvin Lim is the founder of Executive Coach International Pte. Ltd., Asia's leading coaching organization. In 2005, he became the first person in Southeast Asia to receive the title of Master Coach, the highest possible certification in the field of professional coaching. A sought-after coaching specialist for his developmental and transformational coaching techniques, Kelvin has worked with more than 5,000 individuals directly and 15,000 people with his team of coaches indirectly from Europe, China, and many Southeast Asian countries.

The most successful coaches in the world are specialists, not generalists. But what if you don't know how to find your own area in which to excel? Discover exactly how to choose the best specialization for you, create your own "secret formula," and develop a formidable reputation in your niche.

In Chinese medicine, there is a unique and highly specialized form of acupuncture known as 时针 (shizhen) or "timed acupuncture." When you hear "acupuncture," most people think of lying down and having someone fill your back with dozens of needles. With a deep and specific understanding of how energy flows in the meridians of the body, this special technique allows the acupuncturist to apply only a single needle at exactly the right point. Your ailment can be resolved with just this single needle. This form of acupuncture beats everything else hands down!

You need to be that needle. Your clients come to you because they want to resolve their issue as quickly and as painlessly as possible. If you're the coach who can solve their problem with one needle rather than fifty, word about your skills will quickly spread.

I started out as a coach at twenty-six. Unlike older coaches, I couldn't rely on wisdom or experience. I had to rely upon my person-to-person ability to create change. I had to be faster and more efficient than anyone else. I developed a reputation for my technical ability to cause results. For instance, I designed workshops and courses that brought forth specific behaviors that my clients desired and became a consultant executing on-the-spot coaching in tricky interorganizational negotiations. I was part of the research team of Thomas Leonard, the founder of Coach U and the International Coach Federation. Back in the early 2000s, we created many of the coaching techniques and models that are still being used today.

Through my trainings and with the help of our research, we produced coaches who gained reputations for quickly creating powerful changes. Part of the reason for this is that we didn't produce generalists. We produced specialists. We wanted coaches to be able to place that one needle in the perfect position for their clients.

To leave your mark and achieve the kind of success as a coach you strive for, you have to specialize. You need to find a specific problem that you excel at resolving, or identify a benefit that you provide, and then become a leading expert in this specialized area. Choose an area that you are passionate about. From a commercial point of view, this is called defining your niche. A niche in coaching would be an area where you are best able to deliver the best results and be known for it.

Some examples of defined niches include leadership coaches specializing in the healthcare industry and relationship coaches specializing in designing reconciliations between between feuding business partners or helping couples develop or increase intimacy.

Within your niche, deliver tangible results that will create a reputation for you within your community. This reputation can then be taken in any direction you choose. You can expand and apply your skill set to a broader range of problems and clients. You can teach. You can write. You can franchise.

Once you have a strong reputation within a specific niche, the possibilities are endless. In this chapter, we'll look at the early steps that will set you up for an incredible coaching career.

QUESTIONS TO DEFINE YOUR NICHE

Most of us begin our journey with a fairly incomplete idea of who we are, what we are capable of, and what we are going to do with our lives. As long as we cannot answer such questions, we will not able to define our own success. We would mostly be reacting and responding to the external environment, as opposed to focusing on our own desired direction and journey.

In order for us to find out where we want to go, we have to look within ourselves and go through a journey of discovering what matters to us. This includes examining our talents, our preferences, the paths we took, what we attract **to** us, and the times when we feel most fulfilled.

The questions below will help you focus your energies and find success as a coach. You may not have all the answers at the moment, but it's important to think through the process. Defining your specialization is going to be one of the most critical decisions you ever make on your coaching journey, so it's worth taking the time to get it right.

Your Current Skill Set:

No matter where you are as a coach—established or just starting out—defining your specialization begins with an honest assessment of your current abilities.

- What skills do you have that are relevant for a coach?
- How have you acquired these skills?
- What experience do you have?
- What are the areas of knowledge in which you thrive?
- What natural abilities do you have?

Your Natural Attraction:

Once you've assessed your strengths, the next area to examine is natural attraction. This is not so much what *you* are attracted to, but more what you attract *to* you.

- What comes to you naturally and easily?
- What kind of people are attracted to you?
- What kind of opportunities come to you?

What Do You Want to Create as a Coach?

As you look at your skills, your experience, your knowledge, your abilities, and attractions, start asking yourself, "Who can I best serve, and in what ways?" There should already be a clue, a connection between your abilities and the kinds of things that come your way.

Making a difference is about being able to concentrate your energies and figure out exactly *where* and *how* you would like to make a difference. Is there a specific group of people for whom you would like to make a difference? How does your niche link up to that kind of impact down the road?

Exercise: Visioning to Define Your Future

If you're having trouble zeroing in on the difference you want to make, I invite you to go through a visioning exercise. This is simply about sitting down and dreaming about your future.

Find a quiet place where you can enter a dreaming, meditative, or contemplative frame of mind. Once you are comfortable and relaxed, examine your state of fulfillment right now. Look at the areas in your life where you find fulfillment. And look at the areas that are not yet fulfilled. Once you are in this state of seeing or experiencing your fulfillment, ask yourself the following questions:

Fulfillment Questions:

- In which areas of your life have you attained fulfillment?
- In which areas are you now seeking fulfillment?

- Visualize yourself ten years into the future, being fully fulfilled, and write down what it is you are doing, being, or having that provides this fulfillment.

The following questions require you to project yourself into your successful future.

- Which areas in your life provide your fulfillment in this vision?
- What have you accomplished?
- What knowledge have you imparted?
- What strengths have you built?
- What contributions have you made?
- What legacy are you providing to the world?
- What path have you chosen that will enable you to reach this place of fulfillment?
- What choices or decisions did you make ten years ago (today) that caused you to embark on this powerful journey?

What Else Is Out There in Your Niche?

Now that you're starting to get an idea of how you want to serve and the kind of coaching practice you want to build, you can begin to look at what already exists in your chosen field. Think about the top five experts who are currently in your field, and ask yourself:

- What are these experts talking about?
- What do they offer?
- How are they perceived—how do other people label them?
- What is it that makes them the leading experts in your field?
- What can you learn from them?
- What if there are no such experts, and yet the need exists? (That's great news! It means you might be the pioneer in this area and you're in luck: It would be far easier for you to establish yourself as the leader within this niche.)

What Makes You Different?

Once you have a clear idea of who is already serving your niche at the highest level, you can begin to draw the contrast between you and them. To stand out, you don't want to be operating in their shadow. You want to stand alone, distinct and unique.

- What do you do that is similar to those top experts you've identified?
- What do you do that is different from those top experts?
- What is your angle—how are you going to *package* your unique offer?

At this stage, you may be thinking you have something. There is an area you want to work in and a group of people you want to serve. You're thinking about what is already out there and how you can stand out as unique and noticeable. Now comes the fun part: defining your secret formula.

YOUR SECRET FORMULA: BUILDING A FORMIDABLE REPUTATION AS A COACH

Your secret formula is the summary of what is special about you and the *offer* that you can make to your clients. This will be the distillation of your unique trainings, the core of the impact you make on your clients, and the source of your reputation as a coach.

As with the questions above, only you know the answer to this, and it may not hit you right away. Like a light in the distance, make your secret formula a goal to navigate toward. The sooner you can define this, the sooner you can shine as a coach.

How I Discovered My Unique Value as a Coach

If you're confused at this stage and aren't sure how to move forward, you may be reassured to know: I, too, started off without much of a clue and only a vision.

When I was younger, I only knew I wanted to get "there," but I had no idea what "there" was. I knew I had to become important, I knew I had to achieve some kind of rank in society. I knew I had to achieve some kind of financial success, and I had vague notions that I wanted to be a millionaire holding an important position in a big company. This was how I began: with huge and vague ambitions and no measurable skills.

At the age of twenty-one, I began to see how the rapid growth of technology was going to cause the replacement of human jobs. I realized that to have a successful career, I needed to develop a specialization that wasn't going to be made obsolete by a computer or machine. I decided to focus on what machines could not do. And that was to develop my ability to grasp the unpredictability and complexity of human beings, what makes them tick, what motivates them, what inspires them, etc. I wanted to know how people lived, breathed, loved, cried, and died (inside).

I took a huge liking to the idea of human development. Back then, the most accessible expression of this motivation was to become a trainer. Being a practical person, I did what anybody would do—I started offering training services. If you want to learn something, you go out and do it, which is what I did.

As a human specialist, I focused on behaviors, patterns of thinking, processes, mechanisms, and how all these things work in different environments. I eventually worked with thousands of people and came to understand how certain things that they do bring them success and fulfillment, and how certain things bring them unhappiness, failure, or stagnation.

In time, as my understanding of these processes became more refined, I was able to create a body of my own knowledge. I tested these formulas with individual clients and noticed how they learned my techniques, applied them in their lives, and obtained results. I refined, experimented, and tested different variations. The results began to build, until I could clearly define my own methodology.

This became my *secret formula* as a masterful coach. Over time I was able to see how breakthroughs affected people at the broader level. I was then able to stabilize and standardize my formula, and then apply it at higher and broader levels.

In Practice: Specialize, Experiment, and Create Tangible Results

Your secret formula rests on your ability to create tangible results for your clients. Creating a tangible result such as producing a product, having a book reach best-seller status, increasing performance so that it leads to a record-breaking profit, or increasing a client-quantified difference and improvement in a relationship, creates a visceral experience for the client. Such a visceral experience alters the experiential and evidence-based reality for the client. To become a top expert, you need to have a noticeable, measurable impact. By creating unique results in a unique way, you can expand and grow far beyond your original specialization. But before you expand, you have to start with a narrowly focused and well-defined area, test, experiment, and refine.

The most important aspect of both creating tangible results *and* being seen as an expert is your own credibility. There are two levels of credibility for coaches: your ability to create results for yourself, and your ability to create results for your clients.

BECOME LIVING PROOF OF YOUR OWN METHODOLOGY

Your backstory as a coach—to use in your marketing material and with your clients—should show how you have become living proof of your own secret formula. Your story is a testimonial to how you have experimented, distilled, and discovered your success formula and applied it to your own life. People are unlikely to have confidence in your ability to help them until you yourself become proof. You need to make your acquired knowledge and skills work for you before your knowledge and skills can be made to work for them.

In the early days, I gave sample coaching sessions to people I knew, people I met, and clients who hired me for other services. I worked odd jobs to make a living. At the same time, I continually tested and applied this method on myself in order to accelerate my ability to gain more clients. Doing this also helped me gain more insights into my applications of coaching, which helped me make my clients more successful. Within two years, I built a base of clients who could attest to the effectiveness of my coaching with their results.

Make Sure Your Formula Works for Others, Too!

Once you've defined your own success, happiness, or fulfillment as a result of your secret formula, you need to establish with certainty that your formula works with others. What evidence do you have of other people applying your methodology and achieving results? You want your clients to prove to you that they are successful because of your work.

For example, you may be an expert networker, able to skillfully relate to people and form lucrative business relationships. By reverse engineering your success, you work out your secret formula that makes you such a great networker. You deliberately apply this formula to test it and prove that it creates results for you. You then teach this formula to your clients and see how it works for them. If they too are successful, you have a proven secret formula, which creates tangible results for you *and* for your clients.

Deliver Beyond Expectations

You have defined your specialization, and you now have a formula that works. Now the question is, how will people hear about you? They have needs, problems, and desires. You have the formula that will solve this for them. Now you just need to bridge the gap and ensure the right potential clients find out about you.

The most effective way to create a formidable reputation is simple: deliver beyond expectations. There's an equation that shows you how this works:

- Disappointed customers at best will refuse to do business with you ever again, and at worst will tell others of their disappointing experience with you, which could diminish your reputation.
- Satisfied customers *might* continue doing business with you.
- Delighted customers become your fans or advocates and tell *other people* to go out and do business with you.

Deliver beyond expectations to create as many delighted customers as possible, and plant the seeds for a stellar reputation.

Cement Your Reputation

Reputation is a function of your reliability. People know they can turn to you, and you'll create powerful results for them. You become known for certain qualities. It is about creating consistency. You get results, and people trust you to achieve this for them.

When developing your reputation, you will start to realize that there are certain things that are more important than others. It is a process you go through to define what matters to you and what is at the core of your business.

For example, one of the most important things to me is creating results efficiently. To prove my own consistency and help cement my reputation, I recently decided to set a world record for the number of clients coached consecutively over the course of thirty days. With the support of a great team, we were able to coach 522 clients in one month. This proved our efficiency and spread our reputation far beyond my home base of Singapore. Because of this exercise, we landed a major government job and helped educate thousands of people about the value of coaching.

Action Steps: What Do You Know about Your Clients?

To discover how to *deliver beyond expectations* and create a reputation in your niche that will serve you for life, ask yourself this question: What do your clients expect from their coach? Think about their core need and then find out how to gauge your own success. Do you judge your impact as a coach based on your own personal standards, or are you looking at what the marketplace is offering?

Get clarity on how things stand, and then disrupt them. *The current expectations of your clients are the starting line, not the finish line.* You have to see the expectations, and you have to *surpass* them. You have to stand out by understanding what your clients expect, delivering on those expectations, and then exceeding them.

Transcend what the market expects of you, and you'll begin to form a loyal community of clients that will grow organically and exponentially.

Long-Term Goal: Create Brand-New Material

The process so far has been about taking something and testing it, proving it, and demonstrating your value to the people in your niche. All this time your community is improving. Your market size begins to grow, your following begins to grow, and that's when you are ready to truly stand out.

To grow beyond your own community, you need to establish new material that you can teach, share, and broadcast. You can use this material to train other coaches as representatives, to create online courses, and to establish a global reputation.

New material doesn't appear out of a vacuum. Like discovering your specialization, it requires incremental improvements that eventually lead to a breakthrough. It's about understanding what makes you and your clients successful and creating a marketable, replicable formula that enables you to create this success over and over again.

Summary and Your "To Do" List

The most successful coaches in the world are specialists, not generalists. Your chosen niche will depend on your skill set, your values, and what gives you the greatest fulfillment. Only you can answer this question, so take the time to get it right.

- **Choose your niche:** Look at your own talents, preferences, things you attract to you, and the things that make you feel most fulfilled. Explore your skill set and your natural abilities, as well as the things you are naturally attracted to. Let this information guide you to your niche.
- **Establish your contrast:** Research the existing experts in your field. Consider what they're doing, what they offer, how they're perceived. See what you can learn from them, and then explore things you do that set you apart from them.
- **Develop your reputation:** Distill your methodology down into a secret formula that makes your approach special.

- **Overdeliver:** Understand the expectations of your marketplace, and then rise above them. Deliver more than people expect and you'll begin to attract a community of loyal clients around you.
- **Start narrowly, grow broadly:** Start with a narrow, specialized focus. Concentrate on an area where you can make a big impact and build a foundation of skill, experience, and reputation. Then, scale up and take your business in any direction you choose.

Coaching Executives and CEOs

5 Changes You Need to Make

MARSHALL GOLDSMITH

Dr. Marshall Goldsmith is the author or editor of thirty-five books, which have sold over 2 million copies, been translated into thirty languages, and become best sellers in twelve countries. He was ranked World's No. 1 Leadership Thinker by Thinkers50, and he has received awards, accolades, or recognition from almost every professional institution in the field of business management, including the National Academy of Human Resources and the American Management Association.

*He's been called the world's No. 1 executive coach, so Marshall Goldsmith knows a thing or two about coaching in the big leagues. Discover **five changes** you need to make to reinvent yourself as a high-paid executive coach.*

Most coaches I meet are great coaches but horrible businesspeople. They believe that if they do their job well and their clients like them, success and recognition will inevitably come their way. This pervasive belief is one of the reasons that so many good coaches are struggling when they should be thriving. In the real world, it simply doesn't work like that.

To succeed as a coach, you've got to learn the business side of coaching. You need to know how to:

- Communicate with executives and CEOs in their own language
- Define a clear specialization
- Market yourself effectively

You need to be willing to do the work and take pride in every aspect of the coaching process.

My journey to coaching began when I was a nineteen-year-old university student in Indiana. Back then, I had never heard of executive coaching—it's possible the profession didn't even exist! I was trying to figure out what to do with my life, and I stayed up all night asking myself big questions and thinking about what I wanted. Dawn broke and I looked out of the window at all the people miserably trudging off to work. I realized I didn't want to be like that.

Almost ten years later, I was the protege of an extraordinary coach, Dr. Paul Hersey, the cocreator of Situational Leadership™. Paul's job was giving talks to business leaders. One day, he found himself double-booked, so he offered me $1,000 to give one of the presentations for him. I was nervous, but I did it. My presentation was well received, so Paul started sending me out for more appointments. My career in the executive coaching space had begun.

After fourteen years of success as a speaker on business leadership, I found that I was no longer growing. I was coasting on the success I had already achieved. It was time for a shift. I started focusing on creating original ideas, doing research, and writing books. It has now been nearly fifty years since that night in Indiana. Over that time, I have met thousands of coaches, some thriving, others struggling.

Based on my experience, I believe there are **five changes** most coaches need to make to become successful and work with top-level clients. Making these changes may require you to unlearn some of the things you were taught when you first became a coach and to change beliefs and attitudes that you may have been carrying for years.

The Five Ways Most Coaches Need to Change

1. Change how you're paid. This goes to your *business model* and the deals you make with your clients.
2. Change your attitude to work. It is possible that you may just get lucky and become incredibly successful without having to work very hard. Don't count on it.
3. Get over your fear of promotion. Many coaches are terrified of promoting themselves, but your business *will not* succeed without marketing.
4. Become a specialist, not a generalist. I'm not an expert at fifty things, but I am **the expert** at one thing.
5. Get coaching out of the shadows. My clients are proud to have me as a coach. Yours should be proud of you, too!

Let's have a look at these five changes in more detail.

ONE: CHANGE HOW YOU'RE PAID

I am frequently embarrassed by how little most coaches earn. Some coaches would increase their revenue if they abandoned coaching in favor of bagging groceries! Fortunately, the reasons for this are simple and easily fixed.

Most coaches get paid based on two incredibly bad measures:

1. How much *time* you spend with your clients
2. How much your clients *like* you

This is a poor foundation for a business model, and not one that will appeal to CEOs and business executives. If you want to work with business leaders and charge high fees for executive coaching, you need to **charge for results**.

My first coaching assignment came about because of a conversation with the CEO of a large company. He said, "We have this young guy on our team who is amazing, but he's a jerk! It would be worth a fortune to me if we could change his behavior." I said, "OK, I'll work with him for a year. If he gets better, pay me; if not, don't."

CEOs are busy people. They like a straightforward, direct offer. "If this is achieved, do I get this money?" It's that simple. When you're playing at a high level, even the slightest measurable improvement in your client's behavior can be worth millions of dollars to the company. A small slice of this will be a handsome reward, but you will not get it if you are not willing to risk getting *zero*.

I've had a guaranteed base salary of $0 for the past thirty-eight years. I tend to get results, so I get paid. Most coaches are afraid of charging for results because it seems risky. The fact is, if you want to be successful, you're going to have to take some risks. If you believe what you say, *bet on it*. Show some guts, be willing to take a chance, and you may just get paid more.

What about Helping Others?

Many coaches are driven to the profession out of a desire to help others. Helping those in need is a worthy endeavor, but it is not a pathway toward wealth. I draw a clear distinction between the work that I get paid for—helping CEOs and business leaders—and my charity work.

About 30 percent to 40 percent of all the coaching work I do is *pro bono*. I've worked with charities like the American Red Cross and lent them the benefit of my expertise. I frequently give back and work with those who cannot afford it. But this is not how I make my living.

TWO: CHANGE YOUR ATTITUDE TO WORK

A couple of young people came up to me recently and said, "Marshall, we want to be like you one day." I said, "What do you mean?" They said, "We want to coach CEOs." While I love their ambition, I've published thirty-five books and flown 11 million miles. If you want to be me, it may take a while. You're going to have to pay some dues.

I've frequently heard coaches say something to the effect of, "I want to coach CEOs, *but*." That "but" is normally followed by what they are *unwilling* to do: "*but* I don't want to travel," "*but* I don't want to work weekends," or "*but* I don't want to write a book—that sounds hard!" The fact is, you will not achieve high levels of success as a coach without putting in the hours. It just isn't going to happen.

When we look at top coaches and successful businesspeople and consider them lucky, we are normally mistaken. Apart from the odd fluke, what seems like "luck" from the outside is the result of years of preparation, planning, and experience. The good news is, this hard work need not be painful.

When my friend and mentor Dr. Paul Hersey received an honorary doctorate, he told the graduating students: "Looking back on my career, I don't feel like I have ever worked a day in my life. If you really love what you are doing, it all seems like fun!" Hold fast to the passion that drove you to become a coach in the first place. This passion will see you through the long-haul flights and early mornings, and it will make each hour seem worth your while.

THREE: GET OVER YOUR FEAR OF PROMOTION

There's an endemic fear of self-promotion inside the coaching profession. In the same way that many coaches are afraid of *asking* for money in exchange for results, coaches are also afraid of marketing their services. They believe that if they do good work, then clients will simply come to them automatically. This sort of wishful thinking is the ruin of so many good coaches.

It's a mistake to believe that refusing to market yourself is somehow modest or humble. It is, in fact, the height of arrogance. By choosing not to promote yourself, what you are actually saying is, "I'm so good I shouldn't have to lower myself to do marketing." Well, most people who say this are so good, they're broke.

Creating a Mission for Your Coaching Business

You may find yourself more comfortable with your marketing efforts—and more successful—if you let yourself be driven by your mission. This mission is the North Star of your coaching business. It's why you exist. This will give your marketing soul as well as a bite. You won't feel like a huckster, because you'll be coming from a place of passion and sincerity.

My own mission is simple. *I want to help successful people achieve positive, lasting change and behavior.* It's right there on my website for anyone to see. Peter Drucker, the legendary management consultant, once told me that companies should be able to "put their mission statement on a T-shirt." The same is true for coaches.

Your mission must be specific. Your clients know that you're not an expert in everything. They will find it easier to believe that you are *the* expert at *one* thing. To define your mission, think first about *who* you are helping, and then consider *what* you are helping them to do.

For me, the *who* is successful leaders, the *what* is "achieve positive, lasting change and behavior." Your mission could be to help *top athletes* achieve *measurable improvement in performance*. It could be to help *technology executives* to *achieve more with less time*. The more specific, the better.

This brings us to the fourth change I want to discuss.

FOUR: BECOME A SPECIALIST, NOT A GENERALIST

If you look at the Thinkers50 list of the top business thinkers in the world, you'll notice one thing in common: They are all *specialists*. To succeed as a coach, you have to clearly define a market specialization that separates you from other coaches. This specialization goes hand in hand with your mission, making it clear why you are different from all the other coaches out there.

Great entrepreneurs provide products and services that everyone wants but no one else is providing. Look around the coaching space you're in, and look for pressing needs that are not currently being filled. Be creative here. Your specialization is one of the most important business decisions you'll ever make. It's worth taking the time to get it right.

Once you've narrowed down your specialization, the real work begins. You don't just want to be *an* expert in your chosen field. You want to be *the* expert. It may sound daunting, but achieving world-class expertise in a narrow field is not as hard as it sounds.

If you have narrowed down your specialization sufficiently, just a few years of work should be enough for you to acquire serious knowledge and stand head and shoulders above those who merely dabble. You will never become the world's expert in *everything*, but you can definitely become an expert in one thing.

FIVE: GET COACHING OUT OF THE SHADOWS

It seems like many coaches think of the work they do as somehow secretive or shameful. They are afraid of announcing their clients to the world, thinking that their clients must surely be *embarrassed* by the fact that they need coaching. Nothing could be further from the truth. The best tennis players in the world need coaches. Everyone knows that. They're not ashamed. Why shouldn't businesspeople be able to seek help as well?

This macho nonsense that it is somehow wrong to admit that we have a problem or seek help damages us both as coaches and as human beings. My clients are proud to have me as a coach. This is important for the business side of what I do. It means I can write about them in my books, quote them in articles, and announce to the world that these respected leaders have chosen me as their coach.

Many coaches keep their client lists secret. If a client of mine ever told me that I wasn't allowed to mention their name, I would politely show them the door, no matter how famous they were or how much they wanted to pay me. If we want to succeed as coaches and lift our entire industry, we need to get coaching out of the closet.

I'm the world's No. 1 executive coach, and yet I still need help. I pay someone to call me every day. I'm not ashamed of this. The dancer and choreographer Twyla Tharp is a friend of mine. She's had the same personal trainer for twenty-five years. There's nothing new that this trainer can teach her, but she still needs someone for the support. If we had the courage and discipline to continue alone, perhaps we would. We don't. Few people do. And that's okay.

It's okay to admit you're a human being. As long as the client believes that the coaching process is in the closet, and as long as you agree with them, they won't get better. The business leaders I coach need to admit that they have a problem. They need to acknowledge the fact that they can improve, that they are ready and willing to change. This improvement needs to be measurable for the world to see.

When I met with Soon Loo, one of the clients from Patryk and Kasia Wezowski's movie *Leap*, I told him something that I tell all of my clients: "You won't succeed because I'm a great coach. You will succeed because *you* are a great client." Be proud of the work you do, and encourage your clients to be proud of it as well.

Summary and Your "To Do" List

If you want to coach CEOs, then you have to change your attitudes and business practices. You need to know how to communicate with executives and CEOs in their own language. You also must define a clear specialization and market yourself effectively.

- **Change how you're paid:** Even though it sounds risky, charge for results. If you want to be successful, you need to take some risks. If you believe what you say, bet on it.
- **Change your attitude toward work:** Embrace the idea of paying some dues. Hold fast to the passion that drove you to become a coach. This passion will see you through the work that success requires.
- **Promote and market yourself:** Refusing to market yourself is not modest or humble. It's arrogant. Let your mission drive your marketing. That way, you will come from a place of passion.
- **Become a specialist:** Clearly define a market specialization that separates you from other coaches. This specialization should go hand in hand with your mission, making it clear why you are different.
- **Get out of the shadows:** Be proud of the work you do and encourage your clients to be proud of it as well.

Like my friend Peter Drucker, we want to look back and realize that we never really worked a day in our lives. If you love what you do and have a passion for being a coach, then I believe these five changes can help you accelerate your success and become better rewarded for the work that you do.

The LinkedIn Coach

How to Use LinkedIn to Generate Leads, Customers, and Clients

MIRNA BACUN

Mirna Bacun is a LinkedIn Lead Generation and Marketing Specialist who discovered the potential of LinkedIn as a marketing tool when she was winding down her software business and struggling to make sales. After cracking the LinkedIn code for herself and successfully getting out of debt, Mirna used LinkedIn again to start her second business—helping coaches, marketers, and entrepreneurs tap into the potential of the network to grow their business by finding and connecting with the right people for their high-end services.

Most coaches struggle to find clients for their business. One answer is LinkedIn. Discover exactly how to use LinkedIn to find, attract, and convert leads to clients and customers for your business.

Many coaches reading this will shudder at the very idea of social media. Around the world, good coaches are stuck in marketing hell, spending hours hustling on sites like Facebook and Twitter without seeing any significant increase in clients or revenue. If this is you, then take heart: You aren't doing it wrong. You're just in the wrong place.

I started using LinkedIn while working in my first company, which was a B2B software business. My company had almost no marketing budget, but we needed sales. I started using LinkedIn, figuring it out as I went along. As a result, I made $47,000 for the software company purely from this platform. Despite the fact that sales were looking up, I realized that I was unhappy as a CEO. I wanted more freedom, and I knew how to get it.

I left the company and started a LinkedIn consulting business so I can teach other people how to put LinkedIn to work for their business, too. Appropriately, I promoted my course and coaching programs on LinkedIn itself, and I made $45,000 in revenue within nine months.

Today, I make over $100,000 (and growing) with two different business by using LinkedIn.

If you're a coach looking for clients, you need to be on LinkedIn. Unlike *social* networks like Facebook and Instagram, LinkedIn is a *business* network. The people there are players and decision makers—CEOs, executives, entrepreneurs—and they are ready and willing to connect with people who can help move their business forward.

Because LinkedIn is a different animal than Facebook or Twitter, you need to approach it with a different strategy. In this chapter, we'll look at exactly how you can use LinkedIn to find and attract high-quality leads and convert them to clients for your coaching business.

FIND: DISCOVERING POTENTIAL CLIENTS

LinkedIn has more than 450 million users worldwide. No matter how specific your niche is, you're likely to find a lot of potential leads on this platform. Before you jump on the Internet and start searching, make sure you know exactly whom you're trying to find. Ask yourself: *Who is the ideal client for my coaching business?*

The search features on LinkedIn make it easy for you to zero in on the exact people you want to work with. You can use these filters to find your *LinkedIn target market*. The clearer and more specific your niche, the easier you'll achieve results. (If you're new to coaching, see Kelvin Lim's chapter for advice on choosing and honing your niche.)

Focus on Position, Not Demographics

If you've already attempted to use LinkedIn to grow your coaching business but haven't seen results, chances are it's because you've been applying a Facebook way of thinking. When you advertise on Facebook, demographics and interests are key. Are your potential clients men or women? Where do they live? How old are they? What books do they like?

A Facebook client profile would read something like: *male, 30–40 years old, based in U.S., interested in start-ups and entrepreneurship.* On LinkedIn, that kind of thing won't get you far. Remember, LinkedIn is a business network frequently used by recruiters, so think like a CEO searching for your next hire.

Focus On:

- What is their job title? CEO? HR manager? Marketing manager?
- Are they the decision maker, or are you targeting someone lower in the company?
- Are they self-employed?
- What industry do they work in?
- What is the size of their company?
- What is their annual revenue?
- What LinkedIn groups do they hang out in?

These are the questions you should ask yourself if you want to define your LinkedIn target market well.

Defining your target market correctly is the "Step Zero" and the key to your success on LinkedIn. If you don't get this right, you probably won't have much success with the platform later on.

Example: Finding Clients for a Wellness Coach

If you're a wellness expert who wants to work with busy technology executives, focus on the kind of person who is likely to be working long hours and in need of some health and lifestyle advice. In this case, you'd search for CEOs, executives, or managers in large, competitive technology companies, as well as the owners of tech start-ups—positions that demand sacrifice and long hours.

Run a few practice searches to get the hang of it. Start with the search bar and LinkedIn will direct you to the search part of the platform—then choose the "People" tab. Zoom in on the job title (under the "Keyword" filter), the industry those potential clients work in, and the "Country" filter. Spend some time reading the profiles of the people who could become leads, clients, or customers. Get a sense of who they are. This will be essential information for the next two steps: *attract* and *convert*.

The more specific your targeting, the better results you'll have—so don't focus on the quantity of results, but quality. I advise my clients to focus on just *one* product and *one* market on LinkedIn. After all, if you seem like the generic coach for *everyone*, then you're actually the coach for *no one*.

ATTRACT: CREATING A PROFILE THAT GETS RESULTS

Now that you have a good idea of who you're searching for on LinkedIn, it's time to create an amazing profile that will help you connect and eventually convert total strangers into loyal clients or repeat customers. It's important to get these steps in the right order, because creating a good LinkedIn profile isn't about *you*, it's about your target market.

Most people think of Facebook as a playground and LinkedIn as an online resume. As a coach looking for clients, however, it's more useful to think of LinkedIn as a relationship-building *page*. Your potential clients aren't interested in how many years you spent at university; all they care about is what you can do *for them*—and that's what you need to communicate on your LinkedIn profile.

Choose One Thing to Sell

Many coaches on the platform struggle to convert the leads they've attracted to their LinkedIn profile because they lack a clear, specific goal. You can't *find* people on LinkedIn until you know who you're looking for. Likewise, you can't *attract* or *convert* people into clients or customers until you have decided **exactly what you're selling and what you want those leads to do once they've visited your LinkedIn profile**.

If you have just one product or coaching package, then this is easy: Your goal is more clients or customers for your program. If you've been around for a while and have multiple products across different niches, then narrow down. Choose just *one* of your products or services, and focus exclusively on this. Run with your most lucrative program, or the niche in which you have the most knowledge and feel the most comfortable. Later, once you've *converted* your new connections, you can upsell your other programs outside of LinkedIn.

Zero In on the Benefits

Forget about optimizing your profile for keywords. Instead, zero in on benefits of the one program you have chosen to focus on.

This is one of the most important marketing questions you'll ever ask yourself as a coach: What are the core benefits of the service or product you provide? Exactly how does it help your clients or customers? If you're a wellness expert, your benefit could be that you help people *stay healthy*, or *lose weight*, or *relax*, or *feel good*. If you're a business coach, you could work with businesses to *double sales* or *reduce costs*.

Just like your target audience, the benefit you provide should be simple, specific, and relevant. What do people in your target group really want, but aren't getting so far? What are their needs, wants, and desires? What points of pain are they experiencing in their lives or business?

A great way to keep yourself disciplined and benefit-focused is to stop saying "I" and instead say "you." Instead of, *"I have ten years of marketing experience in the technology sector, so I know how to help companies dramatically increase their online revenue without significant effort,"* say, *"With a few simple changes, it's easy to dramatically increase your online revenue."*

As you're writing, imagine that one of the potential clients you researched in the first step above was standing over your shoulder, shrugging, and asking, "So why do I care?" Constantly explain what's in it *for them*, why they should work with you.

Create a Compelling Headline

The headline is the part of your LinkedIn profile that goes right beside your profile picture. It's by far the most important element on your profile, because it's visible everywhere—on every piece of content you create and every invitation you send throughout the platform. Often, your short, one-sentence headline is all people read before deciding whether or not to actually find out who you are.

I'm constantly tweaking my LinkedIn profile to better reach my target market. At the moment, my headline is:

> I help 6-figure business owners <u>find and convert high-quality leads</u> with LinkedIn.

The underlined section explains who I specifically work with and the *benefits* I provide to my clients and customers. If you're a wellness expert working with technology executives, your headline could be something like:

> Executive wellness expert. I help hardworking business leaders in the technology space <u>reduce stress, sleep better, and feel healthier</u>.

An effective headline reads like a one- or two-sentence *elevator pitch*. Imagine you just stepped into an elevator with a potential client. You're about to reach your floor, and you have only fifteen seconds to explain exactly why they should work with you and what's in it for them. This is your headline.

Tell a Story That Speaks to Your Target Audience

One of the most important things you can do with your LinkedIn profile is have people *make a connection* with you. You want to focus on benefits and how you help them, but in a way that has you feeling like a human being, not a corporation.

A quick, two- or three-line story at the start of your profile is a great way to accomplish this. The best stories are *relevant* to the benefit and product you're providing, and they speak *directly to* your target audience and the pain and problems they are experiencing.

Here's how my LinkedIn profile currently begins. I'll underline the *benefits* to make them more obvious. Notice how the story makes me seem human, while tying everything together with the *benefits* that I'm offering to customers and speaking directly to *who* my target audience is:

> If you run a six-figure business, then you probably want to <u>find and target high-quality leads with LinkedIn and convert them to clients on autopilot</u> by using a proven system, so you can <u>focus on predictable growth</u> in your company.

> When I started my first company, I had no idea how to <u>get high-quality leads</u> and turn them into <u>paying clients</u>. I just did what everybody else was doing—I tried book recommendations, webinar tips, and every piece of advice I got—but nothing was working.

> And then, out of pure necessity, I started to use LinkedIn.

Like your headline, the opening of your profile is worth spending the time to get right. Let's return to our wellness expert example. Here's how this could read:

> If you are a technology executive or the owner of a tech start-up who works twelve-hour days, then you probably want to <u>keep up your productivity without sacrificing your health</u> and constantly feeling drained.

> When I was an executive at a tech firm, I always felt exhausted and stressed. I had no idea how to perform at a high level at work yet still <u>relax and stay healthy</u>.

> Finally, out of pure necessity, I started meditating . . .

Choose a Call to Action

The final ingredient of a compelling LinkedIn profile is also the one most people forget: a *call to action*. What is the action that you want people to take after connecting with you and reading your LinkedIn profile? This decision will depend on the one specific product or service you have chosen to optimize your profile around and the sales strategy behind this.

Your call to action should be **the first step** toward making a sale or landing a client, not the last step. As we'll see in **step 3**, *convert*, you do not sell on LinkedIn. Instead, you use LinkedIn to make a connection and funnel people into your other (non-LinkedIn) funnels.

How do you normally close clients? If you have an e-mail list that you use to send newsletters and sell products, then the call to action on your LinkedIn profile will be to visit a website and sign up to join your newsletter or download something directly from your profile. If you normally close clients after a phone call that focuses on their problems and the benefits of working together, then your call to action will be to contact you and arrange a free fifteen-minute discovery call.

Whatever your call to action, you want this to be clear in *every section of your profile*. Connect it to the benefits you offer, and give them a compelling reason to take this action. Remember, the reader is constantly asking, "Why, what's in it for me?"

The call to action on my LinkedIn profile is:

If you want to find and target the right leads with LinkedIn and convert them to clients and sales, connect with me here or send an e-mail to me at: mirna@mirnabacun.com.

Returning to our wellness expert example, it could be:

If you want help to reduce stress and feel healthier despite your hectic schedule, get in touch to schedule a free fifteen-minute discovery call. Send me an e-mail at wellnessexpertcoach@example.com.

Action Steps

Spend some time browsing LinkedIn to get an idea of how others have created their profiles. Most won't be good, but some will be. Did any headlines jump out at you and make you want to discover more about this person? Did you feel a connection to any of the stories? Did you end up taking *action* after reading any profiles, such as visiting a website or contacting the person?

Sit down with a pen and paper and write ten different headlines. Choose the best one, and see how it feels for you. If you're not sure which one is the best, ask friends, family, or acquaintances. Choose a true story from your life connected to the benefits that you offer, and spend some time writing this down. Remember, *you*, not *I*. Finally, select your call to action and make sure it is clear, compelling, and visible throughout your profile.

Checklist for a Compelling LinkedIn Profile:

- Include an elevator pitch in your headline
- Tell a compelling, relatable story
- Write "you" sentences, instead of "I" sentences
- Talk about your target market needs, wants, fears, and desires
- Answer these questions in EVERY part of your LinkedIn profile: Why should I care? What's in it for me?
- Weave in small *calls to action* throughout

CONVERT: DON'T SELL, CONNECT

As we discovered when choosing your *action steps* above, LinkedIn is not a place for selling, it's a place for *positioning yourself as an expert and building trust*. Use LinkedIn to build relationships with potential clients, and then direct them off LinkedIn to begin your standard sales process.

The precise strategy you should use will vary depending on your business model. If you're selling coaching packages, then it makes sense to invest the time in speaking to people one-on-one. If you're selling lower-priced products, then you have to reach people in bulk and direct them to an automated sales funnel.

Let's look at a how each process works.

Connecting with Potential Coaching Clients

Here's how to use LinkedIn to convert one-on-one clients for your coaching business. This process requires you to spend time interacting with people on an individual level, which makes sense only if what you're selling is reasonably high-end, such as a six-month coaching package. If you spend a week talking to people on LinkedIn and the result is one extra client that nets you $10,000, that's time well spent.

1. Follow the steps in *Find* above to pull up a list of highly targeted potential clients.
2. Instead of connecting (the LinkedIn equivalent of a friend request) straight from the list, click on each person's individual profile.
3. Then, send a personalized message alongside your request to connect. Most people use this function to send a long and "spammy" message about their product or service. Don't be like that!
4. Remember the golden rule: connect, don't sell. Use this first message to introduce yourself and ask a question about their business. In our wellness coach example, you could say:
5. *Hey (first name). I saw your LinkedIn profile and thought it might be beneficial for us to connect. I'm a wellness coach who works with executives in the technology industry, and I'd love to hear more about you and what you do.*
6. Not everyone will accept your connection request or reply to your message, but some will. In my experience, response rates are normally around 20 percent to 30 percent, depending on the industry you are targeting.
7. When they do reply, *be human, be real*. Ask more questions, engage with them, form a connection person to person. Be natural and congruent. In the messages to follow, you can ask them about their biggest challenges, share your blog post for executives about how to stay productive and healthy while working long hours, or just share someone else's articles on the topic.
8. In your communication, you need to provide them with benefits, educate them, and position yourself as an expert. The most important thing is to get them engaged and talking.
9. If you feel like you've made a connection and there's scope for you to work together, it's time to direct the person to your *call to action*. You still aren't selling them anything. You're offering something free that will provide a relevant *benefit* to them, such as a free fifteen-minute phone conversation.

10. *Thank you for sharing! Would you like to jump on a free fifteen-minute Skype conversation to discuss how you can reduce stress at the office? I'll share a few tips with you that have helped my other clients, and if you like what you hear we can talk about working together further.*

11. On the actual call, offer real value and deliver on your promises, and then explain your coaching package. If you have a standard sales process, this is when that would begin.

It really is that simple. Connect by asking a question, exchange a few messages, and then direct them *off LinkedIn* so your normal sales process can begin. Be human, natural, and authentic. With practice, you'll get better at this. Persistence is key. Don't try with just one person and give up if it doesn't work. Try connecting with ten people a day for one month, and see what happens.

Connecting with Potential Customers

If you're using LinkedIn to sell lower-end products, rather than one-on-one coaching packages, then you need to vary your approach. Instead of investing the time in connecting with people individually, you want to reach as many people as possible with less duplicate effort.

The best way to do this is to create a LinkedIn group. Like a Facebook group, LinkedIn groups pull together people with similar interests. Being a *business network*, not a social network, LinkedIn groups tend to be niche- and business-focused, a great opportunity to reach potential customers.

Here's how the group approach works:

1. Create a LinkedIn group from within your profile. (The process changes frequently as LinkedIn upgrades their platform.) Go to the item labeled "work" on the right and click "groups > my groups > create a group." If these instructions aren't working, you'll be able to find an up-to-date tutorial on Google.

2. Follow the same rules for naming your group that we explored in *Find* above: Narrow it down, make it specific. If you're a wellness coach, don't make your group "The Wellness Group," make it *"Wellness Group for Tech Executives."* The more niche- and business-specific, the better.

3. Invite your existing contacts to join your group. Encourage people to introduce themselves. Promote discussion by asking questions, as we explored earlier, and answer the questions that other people post. Don't expect engagement to be as high as Facebook groups, and that's okay. There's still value for you in people joining your group even if they don't engage.

4. Search for similar groups, join them, and become a productive member, participating in discussions and building a reputation as an expert. Gently promote your group from within there, not in a "spammy" way but in a polite and helpful way.

5. *Great question. We had a similar discussion in my Wellness Group for Tech Executives [link]. The key takeaways from the discussion were about finding a way to relax in the workplace. Here's a useful technique for that . . .*

6. Use the tools LinkedIn provides to set up an automated message to be sent to members of your group. Use a similar approach when crafting this message that you used for creating your profile: Make it compelling, focused on them, and directed toward your *call to action.* Your call to action will be a sales funnel that's separate from LinkedIn. If you're selling products, you probably already have this. For example, you could invite people to visit your website and join your newsletter in exchange for a free gift, or encourage them to watch a video that gives away tips and promotes your course. Here's an example:

   Thanks for joining the Wellness Group for Tech Executives! I hope to get to know you and help you stay healthy, reduce stress, and thrive in the workplace.

   Over ten years as a wellness coach for busy business leaders, I've discovered that the No. 1 thing tech executives struggle with is finding a way to relax while at the office. I've written an eBook with five techniques to help you easily relax and reduce stress with just a few minutes a day. As a member of this group, you're invited to download a free copy. Just visit: WellnessCoachExample.com/free.

7. Stay engaged in the group and in giving value, and send occasional bulk messages directing people to your call to action and your separate sales funnel.

Whether you're selling products to a thousand people or coaching one person, the principle remains the same: Form a connection, and then direct them *off LinkedIn* to begin your usual sales process. Be human, show genuine interest, and provide real value at every step.

Summary and Your "To Do" List

The best-networked coaches should spend their time on LinkedIn, not Facebook or Twitter. As a coach, it is for me hands down the most powerful tool for finding and connecting with new clients online. Follow the steps to success carefully and be willing to put in the time, and you'll enjoy amazing results.

- **Focus on position, not demographics:** Choose one specific product or coaching package to sell to one specific group of people. Find potential clients by focusing on position, not demographics. The more specific and business-oriented, the better.
- **Attract with benefits:** Emphasize the *key benefit* that your product or service will provide to your target market. Tell stories, build connections, and constantly answer the question, "What's in it for me?"
- **Don't sell on LinkedIn:** Build trust, position yourself as an expert, direct people to a free *call to action* that gets them *off* LinkedIn and into your regular sales funnel.
- **Customize conversion:** If you're after one-on-one clients, connection is key. Reach out individually, open a conversation, and build rapport. If you're selling products, then spread your approach wider. Create a niche group, encourage discussion, and invite group members to *take action* and join your sales funnel outside of LinkedIn.

The Nonprofit Sector

How to Thrive as a Coach by Helping Nonprofits Deliver on Their Mission

PATRICK JINKS

Patrick Jinks has twenty-one years of leadership experience in the nonprofit world. He has been the CEO of two nonprofits during thirteen of those years, one with an annual budget of $10 million. Noticing a leadership gap in the nonprofit sector, Patrick decided to make the leap and become a full-time coach, primarily serving social sector organizations. Having rapidly established a thriving coaching practice, Patrick is passionate about advancing leadership development for mission-focused leaders to drive change in their communities.

Just like corporations, nonprofits need coaching to help them find clarity and enhance their impact. There are 1.5 million nonprofits in the United States alone, with $3.5 trillion in collective assets. By helping nonprofits more effectively deliver on their mission, you can thrive as a coach while making a real impact in your own community and in the world.

In the nonprofit sector, mission comes first. People get up in the morning and go to work with the sole purpose of improving their communities.

161

Unlike the corporate sector, where profit is paramount, nonprofits are evaluated by the *social impact* they make on their communities. By helping nonprofits clarify and deliver on their mission, it's possible to carve out a rewarding and lucrative niche as a coach.

For more than twenty-one years, I've held leadership positions in the nonprofit sector. As the CEO of two nonprofits and a part-time consultant, I quickly discovered that the social sector was lacking in the kind of leadership skill and focus that is so in demand in the corporate arena. With just a small amount of coaching, I could help nonprofit leaders greatly improve their effectiveness and make a bigger difference.

It took a while for me to work up the courage to let go of my long-term employment stability and make the commitment to become a full-time coach. I had to learn that if I still had that safety net—those regular consulting jobs or part-time positions that paid the bills—I would never be sufficiently motivated to make my coaching business a success. About six years ago, I decided to get rid of the safety net, climb out of the harness, and make *the leap*. Since then I've managed to thrive as a coach for the social sector.

Contrary to what most people think, working within the nonprofit arena does not mean you need to greatly sacrifice your income or your lifestyle. While your clients don't work for profit, your coaching business remains a for-profit entity, meaning it really is possible for you to make a significant income even though you're working in the nonprofit sector. In just my first year as a full-time coach, I crossed the six-figure threshold, a milestone even for traditional executive coaches.

As a coach to nonprofit leaders, your job is simple: help them accomplish their mission and make a greater contribution to their community. Inside this chapter, we'll explore exactly how putting *mission first* can help you thrive as a coach in the nonprofit world.

Even if the idea of working with nonprofit organizations doesn't appeal to you (and there's nothing wrong with that—this kind of thing isn't for everyone), inside this chapter you'll learn coaching, sales, and positioning principles that can be applied in almost any industry. If it works for nonprofits, it'll help you in the corporate world, too.

YOUR MISSION IS THEIR MISSION: SOCIAL IMPACT

Everyone who has worked as a coach in the corporate world will know the all-consuming power of the *bottom line*. It's a simple measure: If a company is making more money than it spends, it's doing well. For non-profits, things are more complicated. They operate on what is often called the *Double Bottom Line*.

The Double Bottom Line

- Bottom line one: profit and loss. Like regular corporations, nonprofits still need to bring in more money than they spend. This enables them to pay their bills and invest in growing their operation.
- Bottom line two: social impact. This is why nonprofits exist. It's the *mission* that brings the team to the office every day. It's the *difference* that they want to make. Nonprofits have different ways to measure this, from the number of people helped with true charity to the measured impact on a community-wide issue (like a reduction in homelessness) over a longer term.

The Double Bottom Line is essential for understanding how to function as an effective coach for nonprofit leaders. It's also an interesting thought experiment for you if you work with for-profit corporations. Ask yourself: In addition to making money, what is this company trying to achieve?

If you start treating your corporate clients *as if* they were nonprofits, and judging them by the Double Bottom Line, you may find you can help them better engage their employees, sharpen their focus, *and* make more money.

Social Impact Is the No. 1 Currency for Nonprofits

The Double Bottom Line shows us that nonprofits are judged on the *contribution* they make to their communities, based on the particular value proposition of each organization. The two lines of *profit* and *social impact* go hand in hand, forming a symbiotic cycle. The bigger a contribution a nonprofit makes, the higher their profile. The higher their profile, the easier it is for them to raise funds. The more funds they have, the more they can invest in helping their community. And so the cycle repeats:

The Cycle of Success

> *Make an impact > Raise funds > Make more of an impact > Raise more funds > Make even more of an impact.*

Your Role as a Coach: Help Define and Enhance the Mission

Coaches in the nonprofit sector are most useful when we focus on the second half of the Double Bottom Line: social impact. We serve nonprofits best when we help them sharpen their mission and reach a more profound understanding of *why they exist*. This clarity will help them better connect to donor motivation, allocate resources, and inspire their team—all of which will help them increase impact in their communities.

As independent, external coaches, we have enough distance to ask the hard questions and notice things that people inside of the organization may not see for themselves. I find that the best way to achieve this is simply to have *meaningful conversations*. Ask them what value their organization delivers for their constituents. How would their community be worse off if their organization did not exist? Seek to truly understand where they're coming from and what their *why* really is, and both you and your clients will achieve clarity as they discover their own answers.

The Concept in Practice

Let's suppose a charitable health organization exists to help people in a poor community gain greater access to healthcare. They are doing great work, but they lack focus as to where their resources would be best allocated. Which health conditions merit more attention? Should they focus on school communities or single-parent households? By asking the right questions, you help the charity realize not only the greatest needs, but how their core competencies can best meet those needs. Perhaps they arrive at a program that helps sick or injured workers return to work sooner.

With the insights you have helped them achieve, the organization now has clarity of purpose. The second line of their Double Bottom Line is now much clearer to them: number of injured people successfully back on their feet and in the workplace. Of course, the more coaching is applied, the deeper you can help them go. Are they measuring just the people they help? Or is there a greater economic measure that leads to even greater essence (e.g., job retention, real income, household financial stability)?

With this newfound focus, the health charity can better allocate resources and quantify their success. They can communicate their value to wealthy citizens, business owners, and politicians in their community, who become inspired to donate more (after all, they benefit too from having a healthier, more effective taxpaying workforce). With all the new donations, they can help more people, thus inspiring even more donations.

The symbiotic relationship between both halves of the Double Bottom Line accelerates the charity forward, all thanks to the focus you helped them achieve through your effective coaching!

Stay in Your Lane: Be a Coach, Not a Consultant

Like the corporate world, the nonprofit sector is flooded with *consultants*. There are strategic planners, financial consultants, fund-raising consultants, management consultants, and so on. Once you become established as someone who helps organizations enhance their impact, chances are you will be frequently approached for *consulting* work of this nature. Although it's hard—particularly at the start when you're eager for any clients who come your way—you and your clients will be best served in the long term if you stay in your lane by resisting consulting engagements and focusing on coaching.

Consultants provide *answers*. As coaches, we provide the *questions*. Because *mission* and *purpose* are of such paramount importance in the nonprofit sector, the only answers that matter are the ones that the client supply themselves. They must completely own and believe in their reasons for operating and advancing the mission of their organization. You can help them clarify and better focus these reasons, but as an outsider you cannot come up with these answers for them—it just won't be *real*, and it won't stick.

It will be difficult at the start when new business is tempting, but focus on the long term and stick to your core competencies. Be a coach. Refer the consulting work to others to maintain goodwill and build up connections in your industry. Remember, it's all about the mission.

TIME TO THRIVE: CREATING AND MARKETING A COACHING BUSINESS IN THE NONPROFIT WORLD

One of the most pervasive myths about the nonprofit sector is that *there's no money in it*. In reality, the fact that nonprofits do not set out primarily to make money doesn't mean they don't HAVE money.

In the United States alone, there are about 1.5 million nonprofit organizations who have a combined $3.5 *trillion* in assets. Together, they generate about $2 *trillion* in revenue each year, of which nearly $100 billion is left over as profit. Of the funds that the nonprofits spend, almost $200 billion a year goes toward nonprogram expenses—that is, investments *like coaching*, which aren't directly connected to their mission but ultimately do help them make a bigger impact.

In short, the funds are there, so you needn't worry about whether nonprofits can purchase your services. It's usually more about the nonprofits' appetite for spending those funds on anything other than direct client services. I help my clients understand that investing in themselves will increase their capacity to serve more people. That being said, I personally do charge nonprofits less than I charge for-profit corporations. I do this because my mission is to serve the nonprofit sector with the same caliber of world-class leadership and strategy support as that which is enjoyed by Fortune 500 CEOs, but at rates nonprofits can afford. While nonprofits have money, they certainly don't have the resources of the corporate sector. Still, I easily cleared six figures in each of my first two years after going full-time in my coaching business. Nonprofits, just like any others, will buy when they believe your services solve their biggest problems.

Much as in the corporate world, thriving as a coach in the nonprofit sector is about creating a unique *system* that will make you stand out, and knowing how to sell your services in a way that makes them seem like an investment rather than an expense. In the social sector, these steps, particularly the second, take on their own special flavor. Let's look at them in detail.

Creating Your Own Unique Coaching System

As a coach, your *service* is the coaching you provide, but your *product* is the result they will enjoy. You have to package this in a way that appeals to nonprofits so they know exactly what they are getting and they can clearly see why you stand out.

Instead of just offering generic coaching, create a powerful system that is unique to you and own it like a boss. To do this, start by talking to your clients or potential clients and figure out what it is they are missing. Find out what they have been looking for in coaches and consultants in the past but have been unable to find. Really *listen*, and then design a system to fill those gaps.

From my experience in the nonprofit world, I knew that the *strategic planning* phase was a stumbling block for a lot of nonprofits. The organizations I knew about weren't getting enough support in clearly defining and communicating their mission. Just as importantly, when they did find this clarity, they didn't know how to translate it into action at the organizational level. So, I created a system I named the Coaching Continuum. It's designed to help them achieve clarity and then benefit from this clarity at every level of their organization.

The Coaching Continuum is a distinct, packaged, six-month process, carefully crafted for nonprofit organizations. It begins at the highest level, setting strategic direction during a daylong retreat focused on asking big questions about their mission and purpose. This is followed by strategic planning, putting together big-picture plans with the mission at the forefront of their minds.

After this, we drill down and focus on operational plans, the day-to-day nuts and bolts for implementing this strategy in the real world. During this phase, I work with each of the team leaders one-on-one to ensure they each see their place and significance in the plan. One-on-one executive coaching with the CEO comprises the final phase, so that in the end, the client is not left alone. They have six months of support in helping them build the leadership muscle they will need to successfully execute the plan.

Find out what processes your clients or potential clients have gone through, and then figure out what is alive and working for them. Use this knowledge to design an in-depth system of your own that speaks specifically to their needs and pain points. Then, *give it a name* and own it. Brand it. Make it your own. *This* is what will come to define you as a coach—the unique system that you bring to the table. This is your product and the core of your business.

The Secret to Pitching Your Services: Sell Them, Not You

Some time ago, an executive director of a small nonprofit called me. She said, "I love your blog, and I really want to get you here to help us out. How much will it cost?"

When I quoted her a sample figure, she said, "I understand. That's reasonable, but we're small, and I will need to convince my board that you are worth it."

This is a default response from nonprofits, especially the smaller ones. It may be tempting to sympathize with them and say, "No problem, I understand. How about if we cut that rate in half for you?"

Do not make that mistake. When pricing your services and pitching to nonprofits, remember that, as we discussed earlier in this chapter, *it's all about the mission.* Your coaching will help them better clarify and reach their mission and have a greater impact on their community. Therefore, the question is not whether *you* are worth it. The question is whether *they* are worth it. More precisely, the question is whether *their mission* is worth it.

I told the executive director, "It's not about whether I'm worth it. It's about whether you're worth it. Is your mission worth investing in so that you're impacting the lives of more people?"

Framed like this, you'll be able to overcome many price objections that you will face. If your contact is still worried about what the board will think about your coaching fees, help them out. Clearly explain to your contact exactly how your coaching services will help their charity better fulfill their mission. Focus more on the *benefits* than the *features*. In other words, the end result is more important to them than the process. If possible, consider speaking to the board of directors yourself. I frequently Skype into board meetings of my potential clients to make the case directly. After all, no one knows the specific benefits of your coaching better than you do.

Help Your Clients Realize That They Can Easily Afford You

Let me make sure I have adequately emphasized the following: Never believe it when you are told by a well-meaning CEO of a nonprofit, "We'd love to work with you, but we're a nonprofit, so we don't have money." All nonprofits have money, some more than others. If they didn't, their doors would be closed. The question is how they choose to spend the resources they have.

I work with organizations that appreciate the principle of investing to grow. If your potential client cannot see the value of the investment, then they are not ready to benefit from your services. Remember, you must help them see that they are not investing in your coaching *instead* of their mission. Rather, they are investing in your coaching to more effectively *advance* their mission. Also, remember that the nonprofit sector is worth *trillions* of dollars in the United States alone. Out of that, about $200 billion is spent on nonprogram items, and about $100 billion is left unspent each year. In the corporate world, you'd call that profit.

Your coaching services are a great use of such unspent funds, *if* you can directly connect any offer you make to helping them better deliver on their *mission*. Many nonprofits also have unrestricted reserve funds, which they can spend in any manner they see fit. If annual net income and long-term reserve funds still aren't sufficient, consider that there are funding foundations that exist to contribute funds to help nonprofits achieve their mission through capacity building. Leadership coaching is a perfectly valid use of this. It is capacity building at its finest.

To recap, there are sources of funds nonprofits can access to engage a coach. Here are a few examples:

1. Net income: Funds remaining at the end of a fiscal year
2. Reserve funds: Funds available for crisis, innovation, capacity, etc.
3. Grants: Capacity-building grants from funding foundations
4. Corporate sponsorships: Business partners with the nonprofit that may cover expenses
5. Budgeted funds: I talk with many clients in advance of their budgeting season so that they can budget their normal funds to include my services

All the above are simply to help you understand not only that nonprofits *can* afford to work with coaches, but that they *should!* Your coaching will help them sharpen their focus, align with their mission, and deliver significantly greater value to their community. By engaging you as a coach, nonprofits will have a greater impact and better serve their community. The equation really is that simple.

Be Careful with Donating Your Time

A lot of successful corporate coaches donate large chunks of their time to charitable organizations. This is to be applauded, and if you do most of your work in the for-profit sector, then it's an admirable use of your time and a great way to give back to your community.

If you are a nonprofit *specialist*, on the other hand, you have to be a bit more careful. When you donate your time, you run the risk of devaluing your services. Why should charity X pay you large coaching fees when charity Y gets the benefit of your time for free? I'm not saying you should never do pro bono work. Just be mindful of the impact this will have on your pool of paying clients.

Finding Your First Clients in the Nonprofit Sector

You may not want to hear this, but as with the corporate world, finding clients in the nonprofit sector is all about one thing: *hustle*. Clients are not going to drop out of the sky. You have to do the work. Blog, network, market yourself. Remember, there are 1.5 million charities in the United States alone. Potential clients are out there. You just have to intentionally connect with them.

If you're starting from scratch, begin by following the most basic principle of networking: Find out where your potential clients are hanging out, show up, figure out what they need, build trust through content and service, and THEN sell. Attend charity events and networking dinners in your region, and begin to build relationships with the influencers and decision makers.

Don't come on too strong at first. Take the time to get to know the key players in your nonprofit sector. Ask questions, and seek to understand what they are struggling with. When you have deep coaching conversations with potential clients, you leave them wanting more. When the time is right, explain how you can help them overcome these problems and, of course, better deliver on their mission.

Establishing yourself from scratch in a new industry is never easy, and it seldom happens quickly. You may want to gradually transition from whatever your bread and butter is right now—be it corporate or life coaching, or a full-time job—until you have your first few clients and are beginning to grow a network in your community. Once you have those first few clients and your network is showing promise, then it will be time to take your *leap!* When you do, I hope these tips will help you thrive as you help your clients enhance their impact and change lives in their communities.

Summary and Your "To Do" List

In the nonprofit sector, mission comes first. As a coach in the non-profit sector, you help leaders achieve clarity on their mission and better deliver value to their community. The Double Bottom Line shows the relationship between *money* and *mission*. By helping non-profit clients deliver on their mission, you make it easier for them to raise funds that will make them even more effective at helping their communities.

- **Prioritize the Double Bottom Line:** Ask yourself, in addition to making money, what is this organization trying to achieve? This can help you better engage their employees and sharpen their focus.
- **Define and enhance the mission:** Ask the hard questions and notice things that people inside of the organization may not see for themselves. Often the best way to achieve this is simply to have *meaningful conversations.*

- **Stay in your lane:** Be a coach, not a consultant. Develop your own unique system that provides your clients with what they need but haven't been getting so far.
- **Sell them, not you:** When you pitch your services, *sell them*, not you. It's not about how much you cost. It's about how important their mission is for their community. You help them clarify and double down on their purpose.

World-Class Coaching

How to Develop and Live a Mind-set that Inspires and Transforms Clients

KASIA WEZOWSKI

Kasia Wezowski is cocreator of the film *Leap* (learn more at CoachingMovie.com), the first feature-length documentary film about the coaching profession, the director and producer of the documentary *Impact*,[9] and the cofounder of the Center for Body Language. Alongside her husband, Patryk, she is working toward her goal of inspiring 1 million lives around the world through her work as a coach, film producer, and author.

Successful coaches are role models of change. They inspire their clients not just with their skill set, but also by virtue of who they are. Learn how to grow as a coach by manifesting a life that is a true reflection of who you are, and coach from a place of abundance.

As coaches, we are first and foremost role models for our clients. We are role models of the results they want to achieve and the changes they want to experience. When we are impaired by our own doubts or uncertainties, then our clients suffer with us. The best coaches are walking testimonials for their own methods. Their mere presence and the success and happiness they project provide some of the best marketing available.

Before I could thrive as a coach, I first had to transform my mind-set and overcome the limiting beliefs that had been holding me back since my youth. I first entered the coaching profession after completing a master's degree in psychology and psychotherapy, cognitive behavioral therapy, and neurolinguistic programming (NLP). My approach blended the techniques of coaching with those of therapy, and I found frequent success. Despite my track record, I still wasn't confident in my practice, and at the beginning I refused to charge my clients more than a fraction of what I was worth.

Many coaches struggle with valuing their work, and they experience the exact same doubts that I did in the first years of my practice. *"Am I really worth this much money? Will someone really pay this for coaching?"* Thanks to the help of my own coaches, I finally made the decision to accept and recognize my professional value. Then things changed not only for me, but for my clients as well.

Daring to charge more forced both my clients and me to grow. The higher price tag was a great motivator for clients to try harder and commit to the work. My increased income meant I could create a better lifestyle, which gave me more freedom to develop myself and focus on my clients. Shifting my mind-set helped me not only become a happier person, but a better coach.

Your success and your abilities as a coach are inextricably linked. In this chapter, we'll look at how your mind-set and self-esteem can help you become a role model of change. This will result in a better experience for your clients and, of course, a richer, more rewarding life for you as well.

HOW TO DEVELOP SELF-ESTEEM AS A COACH

Having high self-esteem as a coach will fuel a tremendous increase in success in both your personal and professional life. You will project confidence and assurance, meaning more clients will want to do business with you. You will make better decisions because you'll be happier and more focused on the areas that matter.

To maintain high self-esteem, world-class coaches focus on their strengths, not their shadows. They first become a manifestation of the very change they wish to help their clients achieve, and then endeavor to show clients how it's done.

Many coaches first enter the industry as a way of doing battle with their own personal issues. There's nothing wrong with having problems to work through (who doesn't?), but this becomes professionally risky. When we are walking our clients through issues that we ourselves are currently facing, then we are coming from a place of doubt and uncertainty. This lowers our credibility, and it also creates the risk of us projecting our own issues onto our clients. In this situation, a well-meaning coach could end up doing more harm than good.

While coaching clients to overcome issues that we are currently facing is risky, it's actually beneficial to coach from a place of *personal experience* and lead clients to overcome challenges and problems that we too have overcome in our past. The essence of being a good coach is knowing when we have resolved an issue to the point where we speak from a place of success and experience, versus when we are still dealing with an open wound.

The One-Year Rule to Become a Credible Expert

The One-Year Rule helps us maintain our self-esteem as coaches and coach from a position of strength. It prevents us from using our clients as a proxy for our own personal issues. It works like this: If you have an issue in your own personal or professional life, you should wait **one year** after having fully overcome this issue before coaching others on the same topic. This ensures that by the time you are claiming to be an expert on something, you have already *fully resolved* the problem for yourself.

For example, several years ago I had an issue with eating too much sugar and not maintaining a healthy diet. I made the decision to improve my eating habits to become healthier, and I set out on a journey to change. I tried several diets—raw food, macrobiotic, high protein, low fat—to see if I could firmly replace my old, unhealthy eating habits. Eventually, the changes stuck.

During the process of transformation, I wrote blog posts and articles detailing the diets I was trying and the results of each. It's fine to *write* about an issue you are currently facing as an honest account of your experience. This is likely to be instructive to others. But I did not accept clients who wanted me to help them improve their eating habits until **one year** after my own problems with food were completely in the past.

Your burden of responsibility as a coach is much higher than that of a friend or the author of a blog post. I couldn't have confidently or congruently helped someone correct their own eating habits while I was still experimenting and trying to correct my own diet. Only after one year, when my insecurities and uncertainties were resolved, could I truly claim to be an expert on this particular transformation.

The Rule in Practice

If you battled with confidence problems, overcame them, and want to help others to become confident, *wait one year* to make sure your issues with confidence have, in fact, been overcome. During this year, experiment and educate yourself to make sure the changes you have experienced are indeed the result of solid principles that you can explain and teach to others.

After the one year, you will have the benefit of your own personal experience plus the knowledge that you are well and truly an expert on your subject matter. Clients will see you as a *manifestation of the change* that they wish to undertake, and your advice will resonate with them.

Here's how the process of **becoming a credible expert** using the One-Year Rule works, step by step:

1. Encounter a problem or challenge in your professional or personal life.
2. Engage in the process of transformation to overcome this problem.
3. After you have overcome the problem, spend one year educating yourself about how best to help others through it.
4. After one year, if your problem is truly in the past, then you can consider coaching clients on how to overcome the same issue.

In the meantime, as you are working through issues, coach from your existing strengths to keep your business growing. Focus on your current strengths in your coaching practice to boost your self-esteem and confidently effect change. One useful way to emphasize your strengths as a coach is to create a coaching diary.

The Coaching Diary Technique

In the same way that rushing into a coaching relationship before we have properly resolved an issue for ourselves can cause us to project our problems onto our clients, the reverse happens as well. Clients will sometimes see their coaches as having the very problems they wish to overcome. They may become angry and blame their coaches when it is in fact their own problems they are dealing with, not yours.

Being as certain as possible that you are coaching from a position of strength helps you to insulate against this. To maintain your self-esteem in the face of the inevitable ups and downs of your coaching life, consider keeping a **coaching diary**.

A coaching diary will be a log of all your successes.

- Each happy client whom you have helped to transform
- Each victory you have scored in your coaching practice
- Each problem you have solved

This way, when the low points occur in your career, you'll be able to refer to your diary to give yourself a needed boost of self-esteem, confidence, and motivation.

In the early days of your practice, your coaching diary will also help guide you to realize your own specialization. You may notice that you have a particular knack for helping clients with certain goals or issues. You can then choose to focus on this specialization as a way of standing out as a coach, charging higher fees, and boosting your self-esteem by playing to your strengths.

How This Works in Practice

Let's bring the ideas of using a coaching diary and the One-Year Rule together. Say you're personally dealing with weight loss. You're trying various techniques to lose weight with mixed success. Instead of coaching your clients on how to lose weight, you refer to your coaching diary, and you notice that you have been getting amazing results with clients who come to see you for help with releasing negative emotions. You choose to market yourself as a specialist at releasing negative emotions.

One year later, you may have resolved your issues with weight and could consider accepting clients on this topic as well, giving you another area of expertise and broadening your practice. You could also choose to double down on your strengths and continue to focus on helping clients to resolve negative emotions. Either way, you have managed to prevent your personal struggles from interfering with your work, while defining a marketable specialty for your practice.

Find a Mentor to Guide Your Journey

Every coach, no matter how successful, needs a coach of their own. Someone with whom you can share not just your triumphs, but also your insecurities. It can be anyone with coaching skill, but ideally your mentor will be someone who has experience in achieving what it is you are setting out to achieve—someone you admire and look up to.

One of the easiest ways to find a coaching mentor is simply to *become a coaching client*. Search for the coaches in your area who have the best reputation. Experience a few coaching sessions as a paying client to see if there's a connection. If there is, explain that you are a coach and are looking for a mentor. If they really are as successful and well-meaning as they seem to be, then chances are they'll be enthusiastic about entering this kind of relationship with you.

A mentor who has been a tremendous help to both Patryk and me is Mark Thompson, who contributed chapter 10 to this book As he notes in his chapter, Mark has been an adviser to some of the biggest figures in business, including Steve Jobs, Sir Richard Branson, and Charles Schwab. We needed his help when finding investors for our film *Leap*. Mark guided us by helping us create a business plan, reach out to the right people, and communicate our mission effectively. We raised nearly $1 million for our film, and Mark played a major role in making that possible.

When you have a trusted mentor, you have not only a source of advice and wisdom, but also a useful outlet for professional stress or angst you may have. You can explain your problems to them in confidence, which is much healthier than keeping it bottled up or unloading it onto your spouse. You can discuss your professional problems in a safe environment while keeping your personal life secure.

To Succeed as a Coach:

- Wait one year before advising clients on issues you personally face.
- Create a coaching diary and use it to boost self-esteem and find your strengths.
- Find a mentor who has achieved what you want to achieve.

HOW TO LIVE YOUR LIFE AS A WORLD-CLASS COACH

Most professionals are capable of drawing clear distinctions between their personal and professional lives. If a banker is overweight, it need not damage his or her credibility. After all, their business is money, not fitness. Coaches are, of course, human beings and have no obligation to be perfect. As we saw in the sections above, we will inevitably have our own issues, and a few simple rules can help us keep our personal challenges from blunting our professional focus.

Unlike other professionals, however, coaches are in the business of *helping people achieve happiness and success.* As such, it speaks to our own credibility if we can achieve happiness and success for ourselves. Coaching is also the vehicle through which we earn a living. Being a coach isn't just our job, it's our career, and more often than not, our business. Therefore, your personal beliefs and emotions around success and money are directly relevant to your professional life as a coach.

As we learned earlier, coaches should strive to become a *manifestation* of the very change your client is looking to create. The more successful you are in your own life, the better you will be at coaching.

Wealth Matters—but Not for the Reasons Most People Think

When I overcame my own limiting beliefs around money and began charging more, my success as a coach immediately and dramatically improved. Daring to charge more reflected a profound shift in my mind-set. Instead of being guided by my insecurities around money and business, I cultivated positive emotions and let these feelings guide my decision making.

Once I made the shift, my increased income helped me create more positive emotions, which ricocheted back into my coaching life. With more money, I could create a better lifestyle for myself. I designed a home in Spain near the seaside and mountains, which provides me with space to work and space to relax. This means that when I meet clients, I am at my best.

Money matters because being financially secure means we have more opportunities to use our skills and thrive as coaches. Many coaches have other beliefs and desires about money that cause anxiety and lead to poor decision making in their business lives. What matters isn't the *wealth* itself, the numbers in the bank, but the *feeling* that this money enables us to create. When we let this positive feeling guide our decision making, we make smarter choices and create the very success we seek.

Let's examine this a little more deeply.

Exercise: The Red Ferrari

Take a moment to think about this question: What symbolizes wealth and business success for you?

Is it you stepping into a brand-new, bright-red Ferrari? Is it a beautiful house? A certain sum in the bank? Whatever concept or image comes to mind, focus on it and make it as real in your mind as possible. Take a moment to really experience this. Live it. Make it real to you with all five senses. What do you see? What do you touch? What do you hear? What do you smell?

Now, focus not on the experience itself, but on the feeling that this creates in you. Make this feeling as big and powerful as possible.

Remember this feeling. This is the feeling that the idea of wealth inspires in you.

How Positive Feelings Cause Immediate Change

Think about that feeling that you created above. Most people think this feeling is the *result* of wealth. In fact, it's the other way around. This feeling of wealth and success that you found in the exercise above will be the *source* of your success, not a reaction to it. The feeling will be your compass, your guide, and it can lead you to *create* the very level of success and satisfaction to which you aspire.

In every moment of your life, you make decisions. Enough choices are made in each hour of your life to alter your destiny. You decide how to interact with your clients, your business partners, your family. You decide what to focus on, what to do, and how to do it.

While we like to think of ourselves as rational agents, research has consistently shown that emotions play an outsize role in our decision-making process. A 2015 review by Harvard University concluded that *"emotions constitute powerful, pervasive, and predictable drivers of decision making."*[8]

Since emotions have such a profound influence on our decisions, it makes sense to deliberately fill our lives with the emotions connected to what we want. By focusing on the feelings that success gives you and bringing it into your life, you are helping yourself to make better, more empowering choices in every situation that you encounter. Some of these decisions will be big, others frighteningly noticeable at the time, but together they will result in major changes to your life and business.

A few years ago, my husband, Patryk, and I took a trip to Bali, Indonesia. It was our first holiday in a while, and for our first week away I was still feeling wound up from work. The traffic was loud and aggressive. The air seemed dirty. The streets looked filthy. The people seemed unfriendly. Without realizing it, the stress that I carried with me from home was causing me to focus on the negative and make choices—small and large—that emphasized the frustration and depression I was feeling.

After a week or so, this gradually began to change. As I swam in the sea and took walks through the forest, I slowly began to relax. The streets were the same streets that had seemed loud and filthy a week ago, but that day they seemed cleaner, gentler. The people were the same people I had felt irritated by before, but now I noticed their smiles, their warmth, their sincerity. What started out as the worst holiday of my life ended up being one of my best vacations ever. Bali did not change during my time there, but the shift in my state of mind and the different *decisions* that this caused led me to have a completely different, more positive experience.

In Practice: Deliberately Cultivate Positive Feelings to Make Better Decisions

The first step toward manifesting wealth, success, and happiness as a coach is to deliberately cultivate the *feeling* that success gives you. Make it a daily ritual to deliberately place yourself in and experience this feeling. Do it first thing when you wake up: Find that feeling and experience it for just a few moments before you start your day. Meditate on this feeling, and return to it whenever you have the opportunity to indulge in it.

The difference that this causes will be immediate and profound, with each small action you take throughout the day bearing the influence of this new, positive feeling that you have deliberately introduced into your life. You may find yourself being kinder to your spouse and your children. The little things that would have annoyed you before will now just slide off because you will be *feeling* better and therefore focusing on what you love, not what bothers you.

At work, you will be smarter and more focused. Instead of being distracted by fear and negative emotion, you will act deliberately in pursuit of this positive feeling. You'll begin to learn the difference between choices that will lead you *toward* this feeling, and choices that will lead you *away* from it. This may affect decisions that you make about your finances, your marketing, how you deal with your clients, even how many hours you choose to work.

As you practice deliberately cultivating this feeling and its effects are felt in your work, it will become easier to make this feeling part of your life, and you may even end up in the exact situation that you visualized in the exercise above. But when you do, you'll know that it doesn't matter whether or not you have that red Ferrari or that beautiful penthouse. What matters is the *feeling* that you set out to pursue. You'll realize that you can have the same level of satisfaction with or without the external symbols.

This is the coach's path toward wealth. In the same way that your coaching diary enabled you to deliberately cultivate self-esteem by focusing on your successes, this daily habit enables you to deliberately cultivate the **feeling** of success in your life. This feeling will cause you to make better, positive choices. The result of these choices will be the very wealth and success that you set out to pursue in the first place.

You will have become the manifestation of the change that your clients seek to create, making you not only a happier, richer person, but a better coach as well.

Summary and Your "To Do" List

Your success and your abilities as a coach are inextricably linked. The more successful we are in our own lives, the more credible and convincing we will be in our work. Your mind-set and self-esteem can help you become a role model of change. This will result in a better experience for your clients and, of course, a richer, more rewarding life for you as well.

- **Apply the One-Year Rule:** Do not use your clients as a proxy for your own issues. If you have an issue in your own personal or professional life, you should wait **one year** after having fully overcome this issue before coaching others on the same topic. This ensures you have *fully resolved* the problem for yourself.
- **Keep a coaching diary:** Log all of your successes in a coaching diary. Each happy client, each victory, each problem solved. When low points occur, you'll be able to refer to your diary to give yourself a needed boost of self-esteem, confidence, and motivation.
- **Find a mentor:** Search for coaches in your area who have the best reputation. Go to a few sessions to see if there is a connection. If there is, explain that you are looking for a mentor.
- **Cultivate the feeling of success:** Think about what symbolizes wealth and success for you. Focus not on the experience itself, but on the *feeling* that wealth and success give you. This will help you make better decisions and drive the success you desire.
- **Be patient:** These principles take time and practice to apply, and you should not expect things to go perfectly right away. It's not like flipping a switch. It's about developing the habits and gradually adopting the mind-set of a world-class coach.

Part Three:
Finding Success

Putting Your Mission First

How to Create a Daily Work Life You Love and Become Unstoppable as a Coach

DR. JOHN DEMARTINI

Dr. John Demartini is a researcher, author, educator, speaker, and expert in human behavior. John has also appeared in several films, including *The Secret* in 2006. He is the author of ten internationally best-selling books that have been translated into thirty different languages, including *The Breakthrough Experience* and *The Values Factor*.

When the everyday actions you take to grow your coaching business are aligned with your highest values and your mission, then success and great achievement are inevitable. Learn how to prioritize what matters to you and put your inspired mission first—no matter what.

give about 300 speeches and as many as 1,000 interviews every year. Twelve-to-eighteen-hour workdays are not uncommon. I seldom if ever take holidays. But as far as I'm concerned, my vocation is a vacation. I research, write, travel, and teach constantly, but it doesn't feel like I've worked a day in the past forty-five years. My home is a yacht called *The World*, and I change countries every few days or weeks. I love what I do, and I love to serve, so I never feel like I have to work.

It wasn't always like this. About forty-five years ago, I lived in a tent. I was a hippie surfer. Learning problems had cut short my education, and I felt like I had little ambition and no dreams outside of surfing. A man named Paul C. Bragg, a pioneer in America's wellness movement, inspired me to overcome my learning difficulties, go back to school, and make something more of myself. I made an effort to discover my highest values and wrote a purpose statement defining my mission in life. Since 1972, I've refined and updated that purpose statement seventy times. It is my key inspirer and driver, the core of what I do. Ever since then, my work has been my inspiration, and I've been relentless and persistent in doing what I love.

If your goals are congruent with your highest values, then you're unstoppable. You can learn to live a life that you love based on your purpose and inspiration and delegate everything that you are not inspired about doing yourself. By holding your highest values paramount and refusing to subordinate yourself to the opinions of others, your success and achievement will be inevitable. You will not stop until you get there, and then you will keep going. These are the lessons I learned the past forty-five years, lessons I have practiced every day since.

In this chapter, we'll look at how to create a daily work life that you love by delegating everything that isn't directly connected to your mission. We'll then explore how staying true to your purpose and congruent with your highest values makes you unstoppable as a coach.

WHEN YOUR GOALS AND HIGHEST VALUES ARE A MATCH, THERE'S NO STOPPING YOU

Every individual lives by goals and values that are unique to them. If your goals are not consistent with your highest values, you won't be inspired to take consistent action. When your goals and highest values are aligned, your entire being becomes congruent and takes action toward the same purpose. This means you have access to more vital energy and internal drive, because you believe completely in where you're going and the path you're taking to get there.

Your **goals** are where you're aiming to go in life and what you are strategically planning to achieve as a coach. There are a lot of articles and books about goals. What you read less about is the crucial importance of setting goals that are truly congruent with your highest values. Your highest values are the concepts, ideas, and principles that matter to you more than anything else. You already inwardly know what these are, even if you may not be aware of them yet.

Anytime you're living in accordance with your highest values, your energy soars. There's an abundance of energy when you're doing something that's really important to you. Your highest values are reflected in the things that you are spontaneously inspired to do every day, the things you love to do. For me, this is researching, writing, traveling, and teaching. I love to research, teach, and share ideas with others. I can do this all day—it's what inspires me most, it's living up to my highest values. *What is this for you?*

Action Step: How to Find Your Values

Living according to your highest values means finding what you're intrinsically committed to and then prioritizing your life around that. An exercise that I performed early in my career is great for uncovering what's really important to you and discovering the areas in which you thrive.

At the start of each day, write down the six or seven highest priority action steps that you would love to get done. These are steps that would help you fulfill what is most important in your life—your inspired mission. Actually do them, and then reward yourself for it after the fact. Keep a record of each day's list of priorities. After one hundred days, go back through each and every action step you wrote down and notice the ones that keep coming up over and over again. Choose the three or four from which you get the most fulfillment and satisfaction. Work toward gradually delegating the rest. In my case, the top four were most commonly: teach, research, write, and travel. The delegated ones were: manage the staff, delegate further responsibilities, and initiate new market contacts.

Do What You Love and Delegate the Rest

I have a team of thirty people who handle all the detailed aspects of running my business that are less fulfilling and less financially productive for me. I don't do marketing. I don't do accounting. I don't do scheduling. All these things are important for my business, but they aren't the things that are most connected to my highest values. I don't receive the greatest fulfillment or satisfaction doing them, which means I would do them less enthusiastically than a more qualified hired professional. My time is more wisely and profitably spent on the three or four daily activities that are congruent with my true highest values: researching, writing, traveling, and teaching.

Arriving at this point in my business didn't happen overnight. It was a steady, slow delegation process that began with a simple realization: You can't live an inspired life if you're doing desperate things. If you're constantly running around doing your books and marketing and scheduling, you probably won't be able to thrive as a profitable coach. You'll be exhausted, spending your energy on activities you do not love, which are not congruent with your highest values and do not produce the highest number of dollars per hour.

Use the exercise above to figure out what it is you're truly inspired to do. Dedicate yourself to that. Everything else, delegate. True leadership is you putting your time and energy into where it's needed most. Prioritize and delegate.

PUT YOUR MISSION FIRST, NO MATTER WHAT

When you're aligned with your highest values and taking only those actions that are congruent with your highest priority, there's no such thing as an obstacle. Obstacles are just feedback mechanisms to help you hone your approach to what is truly most important. Nothing will ever truly make you stop, because, as I say at the top of my blog, "When you are truly inspired by something, you cannot fail because you never give up."

If you're inspired, you will move forward no matter what. When the "why" is big enough, the "hows" will take care of themselves. To succeed as a coach, your vision has to be greater than the challenges and obstacles the world throws at you. As a coach, your innermost drive has to be to serve and help others. If this is true, then you will become relentless and succeed.

Inspire Others with Your Vision

As a coach, you need to care enough about others to serve them no matter what. When you are presented with challenges, focus on your mission, *not* on the criticism or obstacles thrown at you. A lot of people fear public speaking, and many coaches have a fear of failure or rejection. At the root of this fear is the habit of subordinating yourself to the opinions of others. Your inspired mission has to be *bigger* and *more important* than other people's opinions.

If you're worried about what people think of you, then you're letting their opinion get in the way of your innermost dominant thought and dream. Don't subordinate yourself to other people's opinions. I'd rather on occasion annoy a few other so-called well-meaning people than sacrifice my most inspired dream of global service. This attitude alone was a key driver behind the success of my coaching. A man on a mission doesn't have time for trivial, projected opinions or distractions. Things come into your life according to what you're focused on. If you're focused on your mission every day, it's impossible for you not to eventually fulfill your dream.

How I Applied This Attitude to Create My Coaching Business

At the start of my career, I would speak *anywhere* and take every opportunity to share my most inspiring ideas and insights with anyone who would listen. Friends of mine found me on numerous occasions in elevators or restaurants giving speeches to strangers who were sharing the ride or sitting with me! When I did these speeches, I didn't fear their judgments or rejections. You only get rejected when you're self-righteously projecting your attitudes and assumed values onto others. Show up sincerely to help others and they will respond to this with open hearts and minds. Focus on *their genuine needs*, not on your projected assumptions of their needs, and ever growing numbers of people will respond to your sincerity. One man I encountered was frustrated with his current career and wanted to start his own business, so I shared with him how he could more smoothly make such a transition by questioning and clarifying his new career path and by linking his current career responsibilities with his new path so it would be seen as *on* the way and not *in* the way.

When I really began building momentum with my teaching and coaching services, I was also a practicing health professional. When I opened my professional practice, I was just twenty-seven years old, not long after my Hawaii hippie surfer days. I had rented an office space near a local mall, but I needed more room to present my growing health education and awareness lectures and presentations. My patient roster kept swelling. I tried to lease an empty space next door, which I envisioned as my new lecture hall and daily events center. This space was no longer being rented, but the leasing company that owned it never returned my calls. People I had met through my restaurant seminars, networking efforts, and promotional activities were coming to hear me speak, but I had no venue to accommodate them.

Remember, when your mission and vision are powerful enough, when what you're doing is aligned with your highest values, there are no obstacles. So, I hired a locksmith to open the door of the center next to my office, and I fixed the place up from scratch in just a few days. I rented giant loudspeakers and massive searchlights and placed them out into the shopping mall parking lot, broadcasting advertisements for the evening events I began presenting. My new lecture hall became packed. Soon the public and other doctors started attending events to hear my tips about growing a health practice, and eventually I transitioned into a full-time consultant, working out of a high-rise office. By the way, the leasing company weeks later offered me an incredible deal on the rental space and wanted to know if I wanted to franchise my business and open up in some of their other retail centers.

Don't Wait for Opportunities: Make Them

Many coaches sit around during part of the day, tapping away at social media, hoping an opportunity will fall into their lap. The key is, when you're committed to your mission and congruent with your highest values, the whole world can become your opportunity. You don't wait for opportunities, you make them.

Even when I started to become busier and busier as an international coach and teacher, I never stopped creating new opportunities to share my ideas and visions with ever greater numbers of others. I'd speak in restaurants, standing up and giving an impromptu lecture about achieving your personal or professional dreams that engaged more and more people. People generally assumed that I was hired by the manager or was part of some kind of function. They gave me their attention, and many went on to become clients. I went to high-end hotels to find conferences. On one occasion, I found a huge conference that was just wrapping up. About 5,000 people were getting ready to leave. I stood up on a chair and just started speaking about action steps they could implement that would help them build a more successful business.

I did what most other coaches and teachers were not willing to do. My mission was greater than other people's opinions of me. I hired public relation specialists and went on to do hundreds of radio and television interviews, wrote countless articles and books, and made daily presentations to the highest-priority networking or business groups I could initiate.

As Long as You're Providing Value, People Will Respond

When you deliver more than what people expect, give value, speak to their actual needs, and make sure they are *inspired*, then they will respond to and help you. The key is looking at people honestly and truly serving them, not projecting your own assumptions on them. When you are truly in alignment with your mission and are there with the intention of serving, people will read this in you. There is no such thing as a fear of public speaking, there is only the fear of the opinions and judgment of others. If you hold your mission in higher esteem than other people's opinions, then the fear melts away and your greatest service begins.

Whenever you communicate with others, focus on meeting their genuine needs. Don't make assumptions or project your own needs onto them. Provide true value, and enthusiastically convey a feeling of inspiration. If obstacles come up, this relentless focus on serving in alignment with your highest values and mission will prevent you from getting derailed. If I'm giving a speech and someone resists, I don't even focus on that. I'm focused on my mission. I'm focused on serving. The one person resisting my message is not highly relevant to me—the only thing that matters is fulfilling my mission, my highest values, my desire to serve ever greater numbers of people, and the congruence bringing this all together.

When They Benefit, You Benefit

Because you're a coach, the genuine intention to serve others is probably connected to your mission and the activities you most value. I like researching, writing, traveling, and teaching because they enable me to have a meaningful impact on other people's lives and fulfill my lifetime dream. We all have both an altruistic side and a narcissistic side. When you're aligned toward your purpose, these two sides are in balance: If you help other people get what they want in life, then you will also get what you want in life.

Once you have delivered value and met the needs of the people you are communicating with, you can ask for something in return. Hand out your business card and invite them to contact you and become a client. I would often end my public presentations by upselling future events or by asking for referrals. I'd simply say, "How many of you have thought about other people who could have benefited by being here? Then tell those people." By putting value out into the world in alignment with your mission and highest values, you open yourself up to receive back that value in return.

Summary and Your "To Do" List

Success comes when you align the small, everyday tasks you do with your highest values, your goal, and your inspired mission. When every part of you is congruently acting toward the same purpose, then you become unstoppable.

- **Inspire others with your vision:** As a coach, you need to care enough about others to serve them no matter what. When you are presented with challenges, focus on your mission, *not* on the criticism or obstacles thrown at you. Create an inspired mission that is bigger and more important than other people's opinions.

- **Put yourself out there:** Be boldly willing to speak and inspire others at every opportunity. Find courage in your mission, which is connected to serving others. When you operate at this level, there's no such thing as an obstacle.
- **Tune out judgment:** If people resist, judge, or criticize you, it has no impact. You're not focused on other people's judgment. Other people's opinions matter less to you than your purpose in life. Your goal is to give, serve, and inspire. When you do so from a place of alignment, your altruism puts value out in the world, which will come back to you.
- **Align your action with your mission:** Make an effort to align every action you take with your mission and your highest inspiration. When you do so, you cannot fail, because you will never give up until you achieve and fulfill the dream that others call success.

The Coaching Business Model

Selecting, Branding, and Selling the Right Model to Maximize Your Impact

HEATHER RAMSEY

Heather Ramsey is the founder and CEO of ReWired WorldWide. Committed to the twin goals of human purpose and planetary sustainability, Heather has helped hundreds of entrepreneurs around the world grow successful businesses. She was appointed to the Ministry of Energy Advisory Council in Ontario, Canada, and has trained more than 1,000 professionals in the master's certificate program in adult training and development at York University's Schulich Executive Education Centre.

Most coaches, let alone most entrepreneurs, only think about what product or service they're going to sell, not their business model. 'Selecting' your business model by default, versus by design, leads to default results. You miss out on major opportunities to optimize every aspect of your coaching practice. Learn how to select the best business model to maximize your results, create a compelling brand, and sell without feeling "sales-y."

C oaches are often so microfocused on getting clients that they forget to ask some important questions about their business. Instead of spending all of your time zoomed in on what you're selling or how to sell, it helps to zoom out and take the 30,000-foot view of what business model you're selling from. Are you offering one-on-one coaching? If so, why? Have you really considered whether or not this is the best model for you to deliver value and shine, or have you just fallen into it by default?

Taking the time to deliberately choose your business model empowers you to deliver the most value to your clients in the most effective way. You can then effectively sell others on your chosen model and increase your revenue with awareness and congruence, without having to feel like that not-so-good kind of salesperson. Before you can know the best model for you, you need to be clear on the game-changing result you deliver as a coach and have a solid understanding of *why* you came into coaching in the first place.

Over many years of self-examination and hard work, I learned that the two dreams that are most important to me and my business are, put simply, human purpose and planetary sustainability. I've been exposed to spiritual ideas since I was seven years old and my mom would send me off to camps and spiritual study groups to learn about dream interpretation, meditation, and concepts like reincarnation. I've translated spiritual principles into success principles while walking the road through the business challenges that I've faced as the founder of six different successful companies and as a trainer of entrepreneurs.

My university degrees are in business and adult education. I've trained more than 1,000 business professionals in an academic setting, and I have practical experience in sales and optimizing revenue streams. For me, coaching was about bringing all this together: business, training, spirituality, and my twin goals of human happiness and planetary sustainability. With this in mind, I deliberately evaluated and chose the optimal business model for my coaching practice. ReWired WorldWide's first phase started as a training company, and we are evolving into the academy model—two business model options we'll explore below—as we equip entrepreneurs with the skills they need to be successful.

In this chapter, you'll learn about four coaching business models and how to choose the right one for you. We'll then look at how you can take your chosen business model and grow it through intelligent branding and apply your skills as a coach to sales.

SELECTING YOUR COACHING BUSINESS MODEL

I once had a conversation with a mentor whose net worth is a cool half-billion dollars, so this is someone worth listening to in matters of business. He said entrepreneurs could be so much more successful and wealthy if they stepped back from the "what are we selling" approach and instead started asking, "What is our best business model from which to sell and serve?"

Most coaches end up in the one-on-one coaching business model by default. There's nothing wrong with this model, but:

1. It's not the *only* way to structure your coaching business.
2. If you're going to operate with this model, you should choose it deliberately. This way you'll have the clarity and insight you need to intelligently grow and optimize it.

The ways you can structure your coaching business are limited only by your experience and imagination, but in general there are four basic models for coaches:

- **The one-on-one coaching model:** Serving individual clients as either a life or a business coach.
- **The training/speaking model:** Your first offering is usually online or offline training seminars, which often leads to private coaching clients.
- **The academy model:** The primary offering is training, often with a wider offering of courses and/or trainers.
- **The team-of-consultants model:** You assemble a team of specialists to deliver results to businesses.

How to Choose the Right Business Model for You

The model that works for you will depend on both (a) the game-changing results you are best at producing for your clients, and (b) what I like to call your "superpower." Your superpower is your biggest strength. You may be a great listener. If so, one-on-one coaching may suit you best. You may be a compelling public speaker, in which case the training/speaking model may work for you. You may be a stellar marketer, in which case the academy model could be for you. You may be a first-class networker or business strategist, in which case, the team-of-consultants model could be your ideal match.

The most important thing is focusing on the *game-changing result* you want to deliver to your clients or customers. How will their lives or businesses be better as a result of working with you? My game-changing result is that entrepreneurs achieve dramatic improvement in the sales, systems, and success of their business, while feeling more secure and deeply satisfied as the entrepreneur at the helm of their business. Yours could be that your clients' marriages are saved, or they recover their health, or they get more done in half the time. It must be big, compelling, and *real*—something that clients actually want to pay for and get because of working with you.

Let's look at the four main coaching business models in more detail and explore the kind of person each model best aligns with. As you read each model, think about the end result you are committed to creating for your clients, and think about which model will best enable you to achieve this.

The One-on-One Coaching Model

This is the business model most coaches choose by default. You see clients one-on-one as a coach and help them achieve positive change or overcome problems in either their personal or professional life. It's a legitimate way of running a coaching business, but if you choose to run your business this way, you should do so deliberately because it matches your goals and your superpower, not just because it's the easiest or you happened into it.

The one-on-one model may be for you if: You like working with a small group of clients, getting to know them and working closely with them to achieve powerful transformation. Your superpowers could be your ability to listen, your compassion or empathy, your ability to understand someone's problem, your skill as a giver of advice, and your technical abilities as a coach.

The Training/Speaking Model

This is the business model that I chose when we launched ReWired WorldWide. I studied business, became a master facilitator and trainer, and am comfortable designing and guiding the right people to the right outcomes, whether that's training entrepreneurs, facilitating executives, or conducting large-scale interventions.

With this model, you run group events and seminars for as many people as you choose, from a handful to hundreds. You teach them skills on a large scale and guide them through transformation as a group. Or, as the title suggests, your expertise could be as a speaker, and therefore you build your business model around that superpower. Whether leading with training and/or speaking, a portion of those clients can and will lead to private coaching, if it's beneficial for them.

The training/speaking model may be for you if: You are comfortable in front of groups and in a public-speaking setting. You know how to amplify your message so you can inspire a room full of people, and you have a passion for designing game-changing experiences, facilitating training, and/or conducting business sessions.

To see examples, look up training seminars in your area with a focus on personal growth and business skills. See who is giving courses, look at the numbers they are attracting, and see what appeals to you from a marketing and content standpoint. Consider attending as a student to get a feel for what is out there, what is missing, and where you can add value.

The Academy Model

The academy model is the training model amplified: usually a wider offering of training and often by multiple trainers. Client experience is often more like that of a school, institution, or academy, rather than just one person offering training. First convert your principles and techniques to online training programs. Then attract and showcase trainers and training programs complementary to yours and market them as a collective internationally. Usually most of this training is accessed online, though live offerings are definitely a viable and exciting addition to the online training.

For a fantastic example of the academy model, see the chapter by Vishen Lakhiani from Mindvalley. He started the business with just $700 and built it up to $20 million selling mindfulness training! Today it is valued at more than $40 million and is an education investment group that builds and invests in education businesses. Their goal is to reach as many people as possible with their training materials, which is why the academy model suits them.

The academy model may be for you if: You want to inspire as many people as possible with your message and/or the training of a collective offering. You are comfortable creating material (videos, audios, or eBooks) that easily communicates your ideas, techniques, and principles to a larger market. You have a passion for marketing, building a following, and using modern technologies like websites, social media, and e-mail to make sales.

If you're not comfortable with marketing but are still tempted by the concept of the academy model, consider partnering with someone else who can publish and market your materials for you.

Recently I became a faculty member of an international success network, which builds the personal and business growth of members while also supporting planetary wellness. There was a great fit between our organizations' values, messages, training offerings, and audiences, so a new academy partnership was born. If you have a specific area of expertise, chances are there's an audience either of your own creation and/or already created that will make a great partnership for you.

The Team-of-Consultants Model

The team-of-consultants model is like the one-on-one coaching model amplified, and it's often built to attract corporate clients, though that's not always the case. It illustrates the whole point of deliberately choosing your model: You may have a passion to achieve client results that require broader expertise.

This model is about forming partnerships with other coaches who have skills that complement yours. Together, you become an elite team that delivers much bigger changes than any of you could individually. A current client of mine has built this model to become successful and provide a much more comprehensive solution for her C-suite corporate executive teams. Even if she doesn't have the specific skills a company needs to improve their metrics, chances are there's someone in her team who does.

The team-of-consultants model could be for you if: You have a corporate or academic background and you are connected to people with a broad range of business skills. For example, if you're talented at marketing, you could partner with someone who is good at project management, or finance, or branding and use your collective expertise to deliver a buffet of options and solutions to your clients.

You Don't Have to Stick with One Model

These coaching models are not mutually exclusive. As your business grows, you may choose to change direction or expand from one successful model into another. For example, you may start with the one-on-one model and expand into building a team of consultants, or you may kick off with your core training and bring on other trainers' curricula to build an academy model. That is what I have done with my own companies. By first choosing a model that best fits my superpower, I was then able to leverage this into two other supplementary businesses. Begin with your strengths, and then you'll be able to channel the resources you create into expanded business opportunities.

You don't have to stay married to your first choice of models for life, but you will not be able to grow and optimize successfully if you do not know:

1. The top results you deliver
2. Your top superpower
3. Your best chosen business model to realize your optimal income and impact

GROW YOUR CHOSEN BUSINESS MODEL: BRANDING AND SALES

Only after you've chosen your business model can you effectively brand and sell yourself to potential clients. If you've fallen into your model by default, it's likely you've also branded yourself by default, rather than by design. Specifically, you're probably struggling with the sales side of your business, and when people ask what you do, you probably answer, "I'm a coach." When you deliberately select the business model that best enables you to deliver your game-changing result, it becomes much easier to brand and sell your coaching services.

Just like choosing your business model, branding is about taking that 30,000-foot view, overcoming the defaults that you may have fallen into, and making strategic decisions that maximize your messaging, marketing, and business growth.

Your Brand Is Your Game-Changing Result

Don't brand yourself based on your job title, such as, "I'm a coach." Instead, brand yourself based on the results you produce. If you're filing your taxes, you don't really want an accountant, you want someone to "optimize your return." When you answer the question, "What do you do?" think about what solutions your potential clients are looking for and willing to pay for.

When I first started working with a business client of mine, I asked her what results she helped produce. She simply replied, "I help executives make decisions." And so our branding transformation began. Graciously, I said, "If I were a potential executive client and you said that to me, I would think I already make decisions, why do I need you?" We stepped back and got a bigger perspective on her results. I interviewed a number of her executive clients, we compiled her qualitative and quantitative results for just five of her executives, and they reported a conservative $4.5 million gain based on working with her. Her new accurate answer to the "What do you do?" question is, "I make and save executives millions of dollars, while raising their reputation in the marketplace." That helped land her next three corporate contracts.

Branding yourself simply as "a coach" may be a tempting default, but it will not compel the majority of your prospects to say yes, nor differentiate your business from all those other coaches. Instead, brand yourself based on the benefits you bring to your clients—the *game-changing results* your whole business model is based around.

The Concept in Practice

Notice the difference between the two statements: "I help executives make decisions," and "I make and save executives millions of dollars, while raising their reputation in the marketplace." See how the second statement contains clear, game-changing quantitative and qualitative *results*? The results you emphasize in your branding will be the same results your business model is optimized to deliver. Think about the *why* of your business and the change that you aim to make for your client, and then brand yourself with the end result in mind.

The key to branding is to focus on the benefit your clients get from working with you, not the process they go through to get that benefit. If you're a relationship therapist who works with couples to help them save their marriage through mediation, don't say, "I mediate couples." That statement is about the process: mediation. Instead, focus on the result, digging deep to pull out the full nature of the difference you make. "I help couples save their marriage, bring back the passion, and start dream building again."

Action step: Read through or watch all the testimonials you have received from clients, and ask your clients how they describe your services to other people. If you haven't yet had any clients, look at your competition and at others who cater to the same market. See if you can find their testimonials and reviews of their services or products online. Look at the core benefits that clients keep bringing up as important to them, and make *that* the focus of your brand.

THE SALES CONVERSATION: SAVVY, NOT SLEAZY

Most coaches can't sell because they think that sales is somehow sleazy or pushy. They may be the best communicators in the world when it comes to coaching or training, but the moment they have a potential client on the phone or in front of them, they freeze.

Most coaches make the sales process about them. They are taught to be dependent on the client and fear losing the sale. Instead, change your focus. Rather than thinking about your products or about how much money you want to charge and make, stay focused on the client. Keep your mind on the game-changing result you deliver, and structure the conversation around finding out how best to deliver on this result. "Be a stand" for your prospects and treat the sales conversation as the first phase in the coaching process. Be as attentive and sensitive as you are with your existing clients. Prospects will love you for it!

At the heart of your business and any business is the ability to match what people want with what you can provide, enrolling and selling people on the solution you are providing.

The Concept in Practice: Goal, Gap, Gold

By staying in character as a coach, you'll enjoy the sales process a lot more. You'll no longer feel the need to run from opportunities, and you will come across as congruent, effective, and likable as a result.

The "Goal, Gap, Gold" method is a framework we designed as a client-centered, right fit conversation. It's a great way for you to apply the skills you have as a coach toward the sales process. It enables you to create a road map of inquiry, keeping you focused on your game-changing result and enabling you to "be a stand" for each prospect. If what you offer delivers on what they want, they will say, "Yes!"

It works like this:

The *Goal* is the reason that your client is looking for coaching. It is the *change* they want to make.

The *Gap* is what has been stopping them from achieving this result for themselves. It's the problem they need to solve, or the obstacle they need to overcome.

The *Gold* is what will fill that *gap* and get them to their *goal*. This is the game-changing result you provide as a coach.

For example:

- An entrepreneur wants to increase revenue while working less. This is their goal.
- They keep struggling to get game-changing results during each working day. This is their gap.

- You can teach them time management and efficiency strategies to help them get twice as much done in half the time. This is the gold.

More specifically, the time when you will often have the opportunity to "be a stand" for your prospects is after they have shared their goal and their their gap, you have shared the gold, and they present some sort of time- or money-based objection. This is not the time to back down, or think, "Poor me, I've just lost the sale." This is the time to step up and "be a stand" for their dream.

The words will vary but the message is the same. Here's an example: "So you shared with me you want to achieve X, and that your commitment to do so is a 10. Yet you're also suggesting that your 10-level dream is not worth an investment of time, money, and effort to achieve it. Have you heard yourself say this before or decline opportunities before? What if after we worked together you would never have to say no because of money again?" Again, the words are secondary, but "being a stand" for them is primary.

Treat the sales process as if it were a mini coaching session. Try to figure out their goal and their gap, and then paint a picture of the *gold* you have to offer them. Ask if they'd be interested in exploring this further with you as a client. Be a coach, not a salesperson, and clients will thank you for it.

Summary and Your "To Do" List

Most coaches arrive at their business model by accident, but this means you miss out on a major opportunity to optimize your coaching practice. Taking the time to deliberately choose your business model empowers you to deliver the most value to your clients. You can then effectively sell others on your chosen model and increase your revenue. Before you can know the best model for you, you need to be clear on the game-changing result you deliver as a coach.

- **Identify your model or models:** Take a step back and make a deliberate decision about your business model. Answer the question: "What is the best way for me to deliver my game-changing result?" Choose the one that is most connected to the *result* you best produce, your *why*, and your superpower. The four main business models for coaches are:

- The one-on-one coaching model
- The training model
- The academy model
- The team-of-consultants model

- **Be flexible:** Your decision doesn't have to be final. These models can feed into each other. For example, students of your training courses might go on to become one-on-one clients.

- **Emphasize your value:** Branding and sales are about staying true to your game-changing result. Create a brand that emphasizes the value you deliver.

- **Focus on the goal and the gap:** When it's time to sell your services, don't take off your coaching hat. Rather than trying to be a salesperson, have a coaching conversation about their *goal* and their *gap*, introduce the *gold* you offer as the solution, and be a stand for them achieving their goal in record time, with record success!

Promoting Yourself as a Coach

How to Get Your Name Out There to Attract Clients and Customers

KIERON SWEENEY

Kieron Sweeney is an international speaker, leadership authority, and author. A specialist at combining mind-set and personal growth concepts with business strategy, Kieron's trainings and digital content have helped more than 500,000 people around the world improve their lives and businesses.

Successful coaches are recognized as experts in their fields. Discover how to make sure your product—the coaching service you offer—is something that people want, and get your name out there authentically and convincingly so that clients come to you.

I've always been passionate about business: creating and bringing to market things that make people's lives better. I had early success as an entrepreneur, but in 1991 things went wrong. I made some poor business decisions, and everything I had built collapsed. At my darkest moments,

I discovered the world of personal growth and dedicated the next two years to improving myself.

Combining my business background with my newfound knowledge of the power of the mind, I went on to build three international businesses, and eventually I became a sales trainer and public speaker. I was able to inspire large groups with my message, but I found that it was with smaller groups where I really made the most difference. Today I work with coaches, executives, and entrepreneurs to help them shift their mind-set and implement business strategies that work in the modern business world.

I firmly believe that 80 percent of business success is promotion and marketing. Most coaches struggle because they lack the ability or willingness to promote themselves. Coaching is a business, and the services you provide are your product. The same branding and positioning rules apply to coaching as to all other businesses out there. To be successful as a coach, you need to have a product that people want and get your name out there in a way that positions you as a credible authority.

In this chapter, we'll look at how you can ensure the coaching service you offer is something people want and are willing to pay for. Then, we'll explore some easy yet effective ways to get your name out there, position yourself as an authority, and develop a reputation that will have clients chasing you, not the other way around.

PROMOTION BEGINS WITH PRODUCT: CREATING, TESTING, AND PROVING THE VALUE OF WHAT YOU OFFER

Promotion is about taking what you have to offer and shouting it from the rooftops. Before you can do this, you need to make sure that your product—the service you offer as a coach—is something people actually *want* and find valuable. Perhaps even more importantly, you also need to make sure *you* are passionate about the service you are offering.

Most coaches don't promote themselves effectively because they have an issue with selling. Many entrepreneurs hate the feeling of being "sold to," and so they are reluctant to inflict that feeling upon others. The solution is passion. If you align what you're offering with your core values, and you firmly believe in your heart that you can impact thousands of lives in a positive way, and if you are authentic and congruent with your message, then you won't come off like a salesperson. You will be warm, likable, and trustworthy, exuding enthusiasm and passion with every word you say. This alone will be the biggest advertisement for your business.

People may not like to be sold to, but they certainly like to buy. If you are sincere and passionate about what you're offering, others will read that in you and respond. Of course, you also need to approach this like a business and bring to the market something that people actually *want*.

Before You Go Big, Test and Collect Data

People don't buy what they need, they buy what they want. An entrepreneur creates solutions for other people's problems. As a coach, you are also in the problem-solving business. If you're an executive coach, you solve specific business or work-related problems. If you're a fitness coach, you solve health and lifestyle problems. If you're a relationship coach, you solve interpersonal problems.

To find out if people want what you're offering, test it on a small scale. This testing phase is something big businesses take dead seriously but coaches tend to overlook. Film producers test their concept with focus groups before hitting the market. Chefs test their new recipes with friends and family before putting them on the menu. Before spending time and money promoting yourself to the world, start small. Collect data.

If your experiment works, you'll hit the marketplace with two assets you wouldn't otherwise have had:

> **One:** The knowledge and certainty that you have something people want. This will help you persevere and stay motivated when things get tough.
>
> **Two:** Data, evidentiary proof that what you do works and gets results. This data will be gold when it comes time for you to promote your services. You won't just be spouting assertions like everyone else, you'll be armed with facts and evidence to back up your claim.

Let's look at how to test both lower-priced products like information courses and more involved, high-priced coaching packages.

Testing a Lower-End Product

If part of your business involves selling smaller products like books or courses—something with less commitment or expense than a one-on-one coaching session—then an easy way to test your offer is to put on a free event in your area.

If you're an executive coach, you could put on a free event at a local hotel on a topic connected to the product you're selling, such as "Time Management Tips for Executives." Promote the free event to your personal network and any connections you may have in the industry, and see how many people show up. Even if it's just ten or twenty people, that's fine. You now have a focus group of real people and potential customers.

At the event, give away some useful information—and then offer a prototype version of your product either for free or at a reduced price. Explain that you're doing this to gather feedback. In exchange for the free or extremely discounted course, they agree to give you feedback and, if they like the course, to give you an honest video testimonial you can use on your website when your product is ready.

Worst-case scenario, you'll get useful information to hone your approach in the future. Best-case, you'll get some rock-solid video testimonials to serve as proof that what you do works, and possibly some paying customers in the future.

Testing a Coaching Program

You can use the exact process above to test a coaching program. You can also skip it and go straight to the offer phase. Reach out to a handful of people you know and offer them a free or an outrageously affordable coaching program in exchange for honest feedback. Be open and sincere: *"I'm starting a coaching business—I've got this great system. Would you be willing to work with me for free and, if you get results, give a testimonial and help me promote it to others?"*

What's essential here is that you clearly define the unique system that you are offering. What's unique about the results you deliver and the way in which you deliver them?

I had a client who was starting a nutrition business. Her unique approach was her focus on removing harmful toxins from her clients' lives, in both the foods they consumed and the cosmetics they used. She reached out to a few people she knew and offered, free of charge, to help them remove the toxins from their environment. In exchange, all she asked for was a video endorsement if they noticed an improvement in their health.

People showed interest, her clients got results, and she hit the market, both confident in her service and armed with powerful evidence (video testimonials) she could use to validate her claims and promote her service to others.

Walk Your Talk

The tests above will help you validate your product or service and collect testimonials and data to prove the value of what you do. This evidentiary proof provided by your first clients or customers goes a long way toward establishing your credibility. Beyond the third-party evidence, however, the most important evidence must come from you. You have to walk your talk.

If you're a fitness coach, then you have to be fit. If you're a coach who focuses on financial success, then you have to have your own finances in order. This should go without saying, but sadly it doesn't. There's a lot of hypocrisy in the business world, and people know that. The data helps, but it won't compensate for a lack of authenticity.

Let's say that there are 1,000 coaches in your city whose services or products broadly compete with yours. You don't just want to be another coach. You don't want to be in the top 100. You want to be in the *top 10*, the top 1 percent, of whatever field you're in. You do this by:

- Having and owning a unique system or product that fills a need and gives people something they want
- Collecting testimonials and data that prove your claims and validate your ideas
- Walking your talk and being an authentic success story for your own method

If you're failing on any of the above, stop and work on it. Follow the advice in the other chapters of this book, each of which addresses part of the puzzle. Most importantly, *get a coach*. I have coaches. Every good coach has coaches of their own. Find people to help you on both a personal level and a business level so that when you hit the world, you're bringing something truly phenomenal with you.

GETTING YOUR NAME OUT THERE: MEDIA AND PUBLICITY

Now that you have a coaching program that people want and the proof to back it up, you're ready to bring your message to the world. It's time to get your name out there and start establishing your reputation as a leading, credible authority in your niche. Here's the good news: By validating your product and collecting proof that it works, you've already achieved the hardest part.

Publicity is no mystery, and while appearing on the radio or even on TV may seem unattainably ambitious if you're just starting out, it's not that hard. All you need is some initiative and, most importantly, persistence.

How to Get into the Media

The principles we covered for creating and representing an amazing product also apply for getting into the media: have something that people want, be passionate, and walk your talk. The media is always looking for people to appear on shows.

Do some research and find the local media channels that may be open to what you offer. Look out for two things: precedence and seasonality. If a local radio or TV network frequently features coaches or experts in areas related to yours, it's a good bet they may be open to what you have to say.

Seasonality also plays a major role. January, for example, is a great time if you're in the health or nutrition space. Look out for local events and see if you can align what you're offering with the local mood. For example, if you're a sports coach, look out for major sporting events and offer to talk about how mind-set determines success.

But the most important thing is to simply put yourself out there. At the early stages in your career, the cable TV networks and radio hosts aren't going to find you. You have to find them. Call them up and introduce yourself: "This is who I am, this is what I have to offer." Let's say you're an executive coach and you've noticed that a local radio station is doing a weekly interview series with a business expert. Call them up, introduce yourself, explain what is unique about your perspective or system, and offer to share some free tips.

This may seem simple—and it is—but by merely having the confidence to put yourself out there, you immediately stand above 90 percent of your competitors. Persist, and you'll be amazed by how many people are willing to hear what you have to say.

Podcasts Are King

If you're finding the traditional media hard to break into at first, it may help to begin with the Internet.

There's a rich and resourceful world of online TV shows and podcasts out there, and they are eager to have experts appear and share free content with their audience. Some of them are small, but others have tremendous reach: I have been interviewed on several podcasts, and I was recently a guest on an online TV platform that has 100,000 paying listeners, and I was interviewed for an hour. Opportunities like this are a fantastic way to broaden your reach and practice your pitch and delivery skills.

Take the same approach with podcasts as I described with local media:

- Spend some time researching podcasts related to your niche by searching Google and iTunes.
- When you find a match, reach out to the host and introduce yourself: "This is who I am, this is what I have to offer."
- Persist!

If you show up and authentically deliver real value, walking your talk, then people will respond, and more shows will be interested in having you on. A client of mine is a musician who's working on building a following and making a living from her music. Appearing on podcasts was a real breakthrough for her. After appearing as a guest on a few music-themed podcasts, she ended up landing her own online show on PocketLive.tv, and now her audience is soaring.

Flip the Script: Become the Host, Not Just the Guest

Starting your own TV channel or radio station is a mighty task, but anyone can start their own podcast. Consider starting your own themed online talk show and interviewing other people with expertise in your niche. Go back to the list of podcasts you researched above, and reach out to a few of the guests you really liked. People love to be interviewed, and you'll be surprised at how readily even big names say yes.

The benefits here are twofold:

One: You get to form connections with these influencers, planting the seed for joint ventures and partnerships down the line.

Two: More often than not, *they will promote the interview you do together.* This will rapidly grow your following, magnetizing more people to your podcast and to your brand.

If It Isn't Working, Correct and Continue

This scenario is unlikely, but possible: You keep trying to put your name out there, contacting radio stations and podcast hosts, local journalists, and cable news programs, only to find your overtures continually rejected. You persist, but after a couple of months you realize this simply isn't working. What do you do?

My rule in these situations is simple: correct and continue. It's incredible how often you find small changes in your approach can cause a major difference in the response you get. A little bit of external help can go a long way. It could be that there's something in your approach hosts find off-putting. Maybe you're not representing yourself as well as you could be. Maybe you've skipped a step, and what you're offering isn't yet ready for the market. Consult a business coach or a trusted friend and mentor, and walk them through your approach. The small shifts they will help you to make could be the difference between no and yes.

One of my closest mentors is Kevin Harrington, a pioneer of the "as seen on TV" industry and an original star of the TV show *Shark Tank*. When I'm striking out with a new product or idea, he's one of the first people I speak to. Normally I find my idea was 90 percent there but just needed a few minor changes so that other people could really see its potential. Sometimes the books I write don't take off at first, but after hiring a professional editor to tweak and streamline the content, they go through the stratosphere.

If you're striking out, persist, but don't keep doing the same thing over and over again. Get a second pair of eyes to help you make corrections; then you're ready to continue.

Summary and Your "To Do" List

Most coaches struggle because they lack the ability or willingness to promote themselves. Coaching is a business, and the services you provide are your product. The same branding and positioning rules apply to coaching as to all other businesses out there. To be successful, you need to have a product that people want and get your name out there in a way that positions you as a credible authority.

- **Offer something people want:** Test your ideas by holding a free event or offering your coaching services to a small group of people in exchange for feedback. If they don't like it, you've gained valuable data. If they love what you're offering, get their testimonial on video to use on your website and lend credibility to your marketing efforts.
- **Walk your talk:** If you're a fitness coach, you have to be fit. If you coach in the financial sector, you need to have your own finances in order.
- **Get in touch:** Research local cable news, radio, and online podcast hosts who have shown that they are interested in your area of expertise. Look out for precedence and seasonality. Get in touch and simply say, "This is who I am, this is what I do."
- **Flip the script:** Host your own podcast show to form connections with influencers and benefit from the reach of their established audiences.

- **Correct and continue:** If your efforts aren't working, seek help from a mentor or coach, and notice how even the slightest improvements in your approach can dramatically improve your results.

Impossible to Normal

Strategies for Building a Visionary Business

VISHEN LAKHIANI

Vishen Lakhiani is founder and CEO of Mindvalley which he launched in 2003 with just a few hundred dollars. Today, Mindvalley is working to revolutionize how people think about education and personal growth, with millions of students worldwide and more than $30 million in annual revenue.

Your business isn't just a company, it's an expression of what you want for the world. Regardless of whether you see yourself as a boutique coach or CEO of a billion-dollar empire, here's how to get started the right way and build a business fueled by your passion.

Your business is an expression of your values and the shift you want to make in the world. It's not just a "job." It's not just exchanging time for money. As a coach, you create change. You make a difference.

When you build a business based on your *passion* that matches your most deeply held values, *there are no limits*. Every day, you're free to focus on your dreams and bring them closer to reality. You can make what was once *impossible* your new *normal*.

I started Mindvalley when I was working in Silicon Valley and going through a stressful period. I had tried to launch my own start-up, but my timing was terrible. The "dotcom bubble" had burst and I'd lost all my savings. I couldn't even afford rent, so I was sleeping on a couch.

Desperate, I'd taken a "dialing for dollars" job selling technology to law firms. I would pick up the phone, call a firm, and convince them to buy our technology. I hated it. I was miserable.

One day at work, I went online and started searching for an answer. I found a website advertising a meditation class. It was an old program that started in the 1960s called the Silva Method. I flew to Los Angeles to take the class. It was fantastic, but I was the only person there.

After the course, I went back to work and started applying what I had learned. Thanks to my newfound focus and insight, I doubled my earnings month after month. Within the next four months, I got promoted three times, and I quickly ended up as director of sales for the company.

This *one-day* meditation class had fundamentally changed my life. The meditation principles, the process of visualizing my goals, the ability to be in The Zone, let me turn on my creativity and intuition. Because of this, it seemed like I always knew exactly what to say to the other person on the phone.

But the thought that struck me was: *I was the only person in this class.* If this is so powerful, why aren't more people doing this? I stayed with the technology company for eighteen months, but I knew that I wanted to do more with my life.

In my spare time, I started a company promoting meditation programs. The first program we promoted was from the creators of the meditation class that I had attended. This was the beginning of Mindvalley.

Today, Mindvalley has over 200 employees and millions of students. The company makes tens of millions of dollars in revenue every year. Our mission is to change how people view education around the world. We are successful because we put our values first, and we are driven by our passion and this mission.

Mindvalley was not an overnight success, and there were a *lot* of failures and struggles along the way. In this chapter, we'll look at some lessons from my journey and how you as a coach can build your own successful, mission-driven business.

YOUR MINIMUM LIVABLE INCOME

A lot of coaches feel pressure to immediately quit their jobs and coach full-time. What I learned in the early days of my business is that this is not usually the best move. Instead, wait until you have reached your *minimum livable income* (MLI).

Your minimum livable income is the amount of income you and your family need to stay alive and comfortable. This is not your target income—in the long term you want to be making a lot more than this—but it's what you need to keep a roof over your head and pay the bills without stress.

Like a lot of entrepreneurs, I started my business by working nights and weekends. In the first month I lost $300. In the second month I lost $800. By the third month I started to break even. I made tiny amounts of money, but I was celebrating every cent.

After about four or five months, I was making a profit of about $4.50 a day. I would go to Starbucks and spend that $4.50 on my favorite cup of coffee. I thought of this little website I was running as a cool way to get free Starbucks in the morning.

A few months later I was making $6.50 a day in profit. Now I could go from *grande* to *venti* with whipped cream! By month seven, it was Starbucks AND a Subway sandwich. Luxury!

I kept celebrating these little victories, and the tiny amounts of profit I made kept growing and growing. My wife and I were working on this business together, and together we decided to calculate our minimum livable income with the goal of eventually sustaining this income through the new business. We lived in New York and knew that if we could make $4,000 a month, we could survive as a couple. We wouldn't be rich, but we could survive.

I was earning double this in my day job, but I knew that with $4,000, I could quit and dedicate myself completely to Mindvalley. In November 2003, I hit my MLI. I quit my job that very month. I went to Malaysia over Christmas and dedicated all my extra time to Mindvalley. By the time I came back in January, the company had grown 60 percent because now I had the extra time to give it. Things have never been the same since.

Action Step: Know Your MLI

Know when you have reached your minimum livable income—and don't quit your job until then! In most cases, it is safest to start your company on the side, while you still have your day job. If you play your cards right, as soon as you get your coaching business to hit your MLI, you can leave your job with confidence.

Your MLI should be simple to work out: How much do you spend per month on *essential* living expenses—rent, groceries, utilities, healthcare? Leave in a little extra, but don't aim for the stars *yet*. Remember, it is your minimum income, not your target income.

ENVISIONING: THE ART OF MAKING THE IMPOSSIBLE YOUR NEW NORMAL

When I started Mindvalley, my goal was to build the No. 1 place to work in the world. This focus enabled us to attract incredible people to work with us from the start. Because we have the right people on the team, we're able to accomplish *huge* things and constantly push to the next level.

I don't really see limits. I'm only motivated by massive goals. If I can't do something that's going to be legendary, I'm just not satisfied. This means that if I start a company, it has to be world-class, it has to win awards.

This practice of *dreaming big* and being free of what most people would consider reasonable limits is what I call *envisioning*.

Make Yourself Obsolete

At heart, coaches are entrepreneurs, and entrepreneurs are artists. We're creators. We don't start our companies because we want to build a business. We start them because we want to make a shift, to create something wonderful and positive that did not exist before.

At the core of the spirit of *envisioning* is constant innovation. We want to make ourselves obsolete. We constantly ask ourselves: What would a competitor have to do to put us out of business? Great, then we're going to do that ourselves before they get a chance!

When we build a product or platform, we keep tweaking, continually innovating to get to the next level. We recently acquired a tech company, and we put all of its developers to work building the hottest online platform for what we refer to as "transformational education."

In 2016, we launched Mindvalley Home, an online learning space. It's beautiful, it's aesthetic. People love it. But within months of finishing it, the vision for the next level came to me. It's a radical new way of learning, and I knew that if I didn't do it, someone else would do it, and they would make us obsolete.

We immediately wrapped up Mindvalley Home and started work on Mindvalley Quest, which we completed in six months. Immediately, the new platform made the old one obsolete. This is the idea of *envisioning* in practice. We keep pushing ourselves to make what is impossible normal.

Action Step

Celebrate your victories, but then establish them as your *new normal*. Keep pushing the ceiling so that you reach the next impossible level. Then, the impossible becomes your new normal, and you look further and envision the next impossible goal.

MAKE YOUR ENTIRE BUSINESS A WORK OF ART

A lot of people think Mindvalley is a marketing company, but we really are a group of artists. We have more designers, filmmakers, UX designers, graphic designers, and photographers on our staff than any other category of employee.

When designing every aspect of your coaching business, it helps to think like an artist. *Everything* should be beautiful, from your website to your business cards, to the systems you use and the techniques you employ. Creating art will help you attract more clients, win referrals, and inspire your staff.

This obsession with creating art extends to the photographs of our authors that we use on our websites. When the photos our authors provide aren't up to our standards, we send world-class photographers—the same people who photograph rock stars and celebrities—to take their photos.

We hire artists and apply this spirit of artistry to every aspect of our business. This makes us shine as a company, and it motivates everyone involved. We are creating something beautiful, so every part of it must be world-class.

Our authors trust us because they know their brand is in safe hands. Because of this, we can attract some of the biggest names in self-help.

Passion Matters More than Money

This relentless focus on quality and pushing ourselves beyond the ordinary carries a cost. There are times when we take a loss. There have been times when we have almost died as a business. The thing that constantly pushes us forward is that this business is a passion project. I want to change human education. That's why I'm doing this. The money is not the primary motivator.

Recently, I spoke to an employee on my customer support team. A customer had asked for a refund on a program, and he talked the customer out of it. He was proud of this. His attitude was, "Yeah, I saved the company money!" He thought this was a good thing.

I said, "No, this is not how we treat our customers!" If a customer asks for a refund, you try to understand *why*. You give them the refund, or you politely give them a free product. You do not protest. What matters is that the customer walks away loving Mindvalley more than they did before. I don't give a damn about the money we'd save by changing someone's mind about a refund—that's not what matters. This particular employee soon understood the value of true customer service.

We are obsessive about creating art, and we are obsessive about how we treat our customers. We would definitely save money if we cut corners on quality and customer service, but our business would suffer. We succeed because of this constant quality, this attitude that our customers are kings.

Apply this attitude to your coaching business. It is not easy. Sometimes it's a massive battle. But it's a fun battle, and in the long term it pays off.

Action Step

Constantly create art with every aspect of your business. Innovate and push yourself *beyond* what you originally planned. Apply this attitude to your coaching technique, your website, your marketing, your books, your products, and especially how you treat your customers.

ARE YOU A VISIONARY OR AN EMPLOYEE? UNDERSTANDING THE THREE LEVELS OF WORK

I recently had the opportunity to talk to business magnate and philanthropist Richard Branson, and I asked him, "Richard, you've started 300 companies; how do you do it?" He said, "You gotta find good people, you gotta give them meaningful work and make them see their work as a mission. And this way you sit back, and you can focus on the vision."

The idea of envisioning is not for everyone, but chances are if you're reading this book, then at some level you are a *dreamer*, a visionary. You want to create art and are not afraid of challenging the limits that others set for you.

In general, there are three categories of work, with *envisioning* as the foundation. Let's look at this in some detail.

The first level of work: Trading time for money. If your work is highly transactional and isn't likely to produce something of value for yourself or humanity, this is the first level of work. If you're at this level now, that's okay, but make a plan to move beyond.

The second level of work: Creating something that will last. If you're writing code, for example, this is level-two work. After you create an app, millions of people will download it, and it will continue working beyond you. You work once and it continues ticking on. Most coaching is level-two work—your clients' lives are changed, and they continue functioning in the world as better individuals after your sessions, so your work continues and has a positive impact on the world.

The third level of work: Multiplying your business. You are not coaching one-on-one or teaching classes to a limited number of people. Instead, you have created a system that allows thousands of students to be influenced by your work without you having to do anything further. This is the level that I personally aim for.

Today, 70 percent of my time is at level three. When I started, a lot of my time was level one. I had to answer customer e-mails and look after day-to-day tasks. Slowly I shifted to level two. The website that I had created worked by itself, and I hired my first customer support assistant to take care of e-mails.

When I was at level two, I taught meditation classes in New York to a few hundred people at a time. Now that I'm at level three, I have meditation apps that are among the highest-grossing wellness apps in their countries, with *millions* of downloads. My apps teach people on their own and aren't limited by the number of people who can fit in a room or the amount of time I have in a day.

Level-three work is the *multiplier* work. You expand your business beyond what you could ever do as an individual. Instead of coaching yourself, you create a panel of coaches who use a system that you have created. People franchise your method and use it around the world, helping millions of people with your ideas and techniques.

Action Step: Dream Bigger!

To get to level three, *dream bigger.* Most people get stuck at level two, and if that's what you want there's nothing wrong with it. I was really happy teaching meditation classes, but I was only able to teach a couple of hundred people a year. I wanted to reach *millions,* because I love humanity and I wanted to get this stuff out to the world.

So, ask yourself, what level do you want to reach? My goal is to shift the lives of *1 billion people.* It's a huge, inspired goal. If you have dreams like this, then focus on getting to level three. If you're happy helping others one person at a time, then that's absolutely cool as well—get to level two, and Own It.

Summary and Your "To Do" List

Your coaching practice is not just a business. Create a movement, make a shift, and focus on your mission. When you achieve impossible goals, celebrate, but make this level your new normal. Keep going and let yourself dream even bigger than before!

- **Calculate your minimum livable income:** Make sure your coaching business reaches this level before you quit your day job. This reduces the fear and stress you will otherwise feel during the early days of your business.
- **Envision the next stage:** Your business is the vehicle through which you make a difference in the world. Make every part of it awesome! There are no limits. Do not be defined by what holds other people back. Let yourself dream bigger.
- **Create art:** Every aspect of your business should be a work of art. Treat your customers like kings and infuse your entire business with a sense of quality and artistry. It's not always the cheapest thing to do, but it pays off over the long term.
- **Understand the three levels of work:** Level one is when you exchange time for money and work for somebody else. Level two is when you create a positive change directly. Level three is when you engineer products or systems that create this change on a larger scale. Both level two and level three are fantastic—just make sure you choose the level you want.

The Super Guru Strategy

How to Achieve International Recognition as a Coach

JACK CANFIELD

Jack Canfield is the creator of the *New York Times* No. 1 best-selling book series *Chicken Soup for the Soul®*, which *Time* magazine called "the publishing phenomenon of the decade." Jack is a Harvard graduate with a master's degree in psychological education from the University of Massachusetts and several honorary doctorates in human development. Jack has been at the top of the personal development world for more than four decades. Based in the United States, Jack has a major international presence, and his books have been translated into more than fifty languages.

Many coaches dream of becoming internationally recognized and building a global audience of fans. Jack Canfield has done it, having created the Chicken Soup for the Soul® *series, which has more than 500 million copies in print. Learn how to get your name out there as a speaker, author, and online influencer.*

If there is anything I have learned, it is that consistent action over time produces results, and those results don't happen overnight. Whether your dream is to become an internationally recognized coach, speaker, trainer, or thought leader, it takes commitment, passion, hard work, self-care, and the constant pursuit of new knowledge in a never-ending quest for improvement.

My journey, which I am still on, has been decades in the making. The essence of my evolution was my passion for helping others, which I first discovered while attending Harvard, when I attended a psychology class in human relations. After graduation, I began teaching high school, and the school where I first taught in Chicago was rough. Most of the students were not motivated, and I soon became more interested in how to motivate my students than in teaching history. Most of the kids in the school cut classes whenever they could, but the kids I was teaching were having a different experience. I started teaching my students principles of success and worked on building their self-esteem. Soon the kids that snuck out of other classes were sneaking into mine.

Because of my success with these students, I was soon traveling around the state and then the country teaching my techniques to other teachers and school administrators. Eventually, a principal at one of those schools said to me, "The employees in my husband's company need what you're teaching." Because I had never worked in a corporation before, I was hesitant. She said, "Come on. They're just big kids in suits; get over there and teach them what you know!" And that's how I started conducting trainings on self-esteem and peak performance for companies like Microsoft, FedEx, and Johnson & Johnson.

A few years later, after one of my corporate trainings, a woman came up and asked me if all the stories I had told were in a book. I told her they weren't. On the flight home that evening, thinking of all the feedback and comments I had received that day, I decided I needed to put the stories in a book. After all, that day's presentation was titled "The 10 Steps to Success," and step No. 8 is Respond to Feedback.

I spent the next four years writing up all the inspirational and transformational stories that I used in my presentations, along with others I had collected from colleagues and friends. I edited and compiled them into a book, *Chicken Soup for the Soul*®, which went on to become one of the most recognized book series in the United States during the 1990s.

The series now has 500 million copies in print around the world, with translations in more than forty languages.

Let's look at how you, too, can become an internationally recognized speaker, author, and online influencer. To do that, you have to begin to think beyond the one-on-one coaching sessions you do with your clients. You have to amplify your success, grow your business, get your name out there, and create transformation on a larger scale.

ALL COACHES NEED TO BECOME TRAINERS

To achieve international standing as a coach, seeing clients one-on-one isn't enough. You must inspire, empower, and transform people in *groups*. Think about it: Would you rather transform one person an hour or several hundred?

When you're speaking to or conducting workshops with large audiences, more people have those "a-ha" breakthrough moments, creating a deeper, more meaningful experience. Those same people are going to go out and tell everyone they know about you and the work you do, giving you the scalability factor you need to grow. Many of these same people you attract to your large group trainings will also go on to become clients in your one-on-one and group coaching practice.

Live speeches, workshops, and training events are a fantastic way for you to:

- Let people really get to know you
- Show people what you and your work stand for
- Enroll people in your message and your personal brand
- Add more people to your mailing list
- Build a following on social media, like Facebook, Twitter, and Pinterest

These people will go on to become readers, clients, customers, and advocates for you and your larger vision.

How to Get Out There as a Speaker

If you're just starting out, you may worry that getting people into a room to listen to you speak is an uphill battle. In fact, it's easier than you think—if you're willing start by speaking *for free* to any group that will listen. If you provide great value, the word will spread and more people will give you the opportunity to address their members or speak at their events.

Look for local organizations in your community that regularly feature speakers, like civic groups, schools, and churches, and ask if they'd give you twenty minutes to share some powerful, practical, life-improving ideas with their members. When you get the opportunity to speak, *give as much value as possible.* Help the people in the room experience a micro-transformation. Use techniques from your coaching tool kit to give people a real, life-changing experience that they're going to remember and tell their friends about. Leave them wanting to hear *more* of what you have to say.

When people realize that you have something powerful and real to offer, you'll start receiving more invitations to speak. When these invitations come, *say yes!* There was a time when I was willing to speak almost anywhere—from the local church to the chamber of commerce, the Boy Scouts, Girls Clubs, teachers groups, and so on. You must be willing to show up, tell your story, and deliver value, otherwise no one is going to hear about you!

Inspire Others by Knowing Your Why

In addition to the material and ideas you teach, one of the most important things you can do when in front of an audience is to inspire them by telling the *real story* of how you came to be there. We all get into coaching for a reason, and there's probably an event in your past that inspired you to begin your journey. Be open about it, and tell your story.

One of the things we do in my Train the Trainer program is teach people how to become more effective speakers. One of my students is a professor of astronomy at Harvard. One of the exercises in the training involves speaking to the group about a cause you care deeply about. His cause was to get more financial and institutional support for women to study science in college. He started off by quoting statistic after statistic about the lack of financial aid for women who wanted to study science, and soon we were all drifting off to sleep.

I interrupted him and asked, "Why do you care so much about women in science careers?" He said, "Because my sister is smarter than me, but she couldn't get a scholarship to study science in college because of the sexism." And then he went on to tell her story with a great deal of emotion. When he spoke about his sister and how he wanted her to have the same opportunities that men had, we were in tears. From that moment on, we were all captivated, and we were totally enrolled in his vision—to the point where we would have written a check right on the spot!

Every speaker needs a story like this. What is your WHY? Why do you care? Make sure you know what yours is and then *share it*. This shows people where you are coming from and gives them a compelling reason to pay attention to what you have to say. For people to trust you, they want to know what motivates you. Is it service or greed? Is it compassion or ego? Once they know your "why," they become more interested in your what.

Don't be afraid to talk about the painful or traumatic experiences that motivated you to get into coaching—the death of a friend; your divorce; your mother's cancer; your midlife crisis; your loss of a job; or your earlier struggles with alcohol, drugs, or depression.

Enroll People, Keep Them Engaged, and Build a Legion of Fans

A lot of people sell, but they don't *enroll*. Give your live audiences the opportunity to get on your mailing list and learn more about what you have to offer. Share free information and sell just enough to convert your subscribers into fans, many of whom will stay with you for life.

There are many ways to elegantly end a live event by inviting people to enroll on your list. Normally it involves giving away something small for free. One technique I used when I was starting my career was to have a large glass fishbowl at the front of the class. I would invite students to place their business cards inside. At the end of the event, I'd pull one card from the bowl and award the owner a free copy of my latest book or a free coaching session. Everyone else would now be on my list and agree to be contacted with updates, news, and offers in the future. With today's technology, you can direct them to your website to download a free PDF file of some techniques they can use to enhance their life, or an MP3 download of a guided exercise, meditation, or recording of your talk.

The rule for both mailing lists and live events is give away enough so people feel the value of what you are offering, but not so much that they think they don't need anything else. Keep the people on your list eager to hear from you again, with more tips and ideas, while offering products and services regularly enough that you increase your revenue and your list. This way your seminar attendees will go on to become lifelong fans, customers, and ambassadors.

BEYOND THE CLASSROOM: CREATING A GLOBAL AUDIENCE FOR YOUR IDEAS

It's almost impossible to achieve international status as a coach, speaker, or trainer if you don't have a book. My original motivation for having a best-selling book, in addition to sharing my ideas with people I might never meet, was to command higher speaking fees, and it worked! I had no idea that having a best-selling book would create a demand for me to speak all over the world.

Every other year I am invited to go on a seven-city speaking tour all over Asia. The tour is organized by a promoter who hires only what he calls "Mega Gurus." And his definition of a Mega Guru is someone who has three or four best-selling books. No, of course, this won't happen overnight, but don't be intimidated by that. It's possible to write books that sell—and if you don't start now, you'll never get there. Early in my career, I was writing about one book every two years. So, let's look at how to write something worth reading.

How to Become a Successful Author

As I said at the start of this chapter, consistent action over time produces results. It is possible to become a best-selling author, but you have to be willing to pay the price, continually ask for feedback, and never give up. Have you ever wondered how many authors actually ask for feedback prior to publishing their book? Or more importantly, how many authors have shared their message time and again to make sure it is something others are interested in before they write a book about it?

The great thing about starting out as a speaker is that you are constantly collecting wonderful stories and anecdotes to make your message more powerful. As I shared earlier, this is how *Chicken Soup for the Soul*® first came into being. Speaking and conducting workshops is also a place to get immediate feedback on the content you are sharing, the way you are explaining it, and the impact it has on people. You are basically being paid to test out your content prior to compiling it in a book.

People think you need to have a major breakthrough in your field in order to become a best seller, but this isn't always true. If you have some unique discovery or method, that is fantastic, but most people out there *don't* have that, and that's okay. You'll come to learn that *your perspective* is unique. The *stories* and content you have to share are uniquely yours.

You can bring something valuable to the world even if you are just putting a new spin on ideas that are already out there. The things you have that no one else has are your own stories and your own experiences. You have your unique WHY. You have overcome challenges and learned lessons that can help others.

My book *The 30-Day Sobriety Solution: How to Cut Back or Quit Drinking in the Privacy of Your Own Home*, for example, is simply the result of my coauthor Dave Andrews' experience of integrating my success principles into his practice as a sobriety coach. While a lot of the techniques we include in the book—goal setting, values clarification, guided visualization, meditation, EFT tapping—aren't new, the way we combined them into an integrated, holistic approach with success stories from our clients is new and uniquely ours.

The Concept in Practice

You may not have invented a new coaching methodology, but chances are you have applied things in a unique way, and you have a story others can relate to. Think about the ways you have used coaching tools in your own life and with your clients. Is there an area of specialization you could expand into a book? For example, you may not have invented emotional freedom technique (EFT), but you may have unique experiences *applying* EFT to the area of parenting, being a manager, being an effective performance coach, creating financial abundance, or overcoming the trauma of childhood sexual abuse.

Recognize that you do have powerful, unique experiences to draw upon, and you have the unique success stories of your clients. Use them, and write that first book!

Get Your Books Around the World

Becoming internationally recognized as an author is not just about writing a good book. You have to get out there, chase down opportunities, speak, promote, and *enroll people* as we discussed earlier.

I've traveled to more than fifty-five countries as a speaker, including Russia, India, and the United Arab Emirates, and sometimes it's grueling, but it pays off. I now have more than 1,500 students teaching my work in eighty-one countries. This didn't happen by accident. In my earlier days, I'd track down the people who had published translations of books that were similar to mine, get them on the phone, tell them what my books were about, and encourage them to publish them. Sometimes that would result in a lucrative publishing deal, sometimes not. But to be a successful author, you have to get out there, make contacts, be willing to speak, and be committed to relentlessly *make it happen*.

Have a Strong Internet Presence

If the idea of writing a book still intimidates you, you can kick-start your international brand online. Just like running live events and becoming a successful author, having a strong presence on the Internet is about telling your unique story in an engaging way and giving value.

One of my students who is based in the Ukraine creates a three-minute video every single day of the year. He started out just shooting them with his cell phone, creating short, conversational pieces that contained a practical lesson. For example, he'd film himself standing in front of the Eiffel Tower in Paris and would say something like, "You can see behind me the magnificent Eiffel Tower. This wasn't created by just one person, it was built by a team. Everyone has to have a team in place to accomplish their goals. Here are some practical strategies for building a successful team . . ."

Most of his videos would be like this—just a quick little tidbit of interesting advice casually filmed in a relatable way. Every three or four videos, he'd casually mention a product he has on sale or a course that he's offering. "By the way, if you can get to Paris on April 5, I'll be teaching a course here on team building, and there are still a few places available. And if you enjoyed this video, please forward it to a friend." When he started this daily practice of video blogging, he was averaging 30 people in his workshops. Now he averages 600 to 800 people.

Action Step

The key is to just get started and *take action* as soon as possible. Commit to creating one compelling piece of content every day, and get the word out to people in your network. In the same way that people will be happy to let you speak at their community center *because you're giving value*, you'll find it easy to motivate others to check out your free advice. Work consistently to build up a following, and every few videos include a call to action that directs people to a specific product, webinar, or live event.

By following this strategy consistently, my student in the Ukraine now has more than *1 million* followers online!

Everything Connects

So far we've looked at three ways to get the word out about your ideas:

- Speaking in person
- Writing books
- Building an online following

In today's world, you really need to do all three to truly achieve super-guru status.

You're probably starting to notice how all three feed into each other. People who see you speak in person will be motivated to join your online mailing list. Followers of your video blog can be encouraged to sign up and pay to attend your live courses. You may want to begin with your strengths, create an established following in the arena that is most comfortable to you, and then leverage this into the other arenas when you're on a roll.

I have several million followers when I combine Facebook, Twitter, Instagram, Periscope, LinkedIn, and YouTube, but these platforms didn't even exist when I wrote *Chicken Soup for the Soul*®. My live training business grew into books, which sold internationally, and has now expanded online. These days, the trajectory for a lot of coaches is likely to be in the opposite direction: an online presence expanding into physical books and live events. Become an influencer in the arena that best suits you and excites you, and then build your empire from there.

Summary and Your "To Do" List

Consistent action over time along with responding to feedback, learning new skills, and being willing to do whatever it takes will bring you the results you want. To become internationally recognized, work on transforming yourself into a compelling speaker, workshop facilitator, trainer, best-selling author, and online influencer.

- **Get in front of audiences:** As a speaker, be willing to pursue all opportunities to get in front of an interested audience. Give away useful information, and inspire people with your "why."
- **Use free offers:** Rather than constantly selling, use free offers to enroll people in your brand and constantly build your mailing list.
- **Stay in touch:** Keep in regular and consistent contact with your subscribers, provide useful information to them to keep them coming back, and then market your products to them.
- **Share your unique experiences:** Remember, you don't need to invent an earth-shattering new methodology to become a best-selling author. You have unique experiences that you can use to add something new to an existing approach or methodology.
- **Cultivate an online presence:** In today's world, you need to have a strong online presence to become recognized internationally. Video blogging is a great way to build a loyal following; get your name out there; and promote your books, speaking engagements, and live courses.
- **Tie it all together:** Your online presence will promote your live in-person events. And during your live events, you'll be able to sell your books and enroll new subscribers for your online offerings.

© 2017 Jack Canfield and Self Esteem Seminars, L.P. All rights reserved.

Coaching, Amplified

How to Take Your Unique Value to the Masses and Build Your Business Empire

> **Roberto Re** has been on the forefront of the Italian personal growth market for twenty-five years. A popular author in Italian with over 700,000 copies of his books sold, Roberto speaks to 30,000 people at his live events every year. A peak performance specialist, Roberto's clients include football stars and gold medal–winning athletes. After crushing it in Italy, he is now expanding his domain to Dubai and the UAE.

Want to go beyond one-on-one sessions and have an impact on thousands of people? Learn how to create meaningful products that sell and bring value to the masses.

It's one thing working with someone face-to-face. It's another thing entirely to create transformation at large scales and via long distances through your products, your books, and your seminars.

I've had a passion for personal improvement and peak performance since I was twenty years old. Back then, there was no personal development market in Italy. There were a few mind-set teachers, but nothing like what was available in the United States.

After trying to learn as much as I could in Italy, I stumbled across a leaflet for a Tony Robbins training in the U.S. It was very expensive for me at that time, but I knew this could be a watershed moment in my life. So I found the money, made the journey, and met Tony Robbins in person.

I became one of his trainers at his Mastery University and soon started delivering Tony Robbins–style events back in Italy. We started off teaching to small rooms with just a handful of students. The crowds grew larger, and I began to create my own products (books, videos, audio programs, etc.) to share my ideas and techniques with self-created visualization and meditation with a wider audience.

What excites me most about my work is seeing the faces of my clients or the faces in the crowd *when they get it*. It's that light in their eyes. I've learned to cultivate an awareness of my audience, of what's going on around me. As I train or work with people one-on-one, I'm constantly asking myself, "What are they thinking as I'm saying this?"

Today, I have a database of more than 400,000 students and followers, and I speak to 30,000 people at my live events every year. If your goal is to reach a mass audience as a coach, the first step is always value: Create a great product that gets results. (More on this topic in just a moment.)

The results you achieve for your clients will be your No. 1 marketing asset. Prove your value to them the *right way* to build your credibility and stand out from the crowd. As more and more people experience the power of your programs, your customers will become your best advocates and ambassadors.

Business is a team sport, and I didn't get to where I am alone. The final, crucial step toward reaching a mass audience as a coach is to put a team in place that will support and facilitate your progress, and let you do what you do best. Ultimately, your business should be able to run itself with little involvement from you!

Let's look at each of these steps in more detail.

CREATE A GREAT PRODUCT

Your products give you potential to be all around the world at the same time. They can be a book, a video course, an audio program. What matters isn't the medium, it's the *quality*.

Creating an excellent product that people love isn't easy, but it's worth it. My first book, *Leader of Yourself*, came out thirteen years ago, and it's still selling thousands of copies every year. You never know who's going to read it today or tomorrow. When you do a great job, it lasts, it will be there for many years.

The key to creating a unique product isn't strictly about unique *content*, it's about delivering it in a unique way.

You don't need to have some earth-shattering breakthrough to create a product that sells. In fact, today, no one really has a truly unique product in the market. Everyone is using something from someone else. There's so much out there and so much competition that, even if you did create something truly original and special, someone else would probably have it in a few months.

This means that you have to have a unique way to *teach* and a unique way to *market* what you offer. Create a technically well-crafted product that feels professional at every level. This alone will immediately help you stand out from the competition. When most people are shooting videos on their cell phones but you've paid for an experienced videographer, everyone will notice the difference.

Create Something That Offers Real Value

Instead of wondering if what you have to say is new and original, the No. 1 question you have to ask yourself is: *Is this interesting?* Can it really change your customers' lives? When they're watching your video or reading your book, are they nodding and saying, "Wow, me too!" Or, are they just going to shrug and say, "So what?"

For starters, focus on that small area of your business in which you really thrive. Use the 80-20 rule: What is the 20 percent of your business that brings you 80 percent of the reward? If you're a performance coach and get the most success and benefit by working with athletes, then don't create a generic program on *peak performance*, create a program specifically on *peak performance for athletes*.

This is what I did for my latest product, "Sport Power Mind." It's a video program for athletes who want to train their minds and be more focused during competition. I've worked with athletes for fifteen years, so I know what they need and what's important for them.

In this business, you cannot be *just enough*. You cannot be average, you have to be *great*. The magic word is *results*. The more you give results to people, the less you need to talk about yourself. Instead, you can talk about the results you help people to achieve—that's what people want to hear! If you're blowing people away with practical, powerful ideas that they can use and apply, they will love you. They will want to tell all their friends, their family, and their spouse about you.

SHOW YOUR RESULTS WITH SOCIAL PROOF

One of the most important elements of any successful marketing campaign is "social proof." This is third-party evidence that what you do works. It can be testimonials (if possible by well-known people) endorsing your product. It can be the size of your social media following, or a recommendation from a trusted friend.

What a lot of coaches don't realize is that *social proof begins in the product*. It's not just something you do during the marketing phase. For one of my courses, I featured interviews with well-known Italian athletes who have been helped by my techniques. This makes the proof much more powerful.

When you show results from your product, you're helping customers *get results* from your material. They'll believe in it more, invest more of themselves, and give your ideas more energy.

Talk about Your Results, Not Yourself

Anyone can say, "I'm great, I'm the best coach in the world." But it's meaningless hyperbole. When it comes to your marketing, don't speak about yourself. Speak about your clients and the *results* you've achieved for them.

When advertising my program, I don't talk about me, I talk about the gold-medal athlete who increased focus and confidence thanks to the techniques I teach. I've been in business for twenty-five years, and I didn't start out with celebrity clients. The fact is, *any testimonial will do, so long as the results are real*.

People want to know how you can help *them*. In a world full of exaggerated claims and unfulfilled promises, they are going to be skeptical. You have to create your own credibility from the ground up. Have your satisfied clients give video testimonials to use on your website. When you're speaking about yourself, it's just words. When someone *else* is speaking about you, it's *proof.*

Your customers and clients should be talking about *you*, and you should be talking about *them*. When you do so, be specific. Anyone can say, "I've worked with many wonderful athletes." You stand out when you specify. Tell us *which* athletes you have worked with and the exact results that you were able to achieve for them. "I helped John Smith run 10 percent faster on the 100 metres after just two months of coaching." That's specific, that's real, and that's so much more powerful than just saying, "I'm a good coach."

The Ultimate Sales Strategy Is to Overdeliver

Coaches often struggle with *selling*. They find the process uncomfortable, they don't like it. Unfortunately, sales is one of the most important parts of any business. People won't buy your products just because you're nice. You have to market yourself. You have to *make the sale*. Other chapters in this book will give you more specific information on sales techniques and strategy. Here, I want to focus on my favorite sales tool: the art of *overdelivering.*

The real power of selling is understanding what is important to the other person. How can you help them? What do they want? What benefits do they need? If it turns out they don't need your service, don't sell it to them. Use your creativity and put everything you have into delivering *more value* to your customers, clients, and students, no matter what.

I had a situation in my business recently when a trainer who worked for me canceled at the last moment. He was a brilliant trainer, and people had bought tickets to the event hoping to see him. The training was supposed to be about neurolinguistic programming (NLP) and communication skills. He canceled just few days in advance, and I had dozens of people about to show up to see him live. I had to find a solution.

I called the Dale Carnegie Institute and asked them to fly over one of their best trainers to fill in and deliver one of their flagship courses. This was worth *double* the price tag of my event. And then I organized an exclusive NLP seminar that I personally delivered. I have a lot of experience with NLP, but I hardly ever teach it. Yet, I made an exception in this case because I wanted to *overdeliver*.

When the event happened, I showed up, explained the situation with complete honesty, and said that if people didn't want to stay, they would receive a full refund. People stayed. They felt taken care of—they ended up receiving more value than they had originally expected.

Instead of complaints, we had passionate compliments and testimonials from the attendees. I told this story on a video, which I uploaded to Facebook. It took off and received over 150,000 views, becoming an incredible marketing asset for my business.

Because I insisted on overdelivering no matter what, my business benefited. Go the extra mile for your customers, and you will share in the rewards.

BUSINESS IS A TEAM SPORT

Life is a team sport, and business is a team sport. You need to work alongside people who are *better at things than you*. Most likely, you will be the *star* of your business, the person on stage, on video, and in the room. But you still need a team that shares your mission, people who are part of the game with you.

Your team has to bring the same passion to their work that you bring to yours. You need a shared vision that is greater than money. It's about contribution—what you are putting out into the world.

As soon as you can afford it, begin to build a team. Choose people who like your products, who love what you are doing. Then, focus on building something together. When your employees share in your vision, they could end up being with you forever.

The CEO of my company has been with me since day one, twenty-five years ago. Having someone like this is like having another version of you—someone you can trust completely, who shares your passion, and with whom you can achieve far more than you ever could alone.

Eventually, Find a Partner

You're not good at everything. You may be a fantastic coach, but are you also a brilliant accountant, a killer salesperson, a great website designer, a meticulous organizer? Before people can appreciate your products, you have to be able to sell them. You need the machinery of a business to deliver your ideas and programs to the world.

If you want to focus exclusively on being a coach, creating products, and teaching, then you may want to partner with someone who can handle the business and marketing side. Find someone to merge with and create a successful business together.

The biggest challenge for me was stepping back and letting my team handle things. My business was like my son, but I had to remind myself that a business, even though it is your passion, is still just a business.

As we've expanded into Dubai, I've been able to step back from my Italian business and leave more things for my team. Because I've known them for years, because we share the same vision, I know that my customers are in great hands.

Summary and Your "To Do" List

To get your name out there to the masses and build an army of raving fans, you have to be *better than the rest*. The first step is value: Create a great product that gets results. The results you achieve for your clients will be your No. 1 marketing asset. Prove your value to them the *right way* to build your credibility and stand out. As more people experience the power of your programs, your customers will become your advocates and ambassadors.

- **Prove your results:** Ask yourself, "Is this useful?" Then, prove your results *within* your product by demonstrating the power of your techniques on real people.
- **Overdeliver:** The ultimate sales and marketing strategy is to overdeliver. Create beautiful, well-crafted products that look and feel professional. Go the extra mile and give people tangible results.
- **Let others speak for you:** Don't talk about yourself. Anyone can say, "I'm great." People won't listen to this. They will listen to stories about your clients and the *results* that you have helped

them achieve. Feature testimonials from satisfied customers. When other people talk about you, it's *proof*.

- **Build a team:** Build a team around you that is aligned toward your mission. Choose people you trust and who can be there for the long haul. If you don't like business and marketing, partner with someone who does, so you can each focus on what you're good at.

Persistence

How to Stay on Track toward Your Vision

MELISSA TIETZ

Melissa Tietz was trained by Bob Proctor, one of the most widely recognized and revered teachers on human potential and success in the world. She is on a mission to help others transform their thoughts into concrete, real-world results. Since 2012, she has served thousands of clients, helping them to stand in their power, overcome their limitations, and bring their vision to life.

Success isn't a secret, it's a system. To get the results you want, you have to persist no matter what. Learn how to align yourself with your goals by taking consistent action, upgrading your paradigm, discovering your uniqueness, and finding mentors who can take years off your learning curve.

Your coaching success is an inside job. Whether you succeed or fail is up to you. Most people start strong, taper off, and quit when they face challenges. They retreat to where they were because things aren't working as they had planned. For you to change your results, you have to look at what's going on inside of you.

Our ability to enjoy a fabulous life and create what we want all depends on our level of awareness. There is a marvelous inner world that exists within each one of us; we just have to tap into it.

How can you expand your level of awareness? Through effective trainings, the learning curve of life, and locking in with a mentor or coach who will set your coaching business up for thriving success. Make it a part of your daily routine to practice the beliefs and habits of success. When you're standing in your power, when you *persist*, you create opportunities and find ways to keep moving forward no matter what.

Like many coaches, my journey began with a decision. I was in an unhealthy marriage, and I made the decision that there was something better for me out there. I pursued a divorce and, newly single, took a leap of faith and enrolled in my first coaching class. I took a position with the same coaching company that certified me, and I taught courses with them as I continued to train and upgrade my skill set.

For a while, I was getting amazing results, and I took advantage of every opportunity given to me. I loved the freedom of being able to set my own hours and doing what I love every day. I also loved having such a huge impact on my clients and other coaches. I was feeling at the top of my game!

Then the coaching company I loved—where I had learned to thrive—folded and shut down. That was the end. Once again, it was time for a decision. Many of my colleagues went back into traditional nine-to-five jobs, even though it was not their passion in the first place. It was tempting to retreat into the familiar, but I had already learned the value of persistence—the importance of living on purpose and doing what I love every day.

With the right mind-set, I knew I could thrive. I was also reminded that we have to experience the upsets in order to fully appreciate our successes. I decided to pursue my passion. I was going to be a coach *no matter what*. My clients were achieving amazing results, and I was having a lot of fun every day, and I wanted to remain in this life-changing industry.

I had learned that failures are not really *failures*—they're part of the journey. Failing is not bad, it just means what you're doing isn't working. With persistence and by holding on to your vision, you just get up and try another path. There are so many great learning opportunities when things don't work out.

As I was sorting out my *why* in life and also continuing with more training, I came across a live stream of a Bob Proctor event. I was captivated. I took action and got connected with the Proctor Gallagher

Institute. I had found my new fit and began my training with the legendary personal development teacher himself.

Through my time as a trainer with this amazing leader, I honed my coaching skills and upgraded my understanding of success. This information made a huge difference with my wealth, health, and happiness. I learned that there's no success secret—success is a *system*. It's all about doing things in a certain way and following a step-by-step process. It's not just about taking more training, it's about *internalizing* the success principles and practicing them every day. Consistent repetition—this will take you where you want to go.

In this chapter, we'll look at how to take deliberate action every day toward your goal. We'll examine the power of patterns and paradigms, and how to make your habits work for you. We'll look at how success comes from you *being you*—not a copy of anyone else. Finally, we'll examine the importance of mentors, and you'll discover how to find someone who will champion you on your journey.

TAKE ACTION EVERY DAY TOWARD YOUR GOAL

Before you start thinking about how to get there, you have to know *where* you're going and, most importantly, you have to know your *why*. Visualization and your burning desire are covered elsewhere in this book. Read those chapters, because everything below depends upon you building a big, clear picture and then focusing on it until it becomes part of you. When you're clear on what you want, you've planted that image in your mind, and you are passionate about making it happen, then you can begin to bring your desires into reality.

The Power of Small Action

To succeed in starting your own business, you have to take action *every day*. All of the effective success strategies, goals, and law of attraction principles in the world will not do you any good if you do not *act*. Sitting home on the couch and visualizing all day will not move you onto your success path. Visualization works. It's powerful. You have to think differently to create differently, but it must be accompanied by *action*.

Little steps are great. Just make sure you're moving every day. Sometimes "getting started" is the toughest part. One of my clients had a strong desire to move to a different residence. She was struggling with clutter and needed a change after living in the same place for twenty-seven years. The small action step I gave her was to start packing one box. That's it! She got inspired and decided to start clearing out her clutter. She donated and consigned carloads of items she did not want. I explained we must take the action and believe it is happening before we will see it. Shortly after her cleaning spree began she was presented with an opportunity to be a property manager across town, in a beautiful new building with free rent! What a difference packing one box has made. Now her focus is starting her online business at home instead of her cluttered apartment where she wasn't feeling good. Taking action doesn't have to mean doing big, crazy, disruptive things. If you want to move, pack a box. If you want to start a health goal, take a fifteen-minute walk outside. If you want a new car, go test-drive one. It's the compounding of the little things that makes the big difference over time. Every step gets you closer to your goal. Most people procrastinate or aren't sure what to do. They talk, but they don't take action. We call this the Knowing-Doing Gap. Instead of being overwhelmed by the size of the mission ahead, break it down into small chunks, and tackle them one at a time.

People make things bigger in their minds than they really are. That's why so many people are unhappy and stuck. In fact, even the smallest action sets up a *reaction*. I used a small step action technique with selling a car. I wrote a statement on paper about how easy and effortless it was to sell this car and get a great price. I visualized the car being sold and took some action with visiting a local car dealership to get a quote on a trade-in price. Within two weeks I removed my note that I was visualizing on. It was sold, exactly what I wanted. Keep persisting. Always see the result of each action you're taking in the context of your goal. Know where you are and where you're going, and trust your intuition to guide you toward the next logical step. When you get an impulse to take action, follow through and do it *now*.

You may have to course-correct on the way, responding to the lessons you acquire on your journey. But know that there are no failures; everything is part of the journey. Have the faith that you will arrive on time, and hold on to a *confidence* that the pieces will all come together.

When you know the *why* and keep moving forward, the *how* figures itself out. Take the actions that feel good. Just take one step, then the next step, and before you know it you're a long way down the track!

Action Step: Take Inspired Action

All the success principles in the world don't mean anything if you don't take *action*. Persist with small actions every day, following your intuition, and with your eyes fixed upon your dream and your *why*.

Each night before you go to sleep, write down three actions that you're going to accomplish the next day no matter what. These are the critical few things that will propel you forward. Success comes daily. Instead of seeing these actions in your mind as a chore or task, view them as the building blocks of your vision of success. Keep moving forward and the "how" figures itself out. These are automatic, feel-good, next-logical-step actions. Imagine them *as if they have already happened*. The next day, follow through and *get them done!*

CHANGE YOUR PARADIGM TO
CHANGE YOUR RESULTS

A paradigm is a mental program that controls your habitual behavior. For example, waking up every day and going to a job you dread even though in the long run you would be happier doing something else. Maybe you continue on this path because your parents wanted you to or because it's what you have always done and it feels safe. Even the thought of making a change makes you feel uncomfortable. This is a paradigm. I'm here to tell you there is no reward without taking the risk. You have to take a leap into the uncomfortable and stretch yourself to get beyond your current level of results. *Most* of our behavior is habitual; paradigms effectively control our life. When you understand what a paradigm is, you can begin to change it. You want to change the habits that aren't working toward your desires because they determine what you manifest into your life.

Before I started my journey, I would take a long time to gather information and make decisions. I have learned that gathering more information and becoming a knowledge bank does not change your results. Procrastination is one of the most common causes of failure. I was going through life waiting for the time to be "just right." That waiting just kept me in the same place. When I was given an opportunity to take a higher-level position, move across the United States, travel to different countries, I took it. My journey has become much richer from it. Start where you are right now, work with what you have, and you will gather more insights along the way. But you have to take the leap—there is never a wrong decision, just course corrections. That's the difference a paradigm shift can make in your life. It did in mine!

Most people wake up and follow a pattern of behavior, and this pattern leads them through life. Paradigms stem from our genetics and our environment—what we learn from our parents and at school, what is programmed into us by the world at large. Paradigms protect us, but they also keep us stuck. Our patterns of behavior, thought, and belief hold us in place. If we act the same way every day, then we are going to get the same results every day. If you want to change the results and create what you want in life, your paradigms have to change.

How to Replace Stuck Paradigms

Breakthroughs come when you learn to think differently, when you replace those negative/limiting beliefs and patterns with positive beliefs. Through consistent repetition, your whole world will begin to change. Because paradigms are deeply ingrained through years of exposure and practice, changing them requires *persistence*. The trick is retelling your positive story. Reprogram your mind and plant more effective habits through consistent *repetition* of the kind of thoughts or behaviors that focus on your ideal life.

Repetition of positive paradigms helps you clear out your old, unhelpful ways of thinking and burn positive, success principles into your mind. When the empowering, uplifting principles and strategies of success are as deeply programmed into you as any lifelong habit, then you will start living your dream automatically and taking inspired action without even having to think about it.

Your thoughts, habits, and beliefs are all stored inside your subconscious mind. One of the beautiful things about the subconscious mind is that it has no ability to tell the difference between what is actually happening in your life right now and what you're simply imagining. The subconscious is very powerful; it runs the show. Over 90 percent of your habits, patterns, and results are stored in your subconscious. This means that if you get a clear vision of success, tap into your burning desire, and practice it in your mind over and over, you can deliberately make these new patterns your present reality.

Once you burn the success principles into your mind, the magic happens. The repetition of positivity changes your thoughts, which changes your behavior, which changes your life.

In Practice: Change Self-Doubt into Self-Affirmation

One of the clearest ways in which you encounter your paradigms every day is through your self-talk. If you're like many people, you go through life under the burden of self-doubt. You may ask yourself questions like:

- Can I really do this?
- How is that going to happen?
- Where is the money going to come from?
- Am I worthy?
- How on earth will I achieve this?

You may have been experiencing this kind of self-talk for years, or even decades, ever since you were a child. Deep in our subconscious mind, we have a perception of who we are, what we are, and what we think we're worth. This is our self-image. It is a control mechanism that determines how well we do and what comes into our life.

It is up to you to change your self-image; you are the only one with that control. The opinion you have of yourself is always reflected in the world around you, in the form of your results. Rewriting this paradigm requires persistence. With conviction, rephrase these questions as "I AM" statements:

- I AM worthy.
- I AM the power in my world.
- I AM increasing my income.
- I AM deserving of the best.
- I AM successful.
- I AM stepping into my power.

Whenever you find yourself questioning your ability or self-worth, instantly rephrase the question as a positive, affirming statement. Over time, these affirmations will become a habit, and you will have replaced your negative paradigm with a positive one. This is where having a coach is key, because forming this habit takes dedication and persistence. Many of my clients have paradigms around not following through and procrastinating. I recommend a high-performance coach or accountability partner to keep you on track with your mind-set training.

One way I've found success with this is by recording myself saying these positive "I AM" statements into an audio recorder. The words "I AM" are very powerful words. You want to use these words with care, so you are only putting out there what you desire and want to create. If you say, "I AM strong," you are pointing divine strength directly back at you. Let this power work for you. Say these affirmations with conviction in your own voice, and play them back to yourself. The sound of your own voice saying these affirming statements with emotion will have a powerful impact on your subconscious, helping you to more easily rewrite your paradigm and move toward your desired results.

BE YOU—DON'T COPY THE REST!

You are an exceptional coach with huge gifts, talents, and abilities. Don't try to be like your favorite author, mentor, or boss. Appreciate yourself for your uniqueness, be kind to yourself, and use positive self-talk. Know that you are worthy of all the good that you desire. Truly believe in and enjoy what you are doing. Be persistent, stay inspired, and remain dedicated to your success as a coach.

It's much easier to persist no matter what when you're *enjoying* yourself. Find the fun in everything you do. Do what you are passionate about, and develop your skills and talents along the way.

Study every day to continually move forward. Listen to your quiet voice within; it will tell you exactly what to do.

Step away from the crowd, make it about your client's needs with a touch of your style. When I was studying to be a coach, I was trained in a specific way of doing things. For example, I was instructed to follow a script when talking to prospective clients. This was helpful for some of the coaches, but it was stifling for me. Every session and every client was different, so I experimented with my own style. I took the script and used it as an outline and added more from what I learned from other trainings to give more value. As a result, I signed on more clients to coach with me, and I stood out in the company.

So many coaches are doing the same thing as everyone else, using cookie-cutter strategies instead of embracing the thrill of doing things in their own way. Well, here's the rub: Most people aren't reaching their full potential. If you do the same thing as everybody else, you're going to get the same results as everybody else. Move away from the masses.

Tap into your mental faculties so you can create using your innate abilities. *Be you!* Take control, gather information, and then make your own decisions rather than asking other people what you should do. No one else knows what is best for you or for your business. Take charge, feel confident in what you are creating, and get more done than anyone else around you. Make a huge impact with your clients, and then watch the ripple effect.

Happiness Creates Success

When you apply these success principles, people notice the change in you. They see you thrive! You will have a different energy about you. When you are *being you*, your life expands, your world grows. You become the best for your clients and the best for yourself. One of my students asked me recently, "You're so happy and bubbly. Are you always like this?" I said, "This is *me!*"

Action Step: Be Creative, Be Unique

Earlier, this chapter explored creating your evening ritual, where you write down three actions to accomplish the next day. Now let's look at a morning ritual. Before you get out of bed in the morning, stay relaxed, and set your intention for the day. Visualize what you are going to achieve, easily and effortlessly, and see it as if it has been accomplished. Be open, and let creative ideas come to you.

Gratitude is another key component to your morning ritual, and it brings more into your life to be grateful for. It puts you on the path to what you desire. Be grateful for things in your life right now, as well as for the things that are on their way to you. Show appreciation now in your gratitude journal, as if it has already happened. Set up these habits to break free from the box—that's when your *leap* is going to happen!

LEARN FROM SOMEONE WHO IS GETTING THE RESULTS YOU WANT

Finding the right mentor takes years off your learning curve. Find a mentor who's been where you want to go, and who has what you want. They should be just a step ahead of you on your journey. A great mentor will see something in you that you may not see in yourself, inspire you to keep moving, and give you essential advice that will help you go *further*, faster.

I have two mentors, one of whom is a senior leader for a company where I currently coach. After several phone conversations and talking with this gentleman for just a few minutes in person, I knew I wanted to learn from him. He's a powerful, strong, sought-after leader, so I knew that he wasn't going to give his time to mentor just anyone who asked.

I had a friend take a picture of this gentleman and me together, and I placed the picture on my wall, where I would see it every day. I also wrote down in my gratitude journal that I was being mentored by him. I persisted and imagined it as if it were already true. When we met again a couple of months later, I looked him in the eye and told him, "I'd love to have you mentor me, and I see myself being an integral part of this company."

The next day, I got a phone call from him. He said, "I'm not quite sure why I'm making this call to you, but I'm going to start mentoring you and bring you on to my sales team." If he only knew I had been looking at this picture every day!

Action Step: How to Find Your Own Mentors

Be on the lookout for mentors who are going to see what is amazing in you, who are going to champion you and challenge you.

Write out a list of five people who have been where you have been and have what you want. Write down the qualities that stand out in these people. Think about ways you can contact them. I was lucky that, after looking at a photo of me and my mentor every day, I could verbally contact him. Meet them in person, call them, e-mail them if you have to; get creative. But if there's one thing you may have picked up from this chapter so far: They won't become your mentor if you don't *take action!*

Summary and Your "To Do" List

Success isn't a secret, it's a system. To get the results you want, you must persist no matter what. You can do this by taking deliberate action every day toward your goal, and by making your habits work for you. Your success comes from you being you—not a copy of anyone else. Set your intention, take action, and change your paradigm—and find someone who will champion you on your journey.

- **Set your intention:** Set your intention and focus, and then *take action*. Make it BIG and beautiful and give it everything you've got.
- **Take daily action:** Translate your positive thoughts and desires into consistent, daily action. Break your goals or challenges down into small chunks and tackle them one at a time. Focus on your destination, and take that inspired, automatic action to move forward every day.
- **Change your paradigm:** Success is the process of *ingraining* in your mind a new, more empowering paradigm. If beliefs, self-talk, or behavior patterns are impeding your success, they must be replaced in order for you to change your results.
- **Stand in *your* power:** Be open to new information, but don't try to be like anyone else. Be you, and stand in your power *as you* and take pride and pleasure in what makes you unique.
- **Find a mentor:** Make a list of five people from whom you want to learn. Form a belief and expectation that they will mentor you and then *take some action* and contact them. Find a mentor who is one step ahead of you on your path. Let them be your teacher and guide you.

- **Align yourself:** If you're going to change your results, then your *intention*, your *actions*, and your *paradigms* have to align. If you want to WIN, you have to bet on yourself. Don't play it safe. Tell yourself, "I'm going to make this happen." The sky's the limit, but it's up to you.

Seven Keys to Scaling Your Business

Forging a Mission and Legacy

PATRYK WEZOWSKI

Patryk Wezowski is the cocreator of *Leap* (learn more at CoachingMovie.com) the first feature-length documentary film about the coaching profession, and the director and producer of the documentary *Impact*.[10] Alongside his wife, Kasia, he is the founder of the Center for Body Language, which has fifty representatives in twenty countries and has trained more than 50,000 students.

Once you've set yourself up as a successful coach, the question then becomes, what's next? What legacy do I want to leave in the world? How do I scale my business? In this chapter, we'll explore how to scale your coaching business and create a legacy you can be proud of.

There's nothing wrong with having a private coaching business and spending your time with clients one-on-one. That's a fantastic way to earn a living and a make difference. But if you're eyeing *bigger things*, if you see yourself leaving a huge legacy and inspiring more people with your ideas, then there are a few things you can do to make that happen. It's about taking the material you have and leveraging it so you extract maximum value from your ideas.

I started small, a Polish kid who grew up in Belgium trying to speak a foreign language. To make things harder, I had a hearing disorder, which meant I was disadvantaged and really struggled to connect and communicate with others. Because I couldn't always hear or understand what people were saying, I started focusing on visual cues like body language, facial expressions, and posture.

This led to a passion for body language, which I ended up transforming into a business. I studied as much as I could in the early days, soon realizing that I had ideas, techniques, and material that would benefit other people.

When I decided to create my first body language training course, I rented a video camera for about $50. I spent a day recording a body language training program in Dutch, which is spoken in Belgium. I thought to myself, "This is never going to work. I'm not well-known—who's going to buy a DVD featuring *me*?"

That one DVD went on to sell enough copies to generate $50,000. Since then, my wife, Kasia, and I have forged a partnership as coaches, body language experts, and now, filmmakers. Our body language business is flourishing in twenty countries, and we raised close to $1 million to create our dream project, the movie *Leap*.

Throughout every step of the journey, I have been driven by my *passion*, the desire to make a difference and leave a legacy to the world. If you aspire to create something bigger than yourself, then these seven "keys," which I developed through my own work, will help you to engineer your own seven-figure coaching empire.

1. JUST DO IT—DON'T WAIT UNTIL TOMORROW

When I started out, I didn't have a company. I had no business experience. I didn't know what to do. I was given the advice that I should create a DVD program or an online course. So, I started brainstorming, thinking about what I could teach others.

At the top of the list was *body language*, which I had been studying since I was a child. My father was an Olympic trainer in fencing, and I'd trained alongside him since I was fourteen. So, I knew about body language, and I knew about training. I put them together and created a body language course.

I read several books on marketing and business, and I had long possessed the goal of creating something independent from me—something that could sell over and over without requiring additional work. This is when I rented that camera for $50 from a friend. I had it for only one day. After twelve hours of almost straight filming, I nearly collapsed from exhaustion.

The DVD I created mainly targeted recruiters, helping them read candidates they were interviewing. I was a consultant to recruiters, so I had contacts and experience in the field. It occurred to me that the material could also be useful for people on the other side of the table, the job seekers.

Because I worked in recruitment, I knew a lot of job seekers. Through these connections, I invited a group of unemployed people to attend a free seminar about job interview techniques. I planned to speak for an hour and pitch my DVD at the end.

That evening was historic for me. I feared that I wouldn't sell one copy. But almost half of the fifty people in the room bought the DVD on the spot. These were unemployed people who opened their wallets, took out $40, and bought my DVD. Wow!

I walked away with about $500 in profit, just from that one speech. It hit me: With just two or three presentations like this a month, I could make more than I earned at my regular job.

Create Your Own Product Today!

If you have an idea for a product, a training program, something you want to *build* and *create*, then start right here, right now. Your first product may not be your best work. It may not be your legacy on its own. But it's a start, it will get the ball rolling. If you continue to wait until you're struck by the perfect idea, there's a good chance you'll be waiting forever.

Make a list of topics you have expertise in, then brainstorm the kind of people who may buy what it is you have to offer.

You will never create your masterpiece if you're not willing to *start from wherever you are right now*. I wouldn't have been able to create my business if I hadn't been willing to start out with that small DVD filmed on a $50 rented camera. This created momentum and helped me build my confidence while realizing, "Hey, I have something to offer that people want!" Follow your idea, and eventually it will lead you to where you want to be.

2. DO THE WORK TO CREATE SOMETHING UNIQUE AND BUILD MOMENTUM

When I met my wife, Kasia, I was the top body language expert in Belgium, but I had a very low profile overseas. Kasia said, "If we're going to have a company together, it has to be international, because I don't speak Dutch!" We translated our materials to English, asking ourselves, "What can we create in the English market that is better than anything else out there?"

We did research. We looked at Google keyword trends in our specialty. We noticed that there was demand for a training program with videos of microexpressions, those tiny little half-second facial expressions that are impossible to fake and which reveal people's true emotions. Nobody else had a microexpression video training program. People were looking for microexpression training, but there wasn't a single course with videos of microexpressions on the market.

Our Micro Expression Training Videos catapulted us into being major players in the body language niche *globally*. They helped us land speaking appearances at TEDx and Harvard University, and we appeared on U.S. TV networks like Fox and CBS.

Create Something Unique That People Want

For your product to succeed, people have to *want it*. Marketers very seldom create desire. Instead, they tap into existing currents and *channel them* toward their products. My new products tend to begin with *research*. Ask people what is important to them, find out what they are looking for. Don't subordinate your own vision to other people's prejudices, but get a sense of the market that is out there.

- Who is your target audience?
- What are they motivated *toward*—what do they want to gain or achieve?
- What are they motivated *away from*—what do they fear?

The best way to know your market and get your name out there is to show up and be in front of an interested audience as much as possible. With the Center for Body Language, we've trained more than 50,000 people worldwide. These days we can charge high fees for our training programs, but in the early days I was willing to talk for free as often as I could. This increased our exposure, and it enabled us to evaluate the audience to see which ideas most excited them.

Be Everywhere You Can Be

In addition to the live trainings, Kasia and I have worked hard to make our body language ideas accessible all over the Internet. We write articles for websites and publications. This started out small and local but recently has snowballed into bigger, international publications like *Harvard Business Review* and *Forbes* magazine.

Whenever possible, we film our live talks and put them on YouTube. Some of these went viral, and our videos now collectively have over 3 *million* views. During the 2012 U.S. presidential election, we approached TV stations and told them we would use body language to predict the outcome, which led to appearances on Fox News and CBS. This gave us huge publicity and, of course, our prediction was correct!

Get your name out there every way you can. Think about how you can package your ideas to appeal to a mass audience. What benefits do people get? What interesting ways can you prove your effectiveness?

Leverage Attention to Build Your Network

When people watch our videos on YouTube or read our articles, they're invited to come to our website to learn more about body language. There, they can receive a free course.

This means that, instead of just reading an article or watching a video and then disappearing, people stick around. They become fans and eventually repeat customers. We get 10,000 leads per year from people signing up for our free body language videos. This now happens purely *on autopilot*, without having to do any more work. Once you've set something like this up, it's done.

Think about what you can offer people who visit your website to get them to stick around. Create a small PDF report or a free e-mail course and offer this to people in exchange for signing up and giving you permission to e-mail them. *Enroll people* into your brand, and you begin to build up a solid fan base.

3. AUTOMATE WHAT WORKS FOR RECURRING PASSIVE INCOME

Once you have a system in place that generates attention, subscribers, and sales, put it on autopilot. We have twenty online courses that are ready made and available for people to instantly download—without us having to do a thing. When people join our e-mail list, the introductory e-mails are programmed in. Our free courses are delivered automatically. This introduces people to our programs. If they buy them, it's also automatic.

With technology like autoresponders, you can effectively clone yourself. You have to do everything just once, and then it can repeat itself without your help.

Automate at the Right Moment

Some tech-savvy businesspeople make the mistake of automating *too early*. There's no point in replicating something that doesn't work. Instead, wait until you have a successful, proven model. If people are reading your content, opting in to your e-mail list, and then buying your courses, you're probably there.

Once you have a working model, break down each stage in the process: What e-mails do your subscribers receive? What is your onboarding process? What sales e-mails are the most effective? How are your products delivered? Then, use an autoresponder to plug everything in and let it run itself.

4. LICENSE YOUR FLAGSHIP PRODUCT TO EXPAND YOUR REACH

Now you have some traction, a fan base in place, and at least one proven product that people love. It's time to start thinking bigger. Real, international success comes when you *franchise* yourself.

First, make sure you have a clear *flagship course*. For me, this was the Micro Expression Training Videos program, a unique course that delivers real value for people interested in body language and communication.

Your flagship course should become an extension of your *surname*. I am "Patryk Wezowski, creator of the METV program." You want your name and your flagship course to be married, so when people think of one, they immediately think of the other.

When you have this level of recognition, systematize your course so that other people can teach it for you. Break down each element, step by step. Then, offer to train other people to deliver this course *for you*. They'll make money by teaching a proven, recognized course. You've done the research, built up the reputation, and created the program. All they have to do is deliver it for you. They win, and so do you.

By training others in your unique methodology, you set yourself up with an incredible passive income stream. You are *licensing* your intellectual property to other people. In exchange, you typically receive a percentage (15 percent to 30 percent) of the revenue they generate from your material.

We now have fifty licensed trainers in twenty countries around the world teaching our body language courses. When they make money using our intellectual material, a portion of their revenue comes to us.

Imagine if you had an army of coaches around the world teaching your ideas for you, and you are getting paid for this! This is not only a fantastic business model, it's also an incredible way to create change. You can't be everywhere at once, but when you train other people to teach your material, you can reach more people, change more lives, and spread the inspiration *further* than you ever could alone.

5. CONNECT WITH PEOPLE ON THE LEVEL OF YOUR *MISSION*

Now that our body language business is practically running itself, Kasia and I have had the opportunity to go back to the drawing board and ask ourselves, "What's the mission now? What legacy do we want to leave the world?"

The idea for the *Leap* film came to Kasia as she was meditating on a beach in India. We had just appeared as coaches in a documentary, and Kasia was thinking about her dreams for the future. She had a vision of a world where 1 million people were inspired after seeing others transformed on the big screen. We came up with a plan for a theatrical movie about coaching that would inspire 1 million lives and amplify the entire profession.

Because our mission drives us, we found it easy to recruit other mission-driven coaches to get on board. When we contacted people like Marshall Goldsmith, Mark Thompson, and Jack Canfield about *Leap*, we were just starting out. We had an idea. We had passion, but that was it.

When we spoke to these people, we didn't talk about money. We didn't talk about getting rich. We spoke about our *mission*. Because they shared a similar mission to ours, they were inspired to get on board and take a chance on us.

Formulate Your Mission in One Sentence

We distilled our vision into one sentence: **To create a film that inspires 1 million people to be more successful in life and business.**

How would you phrase your mission in one sentence? This should be a true reflection of what drives you, your purpose, and the legacy you want to leave behind. But it's not just about you—this sentence should be clear and inspiring to others.

It shouldn't be about you, it should be about the world. Don't say, "To make a million dollars a year." That's a valid goal, but it's not an inspiring mission. Think deep. Go for a walk. Meditate on it. And then cut to the core.

Your Mission Will Drive Your Success

This *mission statement* isn't just about connecting with others, it's also about motivating yourself. On the journey to raise funds for *Leap*, I had many moments of doubt. Once we reached the $100,000 mark, I almost panicked: What if we don't raise enough to produce the movie, and we have to give every cent back? What would that do to our reputation, our careers?

With the help of my coaches, I was able to transform these moments of doubt and stay focused on my mission. It's hard to achieve big things. It's scary to create something, to put some part of yourself out into the world for others to judge and possibly reject. If your vision is strong enough, if you're powered by a compelling mission, then you will get through it, persist, and succeed.

6. GET PAID FOR THE RESULTS YOU CREATE

Most coaches get paid per hour, but this is not a formula for a seven-figure business. If you want to work with people one-on-one and command large fees as a coach, you have to charge for *results*, not *time*.

This strategy is risky: You're opening yourself up to the possibility of working hard and getting nothing in return. But if you're really good at what you do, if you can walk your talk, then you stand the chance of succeeding alongside your clients and creating a huge windfall for everyone involved.

Of course, you'll be at your most effective when the work you do is aligned with your *vision* and *passion*. Kasia and I are passionate about making films. One of the most important phases of filmmaking is fund-raising.

For *Leap*, we ran a successful crowdfunding campaign that exceeded our expectations and gave us the budget to create the film of our dreams. We'd learned from the best and synthesized the advice of different coaches and experts, until we cracked the code and found a formula that worked.

Combining our passion for filmmaking with our crowdfunding expertise, we now consult for other filmmakers and run their campaigns for them. At the beginning, when we were first establishing our reputation in this field, we charged for results only. If the fundraising campaign reached its target, we'd get a percentage of the amount raised.

Among our earliest clients were the executive producers for the movie *THINK*, a documentary based on Napoleon Hill's classic book, *Think and Grow Rich*. We connected with the producers on the level of *mission*—like us, they want to inspire others to be more successful in life and business. We went to work for them and ended up breaking the record for the most-funded documentary *ever* on the popular Indiegogo crowdfunding platform.

Now that we have a proven track record, we can afford to charge up-front fees because people know they're likely to get a result.

Get Results and Think Big

If you're good at what you do, if you reliably get results for your clients, then you can work fewer hours and make more money by charging for results. The key here is to think BIG: big clients, big projects.

Ask yourself who would benefit most from your skill set? Then, think about how you can quantify this value in a clear, measurable way. For example, a percentage increase in revenue. Then walk the talk. There's little risk to the client, so don't be surprised if you start getting some very exciting offers by using this strategy!

7. LOVE WHAT YOU DO, LEARN AS YOU GO

What are you really, amazingly passionate about, and what would you be doing even if you weren't getting paid at all? Kasia and I are really passionate about making movies and inspiring others. Our passion is connected to our mission: We are motivated by the end goal, but we also love the day-to-day *process*.

In the beginning with *Leap*, we were driven by a love of the work and that burning desire to make this happen. We didn't have any delusions about this being the next *Star Wars* installment. Sure, money is nice, but that's not why we went to work on it every day. Our feeling was, *"This must happen—this is our legacy, our lives' work. This is how we make our lives matter!"*

Ask yourself: What would you do even if you didn't have to? It's about taking your vision that we looked at in step five, expanding it, and connecting to your day-to-day life. For us, this is about making the film.

Which coaches can we put on the big screen? Which story lines are going to inspire people most? What can we create to help other people *get it?*

These are the things that energize and motivate Kasia and me. We wake up in the morning excited, charged, and driven. Each day is a chance to make this vision more real, to do more of what it is that we love. We help other people to create a legacy, and their legacy in turn becomes part of *our* legacy. Everything snowballs together, the different parts of our business feeding and empowering each other.

Kasia and I used this process to grow the Center for Body Language internationally. We used this process again with *Leap*, and we are in the midst of using it again for our next film, *Impact*. We help our clients use this process to launch products and build huge businesses. It's a circle that grows over time and gets more powerful each time you repeat it. None of this would have happened if we weren't willing to take action at the very beginning. Now it's your turn to make this work for you. Take the first step, and enjoy the leap.

Summary and Your "To Do" List

Creating a successful coaching business is about three things: vision and passion, starting small while thinking big, and connecting your passion to your mission. When you create things that have meaning and put yourself out into the world, the money will come. You will create a circle that grows over time and becomes more powerful each time you repeat it.

- **Just do it—don't wait:** Start small and create something *now!*
- **Create something unique:** Research, put your name out there, and find out what people want.
- **Automate what works for recurring passive income:** Make technology work for you—once you have a proven system, automate it and let your business run itself.
- **License your flagship product to expand your reach:** Train others to deliver your material for you to increase your revenue and inspire more people.

- **Connect with people on the level of your mission:** Think about the legacy you want to leave the world, and distill this into one meaningful, empowering sentence.
- **Get paid for the results you create:** Charge for what you achieve on projects connected to your mission.
- **Love what you do and learn as you go:** Connect your vision to your day-to-day life. Pursue your passion, and keep going no matter what!

Conclusion: Leaving Your Legacy

KASIA WEZOWSKI

In this book, you've learned the skills, attitudes, and principles behind growing a successful coaching business. From coaches like Marshall Goldsmith, John Demartini, and Marc Steinberg, you've learned about shaping your mind-set, setting goals, and keeping yourself on the path to success. From coaches like Jack Canfield, Kelvin Lim, and Roberto Re, you've learned about making a business plan and marketing your practice.

You may have noticed that many coaches throughout this book wrote about the importance of your *mission*—of creating a change not just in yourself, but in the *world*. Doing something that is powerful and meaningful for you and using your skills, energy, and passion to improve the lives of others.

Like you, and like all the other coaches who contributed to this book, I started from scratch. Creating my coaching business and growing it with my husband, Patryk, wasn't always easy, but this sense of mission kept us motivated and moving forward.

Because we diligently implemented many of the strategies and ideas you've learned in this book, we achieved success with our company, the Center for Body Language. This guaranteed us an income and the opportunity to work with interesting people around the world. We were successful, but we knew we still had a lot more to give.

Many people think that achieving some level of career success is the end of the journey. In fact, for us it was where the most exciting part of our story began.

As Patryk mentioned in his chapter, a few years ago we traveled to India to meditate and reconnect with our mission. This is important to do, as it's so easy to lose touch with your sense of purpose during the grind of everyday life.

While in India, my thoughts turned to the idea of a legacy. The question I asked was: "What do I want to leave behind?" It was time to start dreaming big. Through the Center for Body Language and our other coaching work, we've been privileged to have impacted tens of thousands of lives. *But what if we could turn those thousands into millions?*

We set the goal of inspiring 1 million lives around the world. We'd create a movie that would show the power of coaching on the big screen. People would witness others being transformed and be inspired to change their own lives.

Immediately, we started planning our film: *Leap*.

How We Raised $1 Million to Create Our Film

Despite our business experience, neither of us had ever attempted a project of this size. We had the idea. We had the passion. But that was it.

We knew we'd have to raise a large amount of money to create something of the quality and significance that we wanted. This was to be our legacy, something that would outlast us and continue to inspire people for years to come. Good wasn't going to be good enough. This had to be a masterpiece. For that, we'd need funds.

We contacted our coaches (all good coaches have coaches!), and we tracked down others who had been successful at raising funds for other projects. They helped us refine our plan and come up with an effective strategy. At times this was difficult. We had to question many of the assumptions we had made about raising money and challenge a few limiting beliefs that I didn't even know we had.

Countless hours of research went into creating a list of potential investors—people with the means to contribute to our project, whose business goals were in alignment, and, most importantly, who shared our *mission*.

At every step, this mission statement was front and center. We wanted to *inspire 1 million people around the world to be more successful in life and business.* This is a clear, meaningful statement that others could connect with and support.

We Heard "No" a Lot

It took six months for us to recruit the initial investors for *Leap.* During these six months, we sent out more than 40,000 e-mails to coaches, influencers, and potential investors who were part of our network or who followed our body language programs. This led to more than 1,000 phone calls, which resulted in a grand total of thrity investors.

For every one person who said *yes* and decided to become an investor, more than 30 people told us *no!* If it weren't for our passion and drive, our commitment to creating something that would become our legacy, we may have given up after the first few hundred no's. But we didn't.

We kept going and found that, though many people said no, a lot of big-name coaches—celebrities we admired and studied—not only returned our phone calls but were enthusiastic to get involved.

One of the earliest people to say yes was Marshall Goldsmith, whose advice is featured in this book. He's a giant of the profession, and having him onboard gave us and other investors confidence. Suddenly, it seemed like our dreams were indeed going to come true.

Going Public

Once we had our first investors and coaching stars onboard, we had the confidence to take our movie project public. We created a crowdfunding campaign, and we reached out to coaches around the world to get involved and contribute funds in exchange for rewards like priority access to the film and access to our featured coaches.

Coaches worldwide supported the project and drove traffic to our crowdfunding page. From this point on, things began to snowball. Potential investors saw the excitement that our crowdfunding campaign had created, and they were inspired to come aboard themselves. They also put their weight behind the crowdfunding campaign and sent more contributors our way. A movement began to form, and more than 800 people contributed funds.

In the end, between our crowdfunding campaign and private investment, we raised over $1 million to bring our vision to life. Now it was time to make our movie.

Working with Our Heroes

One of the most exciting things about creating *Leap* was the ability to work with the coaches and mentors whom we most admire. You've met these coaches in this book and have experienced their advice, so you can imagine what it would be like to suddenly meet these people and have them help turn your dream into your legacy!

As we worked with them, and observed how they interacted with the clients profiled in the movie, we paid attention to a few key things. We wanted to know what made them tick, what motivated them, and *what makes them special.*

There were two angles to our inquiry:

1. What makes these people successful *coaches*, able to create change and transformation in their clients?
2. What makes them successful *businesspeople*, able to command fees commensurate with their value as coaches, enjoy financial security, and live their best lives purely as a result of helping others?

It is primarily the second question that this book sets out to answer. The film answers the first.

Witnessing Transformation

Four clients with diverse backgrounds are profiled in the *Leap* film. These individuals had encountered severe obstacles in their lives, but they were ready to change and had a willingness to accept help.

- Precious, despite weighing 327 pounds, had a dream to create a lingerie company to inspire other curvy women to love their bodies

- Soon Loo, a high-flying executive who jets around the globe every month, lacked fulfillment and worried that his talents were being wasted
- Chad, a forty-three-year-oldd virgin, wanted to find love on his own terms
- Rob, an Emmy Award–winning reporter whose life fell apart after one night of drinking, wanted redemption

The film documents the experiences of these four individuals during the course of a year. As they progressed, they did deep work with a team of the best coaches in the world and allowed themselves to be vulnerable. Even if you're an experienced coach, you'll be moved and awed by the level of change they all experienced.

The film is expected to hit theaters in fall 2018. When others watch it, our hope is that they too experience their own transformation. Their limiting beliefs will fall away when they see that through coaching, it really is possible to experience transformation and change.

Leap has been the culmination of my life's work so far. It brings together the skills and attitudes you've learned in this book and focuses them on one big, bold mission. It's opened a whole new way for Patryk and me to give back. Other visionaries and filmmakers now frequently approach us for fund-raising advice, and we've already started work on our next film, *Impact*, which is about communication skills and body language.

After reading this book, think about what legacy *you* are going to leave the world. How you're going to use your unique gifts and talents to create something amazing, something that lasts. It could be a product. It could be an idea. It could be that you live and enjoy your life as an example to others.

I hope this book will help you bring your vision into the world.

It's time for you to take your *Leap!*

Notes

1. 2016 ICF PWC Survey.
2. ICF press release of 2014, as quoted by: Marketdata Enterprises, Inc.
3. 2016 ICF PWC survey.
4. J. Krishnamurti Online. Accessed 4/26/17. Available at: http://bit.ly/2weHTel.
5. http://for.tn/1T3cgwU.
6. Robinson, S., and M. M. Robinson. Holonomics: Business Where People and Planet Matter. 2014, Floris Books, p. 212.
7. "HCI and Multi-Health Systems Reveal Role of Emotional Intelligence in Leadership Development." HCI website. Accessed 4/17/17. Available at: http://bit.ly/2ucIyeW.
8. Lerner, J., Y. Li, P. Valdesolo, and K. Kassam. "Emotion and Decision Making." Annual Review of Psychology. Jan. 2015. 66:799–823. Available at: http://bit.ly/2pYjBBw.
9. Learn more about the movie Impact at: http://impact.film.
10. ibid.

Download FREE Video Interviews with Six Top LEAP Book Authors

If you register on www.CoachingMovie.com/BookGift you will immediately receive the download link to a unique package of videos, so you can learn anytime, anywhere how to grow your coaching business with six selected interviews that served as a base for writing the book. Each interview is around forty-five minutes and the package contains the business secrets of six world-class coaches.

Go to www.CoachingMovie.com/BookGift to redeem.

Find out more about the LEAP movie at www.CoachingMovie.com